HOMELAND

THE ILLUSTRATED HISTORY OF THE STATE OF ISRAEL

P9-ARW-887

NACHSHON PRESS

HOMELAND

THE ILLUSTRATED HISTORY OF THE STATE OF ISRAEL

MARV WOLFMAN
Writer

MARIO RUIZ
Illustrator and Graphic Designer

WILLIAM J. RUBIN
Executive Editor/Concept

GARY SHAPIRO
Chief Contributing Editor

KEITH M. KANTER
Contributing Editor

BARBARA CHANDLER
Director of Project Development

DAVE LANPHEAR
Lettering

DREW STRUZAN
Cover Illustration

BARBARA ROOKS
Administrative Consultant

NACHSHON PRESS COMMITTEE

CHARLES FRIEND, CHAIR • JAY GOODGOLD
ELLEN KENEMORE • FRED LEVY • PAUL SAHARACK
MAX WASSERMAN • AL WINICK

HOMELAND: The Illustrated History of the State of Israel
© 2007 Nachshon Press, LLC

All rights reserved. No part of this publication may be reproduced without written permission from Nachshon Press, LLC,
except for brief quotations in books and critical reviews. For information, write Nachshon Press, LLC, 9175 Gross Point Road, Suite 186,
Skokie, IL 60077.

Catalog in Publishing information on file with publisher.

ISBN 0-9771507-1-2
ISBN 0-9771507-0-4

Sign up at www.nachshonpress.com to be part of the HOMELAND Family and receive complimentary updates
about future Nachshon Press projects, HOMELAND groups and visits to your area by HOMELAND speakers.

INTRODUCTION

In many ways, our family's experiences embody the recent history of the Jewish people and the Israeli nation—their challenges and achievements—which is the focus of HOMELAND: The Illustrated History of the State of Israel. Ilan's father was born in Berlin, Germany to a Zionist family who made aliyah before WWII. His father served in the Hagana and fought in Israel's War of Independence. Ilan's mother Tonia, of blessed memory, after surviving the Auschwitz death camp, tried to reach Israel, but was captured by the British and placed in a camp for "illegal immigrants" in Cyprus. Finally in 1948, she was able to reach Israel's shores.

My own parents came from Turkey with the Youth Aliyah Movement at the age of 15, leaving behind parents, family and community to fulfill the dream of building a Jewish home in the land. As a young man, Ilan became a pilot in the Israeli Air Force and flew many dangerous missions. Some are well-known, such as the attack on Iraq's Osirak nuclear reactor in 1981. Ilan was the youngest pilot in that squadron and his plane was the last to return from the mission. He felt he was helping to prevent another Holocaust against the Jewish people, but also helping to stop a threat to the entire world.

In spite of any difficulties Israel faced, Ilan was always filled with pride about our people and our State. So when he was selected to join the crew of the Space Shuttle Columbia, Ilan understood he was not only representing Israel, but also Jews everywhere. For this reason, he requested kosher food on the mission and brought with him a *mezuzah*, a *kiddush* cup and a copy of Israel's Declaration of Independence.

The crew of Columbia came from different countries, backgrounds and religions, but for all of them, this was a scientific mission that would benefit all mankind. This Columbia crew became a symbol of our global family. From space, they took us to a new frontier of hope, tolerance and peace. For Ilan, as the first Israeli astronaut, it was a symbol of overcoming and surviving the difficult history of the Jewish people and the Israeli nation.

Our long history as a Jewish people stands in contrast to our young age as an independent state. It is essential for all of us to learn Israel's history and look forward to a peaceful future. In Ilan's words, "We have to find a way to bring our people closer together, to show more patience and understanding."

HOMELAND tells the stories of the land, the people and the nation that Ilan loved and served. When Ilan was in space, he quoted the words of the song by John Lennon, "Imagine."

Imagine all the people
Living life in peace…
You may say I'm a dreamer
But I'm not the only one
I hope someday you'll join us
And the world will be as one.

Let us all work together for peace.

Shalom to all,
Rona Ramon

This letter recounting the historical events of Ilan Ramon's life has been reproduced with permission of Rona Ramon. Rona Ramon is the wife of Ilan Ramon, Israel's first astronaut, who perished along with the American crew of the NASA Space Shuttle Columbia, Rick D. Husband, William C. McCool, Michael P. Anderson, David M. Brown, Kalpana Chawla and Laurel Clark, on February 1, 2003/ 29 Sh'vat 5763.

May their memory be for a blessing.

WHY THIS BOOK?

Israel's history, from Biblical times to the present, is unique among the histories of world nations. Israel's history is also largely unknown. There is, to be sure, no shortage of works dealing with the 1948 establishment of the State, or of its struggles for survival today. But the story of the State of Israel goes back long before its founding, and even pre-dates the Zionist movement of the late 1800's. We believe the history of the State of Israel expresses the seamless connections between a people, the Biblical land of Israel and this 21st century country. It is this story, and these connections, we tell here in an engaging and thoughtful manner.

This is a story for all who care about Israel, travel to the Middle East, students 12 and older, as well as adults who want to learn about Israel's complex birth and life and even for those who disagree with Israel's supporters. How the State of Israel came to be, how it survived against all odds and still continues to grow is an amazing story, and it deserves a worthy presentation.

We present this story with the latest graphics and state-of-the-art design techniques. Its compelling text has been extensively researched and academically vetted. Our illustrated format brings a new dimension to this 4,000 year-old story whether you are reminding yourself of your heritage or simply interested in the history of a country that has always been in the very center of Western history.

Additionally, we are inspired by present day Israel and its people. Israelis are everyday people who go to work, raise families and pursue their dreams. They are also, to an unbelievable degree, targets and hunters, heroes and victims. They have had to kill, yet not become killers, to suffer loss, grief and sadness, but not become completely embittered or despondent. They live in a desert with limited natural resources, but have developed the land and its capacity tremendously. Israel presents us with a lesson in fortitude, determination and a sense of mission and purpose on both the individual and national levels.

HOMELAND: The Illustrated History of the State of Israel is a unique overview of a unique land. It is our hope you will be intrigued enough to dig deeper into Israel's fascinating past, challenging present and hopeful future.

These are the reasons Nachshon Press created this book. The State of Israel is a great story. We feel fortunate to be able to tell it, and we hope you will find it meaningful.

--- Nachshon Press

THIS COUNTRY MADE US A PEOPLE; OUR PEOPLE MADE THIS COUNTRY.
-- David Ben-Gurion

THE HISTORY OF THE NEAR AND MIDDLE EAST IS LONG AND COMPLEX, FILLED WITH CONFLICT AND WITH CONFLICTING INTERPRETATIONS OF EVENTS.

THE STORY IS EXCITING, BUT TELLING IT CAN STIMULATE DEBATE. EACH PEOPLE TOUCHED BY THIS HISTORY SEES THEIR INVOLVEMENT THROUGH DIFFERENT EYES.

THE MODERN ISRAELI POET *YONATAN GEFEN* EFFECTIVELY ILLUSTRATES THAT THE WAY STORIES ARE TOLD IS COLORED BY THE TELLER'S VIEWPOINT:

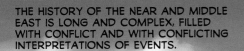

Once upon a time, in a green city, there lived a man, a green man.

The Green Man lived in a green house with a green door and green windows.

He had a green wife and two green children. And at night he would sleep in his green bed and dream green, green dreams.

One day the Green Man got up on a green morning and put on green shoes; he got dressed in a green shirt and green pants.

On his head he placed a green hat and went outside. The Green Man got into his green car and drove down the green street.

On one side of the street the man saw a green sea and on the other side lots of green flowers.

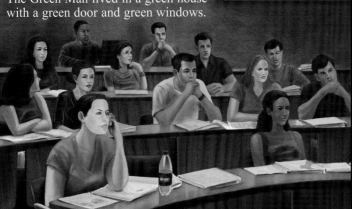

It was a beautiful day, and the Green Man was happy and he sang green songs and smoked a green cigarette with green smoke.

And then the Green Man saw that by the side of the street stood a blue man.

The Green Man stopped his green car and asked the Blue Man:

"Hey, Blue Man, what are you doing here?"

"Me?" the Blue Man said, "I'm from a different story."

SO WE OPEN OUR STUDY OF THE REGION WHERE, BY MOST ACCOUNTS, CIVILIZATION BEGAN. OVER THE NEXT MONTHS WE WILL HEAR SEVERAL DIFFERENT NARRATIVES OF POLITICAL AND RELIGIOUS IDENTITY.

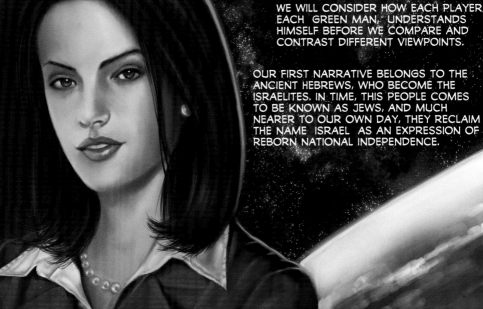

YOU KNOW THAT MANY VERSIONS OF THE SAME EVENTS CAN BE TOLD, BUT AT FIRST WE WILL TRY TO ADOPT AN INSIDER'S PERSPECTIVE ON EACH STORY.

WE WILL CONSIDER HOW EACH PLAYER, EACH "GREEN MAN," UNDERSTANDS HIMSELF BEFORE WE COMPARE AND CONTRAST DIFFERENT VIEWPOINTS.

OUR FIRST NARRATIVE BELONGS TO THE ANCIENT HEBREWS, WHO BECOME THE ISRAELITES. IN TIME, THIS PEOPLE COMES TO BE KNOWN AS JEWS, AND MUCH NEARER TO OUR OWN DAY, THEY RECLAIM THE NAME ISRAEL AS AN EXPRESSION OF REBORN NATIONAL INDEPENDENCE.

THE ISRAELITES BEGIN THEIR STORY

IN THE BEGINNING...

בְּרֵאשִׁית

...GOD CREATED THE
HEAVENS AND THE EARTH.

THE FIRST 11 CHAPTERS OF THE HEBREW
BIBLE FOCUS GEOGRAPHICALLY ON
THE AREA THAT STRETCHES FROM
MESOPOTAMIA IN THE EAST TO
EGYPT IN THE WEST.

THIS AREA HAS BEEN CALLED
THE FERTILE CRESCENT,
BUT CONTAINS SOME
HARSH DESERT LAND-
SCAPES AS WELL.
EARLY CIVILIZATIONS
FLOURISH THERE.

TO THE EAST, THE SUMERIANS BUILD
FORTIFIED CITIES FROM MUD BRICK.
THEY FORGE BRONZE TOOLS AND
PRODUCE THE EARLIEST WRITTEN
LANGUAGE ON CLAY TABLETS.

TO THE WEST, THE EGYPTIANS ESTABLISH
A POWERFUL EMPIRE AND ADVANCE
THEIR UNDERSTANDING OF SCIENCES
LIKE MATHEMATICS AND ASTRONOMY.

LINKING EAST AND WEST IS CANAAN,
A LAND-BRIDGE BETWEEN THESE TWO
IMPRESSIVE CULTURES.

MESOPOTAMIA IS ALSO THE
WORLD OF ABRAHAM.

PROFESSOR, ALL THAT
WAS 4,000 YEARS AGO.
DOES STUDYING ANCIENT
HISTORY REALLY MAKE A
DIFFERENCE TO OUR
LIVES TODAY?

THAT'S A GREAT QUESTION. FOR
ONE THING, LEARNING HISTORY
MEANS PUTTING TODAY'S EVENTS
IN CONTEXT. OUR OWN LIVES IN
THE PRESENT CAN ONLY BE
UNDERSTOOD THROUGH THE PAST.

THINK OF WHAT IT WOULD MEAN
TO WRITE A PERSON'S BIOGRAPHY
WITHOUT COVERING HER EARLY
YEARS. THE STORY OF ISRAEL IS A
UNIQUE DRAMA CONCERNING A
PEOPLE AND ITS LAND.

BUT UNDERSTANDING THIS STORY
CAN TEACH US A LOT ABOUT THE
SITUATIONS WE OURSELVES FACE
AS INDIVIDUALS AND AS A NATION.

ABRAHAM, BORN ABRAM AND HIS FAMILY LIVE IN MESOPOTAMIA'S RICH CAPITAL CITY OF UR, PROBABLY NEAR THE YEAR 1800 B.C.E. (BEFORE THE COMMON ERA).

IT IS A PROSPEROUS LAND, BUT TERAH, ABRAM'S FATHER, MOVES THE FAMILY HUNDREDS OF MILES NORTHWEST TO HARAN. ON THEIR TRAVELS THEY PASS THE FAMOUS TOWER, OR ZIGGURAT OF UR, STILL STANDING TODAY IN SOUTHERN IRAQ.

FOR THE ISRAELITE VIEW OF THIS PERIOD WE TAKE OUR MATERIAL MAINLY FROM THE HEBREW BIBLE. IN GENESIS, CHAPTER 12, GOD TELLS ABRAM

GO OUT FROM YOUR LAND, AND FROM YOUR BIRTHPLACE, AND FROM YOUR FATHER'S HOUSE TO THE LAND THAT I WILL SHOW YOU.

SO ABRAM, HIS WIFE SARAI, AND THEIR NEPHEW LOT LEAVE HARAN AND BEGIN A JOURNEY THAT STILL SHAPES US TODAY.

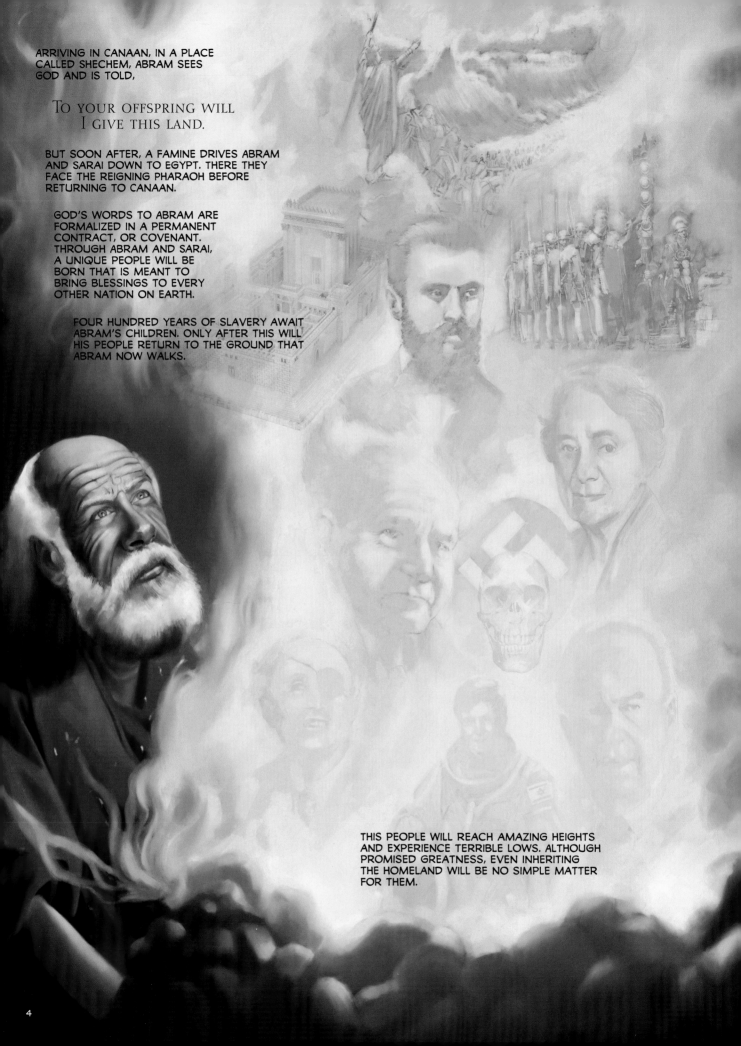

ARRIVING IN CANAAN, IN A PLACE
CALLED SHECHEM, ABRAM SEES
GOD AND IS TOLD,

TO YOUR OFFSPRING WILL
I GIVE THIS LAND.

BUT SOON AFTER, A FAMINE DRIVES ABRAM
AND SARAI DOWN TO EGYPT. THERE THEY
FACE THE REIGNING PHARAOH BEFORE
RETURNING TO CANAAN.

GOD'S WORDS TO ABRAM ARE
FORMALIZED IN A PERMANENT
CONTRACT, OR COVENANT.
THROUGH ABRAM AND SARAI,
A UNIQUE PEOPLE WILL BE
BORN THAT IS MEANT TO
BRING BLESSINGS TO EVERY
OTHER NATION ON EARTH.

FOUR HUNDRED YEARS OF SLAVERY AWAIT
ABRAM'S CHILDREN. ONLY AFTER THIS WILL
HIS PEOPLE RETURN TO THE GROUND THAT
ABRAM NOW WALKS.

THIS PEOPLE WILL REACH AMAZING HEIGHTS
AND EXPERIENCE TERRIBLE LOWS. ALTHOUGH
PROMISED GREATNESS, EVEN INHERITING
THE HOMELAND WILL BE NO SIMPLE MATTER
FOR THEM.

SINCE ABRAM AND SARAI HAVE NO CHILDREN, SARAI TAKES A BOLD STEP. SHE TELLS ABRAM TO TRY TO HAVE OFFSPRING WITH THEIR EGYPTIAN SERVANT, HAGAR. A SON IS BORN, BUT A SHARP RIFT FORMS BETWEEN THE TWO WOMEN AND HAGAR IS DRIVEN OUT.

IN THE DESERT, GOD TELLS HAGAR TO RETURN TO ABRAM'S HOME AND NAMES THE BOY ISHMAEL, MEANING "GOD HEARS."

ABRAM AND SARAI ARE AT ANOTHER TURNING POINT. GOD CHANGES THEIR NAMES TO ABRAHAM AND SARAH AND INSISTS THAT THE CHILD OF THE COVENANT COME FROM SARAH HERSELF, DESPITE HER AGE.

THE COUPLE'S LAUGHTER AT HEARING THIS NEWS GIVES THE BOY HIS NAME: ISAAC, MEANING, *HE WILL LAUGH.*

A YEAR LATER, SARAH GIVES BIRTH AT THE AGE OF NINETY.

AS ISAAC GROWS, FRICTION FLARES AGAIN BETWEEN SARAH AND HAGAR. SARAH WANTS THE TEENAGER AND HIS MOTHER BANISHED. GOD REASSURES ABRAHAM THAT FROM ISHMAEL WILL COME A GREAT NATION.

5

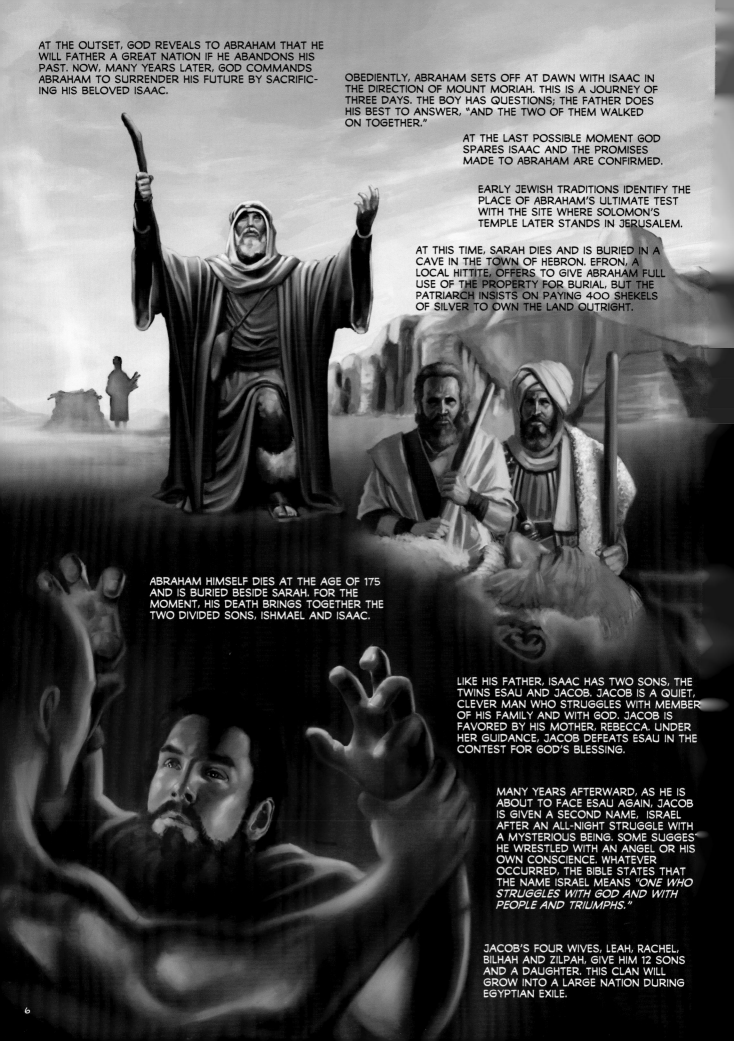

AT THE OUTSET, GOD REVEALS TO ABRAHAM THAT HE WILL FATHER A GREAT NATION IF HE ABANDONS HIS PAST. NOW, MANY YEARS LATER, GOD COMMANDS ABRAHAM TO SURRENDER HIS FUTURE BY SACRIFICING HIS BELOVED ISAAC.

OBEDIENTLY, ABRAHAM SETS OFF AT DAWN WITH ISAAC IN THE DIRECTION OF MOUNT MORIAH. THIS IS A JOURNEY OF THREE DAYS. THE BOY HAS QUESTIONS; THE FATHER DOES HIS BEST TO ANSWER, "AND THE TWO OF THEM WALKED ON TOGETHER."

AT THE LAST POSSIBLE MOMENT GOD SPARES ISAAC AND THE PROMISES MADE TO ABRAHAM ARE CONFIRMED.

EARLY JEWISH TRADITIONS IDENTIFY THE PLACE OF ABRAHAM'S ULTIMATE TEST WITH THE SITE WHERE SOLOMON'S TEMPLE LATER STANDS IN JERUSALEM.

AT THIS TIME, SARAH DIES AND IS BURIED IN A CAVE IN THE TOWN OF HEBRON. EFRON, A LOCAL HITTITE, OFFERS TO GIVE ABRAHAM FULL USE OF THE PROPERTY FOR BURIAL, BUT THE PATRIARCH INSISTS ON PAYING 400 SHEKELS OF SILVER TO OWN THE LAND OUTRIGHT.

ABRAHAM HIMSELF DIES AT THE AGE OF 175 AND IS BURIED BESIDE SARAH. FOR THE MOMENT, HIS DEATH BRINGS TOGETHER THE TWO DIVIDED SONS, ISHMAEL AND ISAAC.

LIKE HIS FATHER, ISAAC HAS TWO SONS, THE TWINS ESAU AND JACOB. JACOB IS A QUIET, CLEVER MAN WHO STRUGGLES WITH MEMBER OF HIS FAMILY AND WITH GOD. JACOB IS FAVORED BY HIS MOTHER, REBECCA. UNDER HER GUIDANCE, JACOB DEFEATS ESAU IN THE CONTEST FOR GOD'S BLESSING.

MANY YEARS AFTERWARD, AS HE IS ABOUT TO FACE ESAU AGAIN, JACOB IS GIVEN A SECOND NAME, ISRAEL AFTER AN ALL-NIGHT STRUGGLE WITH A MYSTERIOUS BEING. SOME SUGGEST HE WRESTLED WITH AN ANGEL OR HIS OWN CONSCIENCE. WHATEVER OCCURRED, THE BIBLE STATES THAT THE NAME ISRAEL MEANS *"ONE WHO STRUGGLES WITH GOD AND WITH PEOPLE AND TRIUMPHS."*

JACOB'S FOUR WIVES, LEAH, RACHEL, BILHAH AND ZILPAH, GIVE HIM 12 SONS AND A DAUGHTER. THIS CLAN WILL GROW INTO A LARGE NATION DURING EGYPTIAN EXILE.

REMEMBER, GOD HAD WARNED ABRAHAM THAT HIS OFFSPRING WOULD ENDURE HARSH SLAVERY IN A FOREIGN LAND. JACOB'S TALENTED SON, JOSEPH, BECOMES A POWERFUL OFFICIAL IN EGYPT AND THE HEBREWS JOIN HIM THERE TO ESCAPE FAMINE. AT THE END OF HIS LIFE, JOSEPH MAKES HIS FAMILY SWEAR TO BRING HIS BONES BACK TO THE LAND OF ISRAEL.

THE STORY OF ISRAELITE BONDAGE OPENS IN THE SHADOW OF DEATH AS THE NEW PHARAOH DECREES THAT ALL MALE NEWBORN BABIES BE DROWNED IN THE NILE. TWO MIDWIVES REFUSE TO COMPLY, AND ONE MOTHER SETS HER SON ADRIFT ON THE RIVER, HIS OLDER SISTER WATCHING FROM THE SHORE.

THE BASKET IS DISCOVERED BY PHARAOH'S DAUGHTER. SHE DECIDES TO RAISE THE BABY AS HER OWN. BUT MOSES IS NOT COMPLETELY SEPARATED FROM HIS BIRTH-FAMILY OR THE STORIES OF HIS PEOPLE, SINCE HIS MOTHER YOCHEVED IS HIRED TO NURSE AND CARE FOR HIM.

MOSES OWED HIS LIFE TO MANY WOMEN: YOCHEVED; MIDWIVES WHO REFUSED TO KILL CHILDREN; HIS SISTER MIRIAM; AND PHARAOH'S DAUGHTER. THE LIBERATION FROM EGYPT BEGINS WITH FEMALE COURAGE.

ONE DAY MOSES, NOW AN ADULT PRINCE, GOES OUT AND WITNESSES SLAVERY FIRST-HAND. HE SEES AN EGYPTIAN BEATING A HEBREW. THE BIBLE DOES NOT DISCUSS WHAT MOSES FEELS AT THIS MOMENT. IS HE TORN ABOUT HIS IDENTITY?

MOSES KILLS THE EGYPTIAN AND HIDES THE BODY IN SAND.

FOR THIS CHOICE, MOSES MUST FLEE EGYPT. HE MAKES HIS WAY ACROSS THE DESERT TO THE TERRITORY OF MIDIAN. HE MARRIES TZIPORAH AND WORKS AS A SHEPHERD FOR HIS FATHER-IN-LAW, JETHRO.

THERE IS A MOUNTAIN CALLED HOREV NEAR WHERE MOSES TENDS SHEEP. MOSES NOTICES WHAT MAY HAVE BEEN A COM-MON SIGHT IN THE DESERT: A BURNING THORN-BUSH. BUT, STRANGELY, THE BUSH DOES NOT BURN UP.

APPROACHING FOR A CLOSER VIEW, MOSES ENCOUNTERS THE PRESENCE OF GOD WITHIN THE FLAMES.

GOD'S MESSAGE HAS THREE PARTS:

I KNOW MY PEOPLE'S PAIN; I WILL BRING ISRAEL BACK TO THEIR LAND; AND YOU, MOSES, WILL LEAD THEM.

BUT TAKING ON THIS HUGE TASK DOES NOT COME NATURALLY TO MOSES. HE RESISTS, HE FINDS EXCUSES. SO GOD PLEDGES TO BE WITH HIM AND TO SEND ALONG HIS OLDER BROTHER, AARON.

MOSES CONFRONTS PHARAOH WITH GOD'S DEMAND: RELEASE MY PEOPLE SO THEY MAY SERVE ME. BUT PHARAOH REJECTS THE AUTHORITY OF THE GOD WHO TOLD MOSES,

"I Will Be Who I Will Be."

SO TEN DEVASTATING PLAGUES COME UPON THE EGYPTIANS, WHILE IN THE GOSHEN DISTRICT THE ISRAELITES REMAIN UNHARMED.

THE RELENTLESS ASSAULT ON EGYPT ALSO SERVES AS A REFUTATION OF THE GODS WORSHIPED THERE. FOR EXAMPLE, THE GOD OF THE HEBREWS BLOTS OUT THE SUN, WHICH IS WORSHIPPED BY THE EGYPTIANS, IN A THREE-DAY ONSLAUGHT OF DARKNESS. POWERFUL SOURCES OF LIGHT ARE SHOWN TO BE NOTHING BEFORE THE WILL OF THE CREATOR.

IN THE FINAL PLAGUE, GOD TAKES THE LIFE OF EGYPT'S FIRSTBORN, AS YEARS BEFORE, PHARAOH PUT TO DEATH ISRAEL'S INFANTS. AT LAST, LITERALLY AMID THE DEAD OF NIGHT, PHARAOH SETS THE ISRAELITES FREE.

IN THE MORNING, MOSES LEADS HIS NATION PROUDLY OUT OF BONDAGE. WITH JOSEPH'S BONES GATHERED UP, THEY HEAD TOWARD THE WILDERNESS.

A FEW DAYS LATER, GOD HAS THEM MAKE CAMP WITH THEIR BACKS TO THE RED SEA (BASED ON THE HEBREW, REALLY THE REED SEA). THIS GETS EGYPT THINKING THAT ISRAEL IS HELPLESS AFTER ALL. PHARAOH AND THOUSANDS OF HIS BEST WARRIORS GIVE CHASE.

GOD DIVIDES THE SEA. THE ISRAELITES CROSS SAFELY ON DRY GROUND, BUT WHEN THE EGYPTIANS TRY TO PURSUE, WATER CRASHES DOWN AND DROWNS PHARAOH'S MEN.

BEFORE WE CONTINUE, LET ME DESCRIBE ONE METHOD JEWS HAVE USED TO READ THE BIBLE, KNOWN AS *MIDRASH.* TRADITIONAL JEWISH SCHOLARS FELT THAT A HOLY TEXT COULD HAVE DIFFERENT INTERPRETATIONS.

FOR EXAMPLE, ONE OPINION CLAIMS THAT MOSES TELLS THE ISRAELITES TO MOVE INTO THE WATER BEFORE THE SEA PARTED. BUT NO ONE MOVED.

FINALLY, NACHSHON, LEADER OF THE TRIBE OF JUDAH, PLUNGES AHEAD. HE ENTERS AS FAR AS HIS WAIST HIS CHEST HIS NECK. ONLY WHEN THE WATER IS ABOUT TO OVERTAKE HIM DOES THE SEA SPLIT.

ANOTHER *MIDRASH* SUGGESTS THAT THE TRIBES OF ISRAEL STRUGGLE WITH EACH OTHER IN THEIR RUSH TO BE FIRST INTO THE SEA.

PROFESSOR, THOSE ARE NICE STORIES, BUT ACCORDING TO JEWISH TRADITION, WHAT REALLY HAPPENED?

WELL, FOR NOW LET'S SAY THAT MIDRASH SEEMS MAINLY INTERESTED IN DISCUSSING THE MEANING OF EVENTS. FOR EXAMPLE, THE STORY ABOUT NACHSHON TEACHES THAT ONE PERSON'S COURAGE AND INITIATIVE CAN MAKE ALL THE DIFFERENCE.

MOSES AND THE PEOPLE CONTINUE THEIR WILDERNESS TREK, BUT OTHER PROBLEMS AWAIT. THE GREAT VICTORY OVER EGYPT DOES NOT PREVENT A DESERT TRIBE CALLED AMALEK FROM ATTACKING THE WEAKEST PARTS OF ISRAEL'S CAMP. THIS UNPROVOKED MALICE CAUSES AMALEK TO BE BRANDED THE ETERNAL ADVERSARY OF ISRAEL.

ALMOST TWO MONTHS LATER, ISRAEL ARRIVES IN THE SINAI DESERT, THE SAME DESERT WHERE MOSES CARED FOR SHEEP.

"NOW MOUNT SINAI WAS ALL IN SMOKE BECAUSE THE LORD HAD COME DOWN UPON IT IN FIRE."

SO BEGINS THE ISRAELITES' FACE-TO-FACE NATIONAL COVENANT WITH GOD. HERE THEY LEARN PRINCIPLES TO GUIDE THEIR LIVES FOREVER. THE TEXT RECORDING DIVINE REVELATION WOULD BE CALLED THE TORAH, THE TEACHING.

LET ME GIVE YOU ANOTHER SAMPLE OF TWO DIFFERENT MIDRASH READINGS. ONE SAYS THAT GOD RAISES UP MOUNT SINAI AND THREATENS TO BURY ISRAEL UNDER IT UNLESS THEY ACCEPT THE TORAH.

ANOTHER OPINION TEACHES THAT ISRAEL COMMITS TO KEEPING THE TORAH EVEN BEFORE HEARING WHAT IT CONTAINS: WE SHALL DO AND WE SHALL HEAR, THE ISRAELITES SAY. GOD THEN SENDS ANGELS TO PLACE CROWNS OF GLORY ON THEIR HEADS AS A REWARD FOR FAITH.

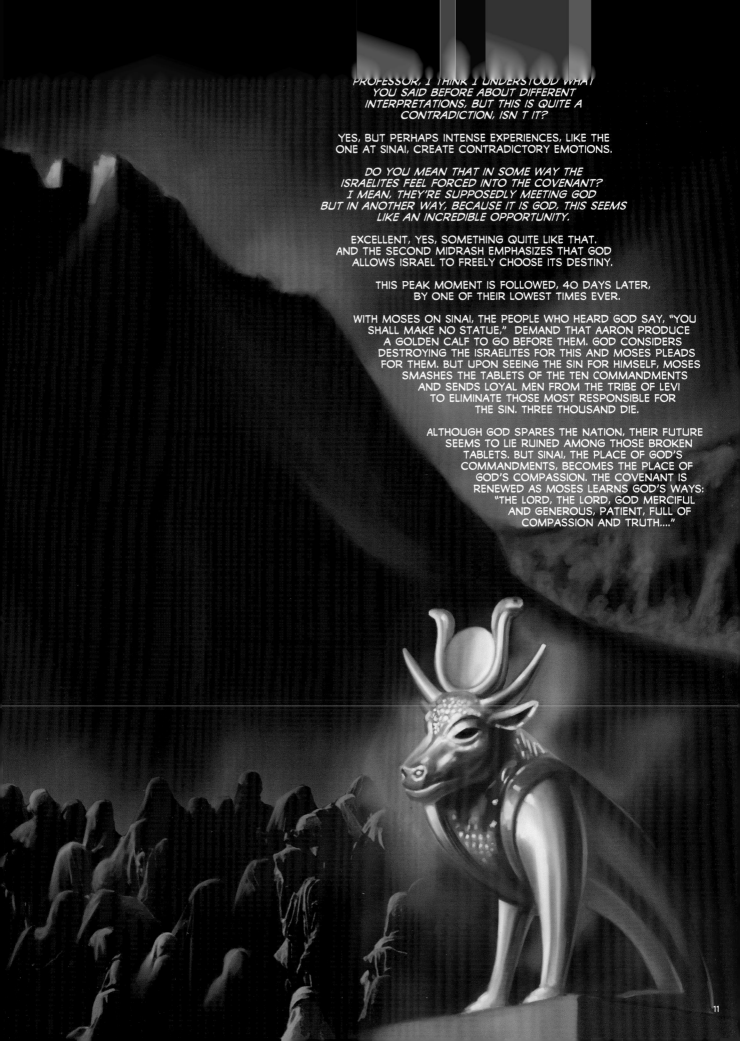

PROFESSOR, I THINK I UNDERSTOOD WHAT
YOU SAID BEFORE ABOUT DIFFERENT
INTERPRETATIONS, BUT THIS IS QUITE A
CONTRADICTION, ISN'T IT?

YES, BUT PERHAPS INTENSE EXPERIENCES, LIKE THE
ONE AT SINAI, CREATE CONTRADICTORY EMOTIONS.

DO YOU MEAN THAT IN SOME WAY THE
ISRAELITES FEEL FORCED INTO THE COVENANT?
I MEAN, THEY'RE SUPPOSEDLY MEETING GOD
BUT IN ANOTHER WAY, BECAUSE IT IS GOD, THIS SEEMS
LIKE AN INCREDIBLE OPPORTUNITY.

EXCELLENT, YES, SOMETHING QUITE LIKE THAT.
AND THE SECOND MIDRASH EMPHASIZES THAT GOD
ALLOWS ISRAEL TO FREELY CHOOSE ITS DESTINY.

THIS PEAK MOMENT IS FOLLOWED, 40 DAYS LATER,
BY ONE OF THEIR LOWEST TIMES EVER.

WITH MOSES ON SINAI, THE PEOPLE WHO HEARD GOD SAY, "YOU
SHALL MAKE NO STATUE," DEMAND THAT AARON PRODUCE
A GOLDEN CALF TO GO BEFORE THEM. GOD CONSIDERS
DESTROYING THE ISRAELITES FOR THIS AND MOSES PLEADS
FOR THEM. BUT UPON SEEING THE SIN FOR HIMSELF, MOSES
SMASHES THE TABLETS OF THE TEN COMMANDMENTS
AND SENDS LOYAL MEN FROM THE TRIBE OF LEVI
TO ELIMINATE THOSE MOST RESPONSIBLE FOR
THE SIN. THREE THOUSAND DIE.

ALTHOUGH GOD SPARES THE NATION, THEIR FUTURE
SEEMS TO LIE RUINED AMONG THOSE BROKEN
TABLETS. BUT SINAI, THE PLACE OF GOD'S
COMMANDMENTS, BECOMES THE PLACE OF
GOD'S COMPASSION. THE COVENANT IS
RENEWED AS MOSES LEARNS GOD'S WAYS:
"THE LORD, THE LORD, GOD MERCIFUL
AND GENEROUS, PATIENT, FULL OF
COMPASSION AND TRUTH...."

A YEAR PASSES AND THE ISRAELITES APPROACH THE BORDERS OF CANAAN. GOD DIRECTS MOSES TO SEND TWELVE SCOUTS, ONE FROM EACH TRIBE, TO REPORT ON WHAT THEY WILL FACE WHEN FIGHTING FOR THE LAND.

THE MEN MAKE THEIR WAY TO HEBRON. THE PATRIARCHS AND MATRIARCHS OF ISRAEL WERE BURIED THERE, EXCEPT RACHEL, JACOB'S WIFE, WHO WAS BURIED ON THE ROAD TO BETHLEHEM.

THE SCOUTS REACH A RIVER BASIN RICH IN NATIVE FRUITS. TO SHOW THEIR BRETHREN THE LAND'S BOUNTY, THE MEN CUT OFF A SINGLE CLUSTER OF GRAPES SO LARGE THAT TWO ARE NEEDED TO CARRY IT.

AFTER FORTY DAYS, THE SCOUTS RETURN. THEIR MAJORITY REPORT IS MIXED. THEY HOLD UP THE HUGE FRUIT, BUT SEEM MORE WORRIED ABOUT THE SIZE OF THE INHABITANTS. THEY SPEAK OF GIANTS LIVING THERE, OF FEELING LIKE INSECTS BY COMPARISON. THE PEOPLE ARE GRIPPED BY ANXIETY.

BUT TWO SCOUTS SEE THINGS DIFFERENTLY: "WE CAN DEFINITELY TAKE THIS LAND!" CALEB SAYS. "DO NOT FEAR THE INHABITANTS," JOSHUA INSISTS. "WE'LL TEAR THROUGH THEM LIKE A MAN TEARS THROUGH BREAD."

GRUESOME DEATH AT THE HANDS OF ENORMOUS ENEMIES, THEY DOUBT EVERYTHING, INCLUDING THEIR FREEDOM FROM SLAVERY.

THIS FAILURE TO TRUST GOD MIGHT HAVE BEEN THE END OF THE STORY. BUT AGAIN GOD FORGIVES. NEVERTHELESS, THERE ARE GRAVE CONSEQUENCES FOR THE ISRAELITES; THEY WILL WANDER ONE YEAR FOR EVERY DAY OF THE SCOUTS' MISSION. EXCEPT FOR THE HOUSEHOLDS OF CALEB AND JOSHUA, EVERY-ONE AGE 20 AND OVER DIES IN THE DESERT.

SO THE JOURNEY RESUMES. WITH CLOUD AND FIRE GOD LEADS ISRAEL, AND NOURISHES THEM WITH A SWEET SUBSTANCE CALLED "MANNA." BY DIRECTLY CARING FOR ISRAEL IN THIS WAY, GOD TEACHES THEM TO RELY ON HIS POWER.

A MIDRASH SUGGESTS THAT FRESH WELL-WATER FOLLOWED THE ISRAELITES THROUGH THE WILDERNESS. THIS WELL WAS LINKED TO THE SPIRITUAL POWER OF MOSES' SISTER, MIRIAM, WHO HAD A LIFE-LONG CONNECTION WITH WATER MIRACLES. IT WAS MIRIAM WHO GUARDED MOSES ON THE NILE AND LED THE WOMEN IN CELEBRATION AT THE REED SEA.

ISRAEL ENCOUNTERS MANY OTHER CHALLENGES ALONG THE ROUTE, BOTH PHYSICAL AND SPIRITUAL. BUT FINALLY THE LAND COMES AGAIN INTO VIEW.

MOSES IS NOT PERMITTED TO ENTER. THE REASON WHY IS SOMEWHAT HIDDEN, LIKE MOSES' OWN SITE OF BURIAL, A BURIAL PERFORMED BY GOD ALONE.

FROM ATOP MOUNT NEBO, GOD SHOWS MOSES WHAT HE MAY NOT TOUCH.

"THIS IS THE LAND I SWORE TO ABRAHAM, ISAAC, AND JACOB."

WE CAN ONLY IMAGINE WHAT MOSES REALLY SEES IN HIS LAST MOMENTS.

13

THE PEOPLE CROSS INTO THE LAND UNDER THE NEW LEADERSHIP OF JOSHUA. AHEAD OF THEM, INSIDE A SMALL ARK, THEY CARRY THE TABLETS OF GOD'S COVENANT.

BUT, PROFESSOR, THERE WERE PEOPLE ALREADY LIVING IN THE LAND. HOW DID THE ISRAELITES JUSTIFY TAKING IT FROM THE INHABITANTS?

THE BIBLE PORTRAYS THIS AS A RETURN, NOT A FOREIGN INVASION. THE WARS WITH THE CANAANITE TRIBES, WHO ARE NOW LOST TO HISTORY, ARE SEEN AS GOD'S WAY OF RESTORING THE LAND TO ITS PROPER OWNERS.

THERE IS ALSO A BIBLICAL CONCEPT THAT THE LAND CANNOT TOLERATE ETHICAL AND SPIRITUAL IMPURITY AND WILL "SPIT OUT" THOSE WHO SIN THERE. THE CANAANITES WERE SAID TO ENGAGE IN IDOLATRY AND CHILD SACRIFICE. NOTE THAT THE BIBLE DESCRIBES THE ISRAELITES THEMSELVES BEING PUNISHED WITH EXILE LATER FOR SPIRITUALLY DEFILING THE LAND.

FROM A MORE SECULAR VIEWPOINT, YOU MIGHT SAY THE ISRAELITES TOOK THEIR LAND THE WAY MOST NATIONS DID, INCLUDING THE UNITED STATES: THROUGH WARFARE AND CONQUEST.

WHAT DO YOU MEAN THE CANAANITES WERE "LOST TO HISTORY"? WERE THEY WIPED OUT FIGHTING ISRAEL?

THE BIBLE IS NOT CLEAR ABOUT THIS. IT'S HARD TO KNOW HOW MANY OF THE CANAANITES WERE DESTROYED OR EVEN CONQUERED. FOR EXAMPLE, THE BOOK OF JUDGES INDICATES THAT CANAANITES CONTINUE TO DWELL IN THE LAND LONG AFTER THE ISRAELITES ARRIVE.

IN FACT, A SERIES OF ISRAELITE CHIEFTAINS BATTLE WITH SURROUNDING CANAANITE ENEMIES FOR MANY DECADES. ONE OF THE BEST OF THESE LEADERS IS A WOMAN NAMED DEBORAH.

FOR MORE THAN 200 YEARS, THE TWELVE TRIBES LIVE IN LOOSE ASSOCIATION WITH ONE ANOTHER. SAUL BECOMES ISRAEL'S FIRST KING AND BEGINS UNIFYING SEPARATE TRIBES INTO A NATION.

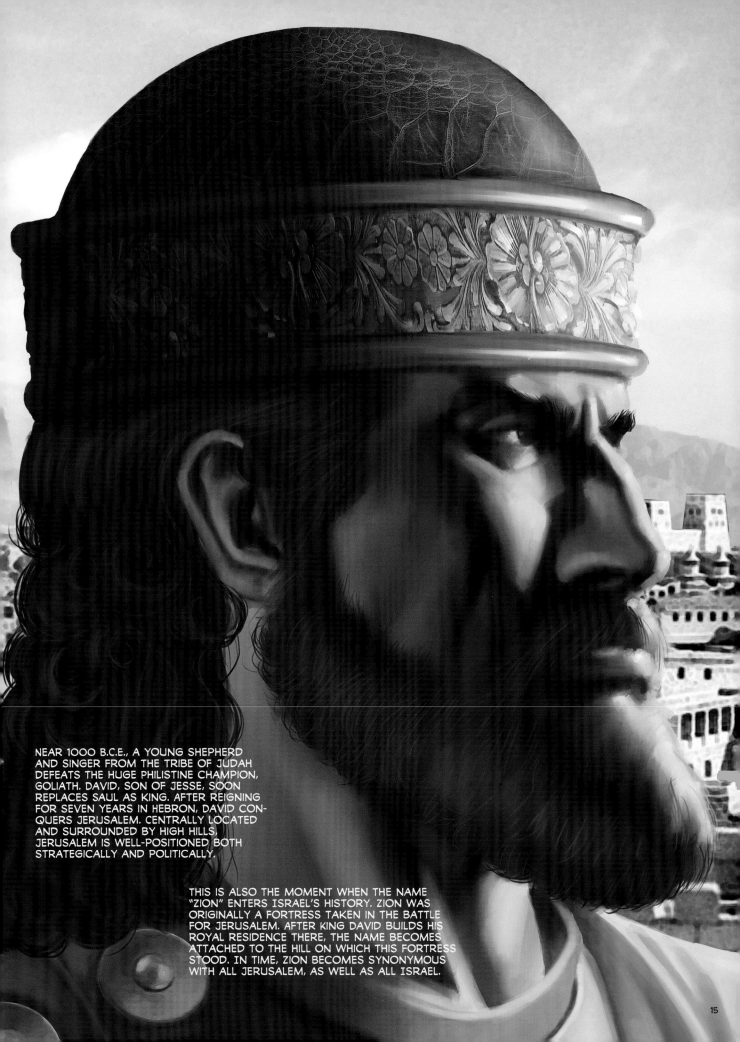

NEAR 1000 B.C.E., A YOUNG SHEPHERD AND SINGER FROM THE TRIBE OF JUDAH DEFEATS THE HUGE PHILISTINE CHAMPION, GOLIATH. DAVID, SON OF JESSE, SOON REPLACES SAUL AS KING. AFTER REIGNING FOR SEVEN YEARS IN HEBRON, DAVID CONQUERS JERUSALEM. CENTRALLY LOCATED AND SURROUNDED BY HIGH HILLS, JERUSALEM IS WELL-POSITIONED BOTH STRATEGICALLY AND POLITICALLY.

THIS IS ALSO THE MOMENT WHEN THE NAME "ZION" ENTERS ISRAEL'S HISTORY. ZION WAS ORIGINALLY A FORTRESS TAKEN IN THE BATTLE FOR JERUSALEM. AFTER KING DAVID BUILDS HIS ROYAL RESIDENCE THERE, THE NAME BECOMES ATTACHED TO THE HILL ON WHICH THIS FORTRESS STOOD. IN TIME, ZION BECOMES SYNONYMOUS WITH ALL JERUSALEM, AS WELL AS ALL ISRAEL.

DAVID ENJOYS AMAZING FAVOR WITH GOD AND PEOPLE. GOD PROMISES THAT ALL KINGS OF ISRAEL WILL COME FROM HIS DESCENDANTS. BUT DAVID SPENDS HIS LIFE AT WAR AND HAS A TERRIBLE MORAL LAPSE WITH THE BEAUTIFUL BATHSHEBA. BECAUSE HIS HANDS HAVE SPILLED MUCH BLOOD IN WARFARE, DAVID IS NOT ALLOWED TO GIVE GOD'S ARK A PERMANENT HOME IN JERUSALEM.

INSTEAD HIS SON, THE WISE AND WORLDLY SOLOMON, BUILDS THE TEMPLE.

THE JERUSALEM TEMPLE BECOMES A NATIONAL CENTER FOR THE ISRAELITES, AND PROPHETS OF ISRAEL SEE IT AS A PLACE OF WORLD UNITY. ISAIAH PREDICTS THAT, "ALL THE NATIONS SHALL STREAM TOWARD IT...NATION SHALL NOT TAKE UP SWORD AGAINST NATION; THEY SHALL NEVER AGAIN KNOW WAR."

THE TEMPLE ALSO REPRESENTS THE CHALLENGE TO LIVE RIGHTEOUSLY. THE PROPHET JEREMIAH TEACHES THAT LIFE IN THE LAND DEPENDS ON GOOD CON-DUCT, NOT BEAUTIFUL BUILDINGS, EVEN THE HOUSE OF GOD:

"THUS SAID THE LORD OF HOSTS, THE GOD OF ISRAEL: IMPROVE YOUR WAYS AND YOUR DEEDS, AND I WILL LET YOU DWELL IN THIS PLACE... EXECUTE JUSTICE BETWEEN A MAN AND HIS FELLOW. DO NOT OPPRESS A STRANGER, ORPHAN, OR WIDOW."

AFTER SOLOMON'S DEATH, HIS SON REHOBOAM SUCCEEDS HIM AS KING. BUT A FORMER OFFICER IN SOLOMON'S WORKFORCE NAMED JEROBOAM BECOMES LEADER AMONG THE NORTHERN TRIBES.

WHEN REHOBOAM REFUSES TO EASE THE ECONOMIC BURDENS IMPOSED ON THE NATION BY HIS FATHER, THE NORTHERN TRIBES REBEL AND THE KINGDOM SPLITS IN TWO: ISRAEL IN THE NORTH, JUDAH (JUDEA) IN THE SOUTH.

FOR GENERATIONS, STRIFE EXISTS BETWEEN THE KINGDOMS. SOMETIMES THERE IS ALL-OUT WARFARE AND AT OTHER TIMES THEY COOPERATE AGAINST COMMON ENEMIES. IN THIS PERIOD, PROPHETS LIKE ELIJAH, AMOS, AND HOSEA DEMAND FAITHFULNESS TO GOD'S WAYS AND PROMISE DIRE CONSEQUENCES FOR SIN.

IN THE EIGHTH CENTURY B.C.E., THE NORTHERN KINGDOM OF ISRAEL EXPERIENCES GREAT SOCIAL DISTRESS. WITHIN 50 YEARS, THE CROWN CHANGES HANDS FIVE TIMES, SOMETIMES BY ASSASSINATION. THE NEEDS OF THE POOR ARE IGNORED. IDOLATRY IS RAMPANT. ISRAEL REBELS AGAINST THE DOMINANT NATION OF THE AGE, ASSYRIA. JUDEA REFUSES TO JOIN THE REBELLION.

IN 722 B.C.E., THE KINGDOM OF ISRAEL IS OVERRUN BY ASSYRIA'S SARGON II. THE NORTHERN TRIBES ARE DEVASTATED. THOUSANDS OF THEIR LEADING CITIZENS ARE EXPELLED AND FOREIGNERS ARE IMPORTED TO REPLACE THEM. A HUGE PORTION OF JACOB'S DESCENDANTS (TEN TRIBES) ARE LOST THROUGH DISPERSION AND ASSIMILATION.

JUDEA LIVES ON, NAMED FOR ITS LARGEST TRIBE. IN FACT, THE WORD "JEW" (*YEHUDI*) COMES FROM JUDAH AND THE JEWISH PEOPLE TODAY TRACE THEMSELVES BACK TO THIS PART OF THE ISRAELITE NATION.

BY THE YEAR 600 B.C.E., BABYLON OVERTAKES ASSYRIA AS THE REGION'S STRONGEST POWER. JUDEA SIDES WITH EGYPT AGAINST NEBUCHADNEZZAR OF BABYLON. IN 586 B.C.E. THIS REVOLT LEAVES JERUSALEM RAVAGED, THE HOLY TEMPLE IN FLAMES, AND MUCH OF THE POPULATION EXILED EAST.

DURING THE SIEGE OF JERUSALEM, WHILE EVERYTHING GOES TO RUIN, THE PROPHET JEREMIAH ANNOUNCES THAT, "YET AGAIN WILL BE HEARD IN THIS PLACE...THE SOUND OF GLADNESS AND THE SOUND OF JOY, THE SOUND OF GROOM AND THE SOUND OF BRIDE...."

ONE EMPIRE FOLLOWS ANOTHER. NOW THE BABYLONIANS ARE CONQUERED BY THE PERSIANS. ABOUT 50 YEARS AFTER THE FALL OF JERUSALEM, KING CYRUS OF PERSIA ALLOWS THE JEWS TO RETURN, OPENING THE WAY FOR RENEWAL IN ZION.

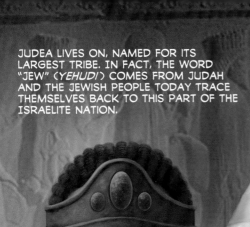

ASSYRIAN EMPIRE

BABYLONIAN EMPIRE

PERSIAN EMPIRE

ABOUT 50,000 JEWS MAKE THE LONG JOURNEY BACK TO THE LAND, BUT MANY DO NOT GO. BABYLON BECOMES A JEWISH "DIASPORA" –A COMMUNITY LIVING IN EXILE.

THOSE RETURNING, TOGETHER WITH THOSE WHO REMAINED IN JUDEA, REBUILD THE TEMPLE. THE BIBLICAL NARRATIVE FINISHES AROUND 450 B.C.E. WHEN TWO SPIRITUAL LEADERS, EZRA AND NEHEMIAH, CONVENE A MASSIVE ASSEMBLY IN JERUSALEM AND THE PEOPLE REDEDICATE THEMSELVES TO THE SINAI COVENANT.

ALEXANDER THE GREAT (356-323 B.C.E.)

- Brilliant military strategist.
- King of Macedonia and Greece at 20; dies at 32.
- Defeats Persians, establishes huge empire from Egypt to India.
- Allows Jews significant religious autonomy.

FOLLOWING ALEXANDER'S EARLY DEATH, HIS GENERALS DIVIDE UP THE EMPIRE. THE MOST IMPORTANT OF HIS SUCCESSORS ARE THE PTOLEMIES IN EGYPT AND THE SELEUCIDS IN MESOPOTAMIA. AT FIRST, THE PTOLEMIES RULE THE CONTINENTAL LAND-BRIDGE IN WHICH JUDEA IS FOUND.

THE GREEK EMPIRE BRINGS HELLENIZATION TO THE ANCIENT WORLD AS NATIONS BEGIN TO LEARN GREEK CUSTOMS, ART, AND THOUGHT. AT THIS TIME, THE GREEKS BECOME AWARE OF THE JEWISH BIBLE, THE TORAH. ACCORDING TO THE TRADITIONAL STORY, NEAR 250 B.C.E. THE PTOLEMAIC KING WANTS A TRANSLATION OF THE HEBREW SCRIPTURES FOR HIS LIBRARY IN ALEXANDRIA, EGYPT. SOME SEVENTY JEWISH SAGES ARE SUMMONED TO BEGIN THIS WORK, KNOWN LATER AS THE SEPTUAGINT (THE SEVENTY).

THIS GREEK TRANSLATION BECOMES A CRUCIAL VEHICLE FOR TRANSMITTING BIBLICAL IDEAS TO THE NON-JEWISH WORLD.

AROUND 200 B.C.E., THE SELEUCID KINGDOM IN THE NORTH GAINS CONTROL OF JUDEA. INITIALLY, THEIR RULE WAS FAIRLY COMFORTABLE FOR THE JEWS: TAXES ARE LOWERED AND TORAH IS RESPECTED AS THE LAW FOR JEWS. HOWEVER, THIS QUIET SOON GIVES WAY TO SELEUCID PERSECUTION AND JEWISH RESISTANCE.

IN 175 B.C.E., ANTIOCHUS IV ASSUMES THE SELEUCID THRONE. HE PLUNDERS THE JERUSALEM TEMPLE FOR ITS WEALTH AND INSTALLS GREEK-SYMPATHIZERS FROM AMONG THE JEWS TO GOVERN JUDEA.

DESPITE THE PROBLEMS, MANY JEWS WELCOME GREEK SCIENCE AND CULTURE, ALTHOUGH JEWS LOYAL TO THEIR TRADITIONS VIGOROUSLY OPPOSE THESE OUTSIDE INFLUENCES.

THE SITUATION REACHES A HEAD AROUND 167 B.C.E. AS A SHOW OF POWER, ANTIOCHUS FORBIDS MAJOR PRACTICES OF JEWISH RELIGION LIKE KEEPING THE SABBATH AND PERFORMING CIRCUMCISION. HE ALSO DEDICATES THE JERUSALEM TEMPLE TO ZEUS.

NORTHWEST OF JERUSALEM IN THE TOWN OF MODI'IN, ANTIOCHUS' SOLDIERS TRY TO FORCE A LEADING ELDER, THE PRIEST MATITYAHU, TO SACRIFICE A PIG AT ONE OF THE NEW PAGAN ALTARS. MATITYAHU REFUSES, AND WHEN ANOTHER JEW COMPLIES, MATITYAHU SLAYS HIM ALONG WITH A GREEK OFFICER.

THIS SPARKS A THREE-YEAR REBELLION AGAINST THE SELEUCIDS AND THEIR JEWISH ALLIES. TWO KINDS OF WAR ARE NOW AT HAND: FOREIGN AND CIVIL. AMONG THE JEWS, THOSE COMMITTED TO THE ANCIENT COVENANT BATTLE THOSE WHO BELIEVE OLD WAYS SHOULD MAKE ROOM FOR THE NEW. MATITYAHU AND HIS SONS, THE MACCABEES, LEAD THE TRADITIONALISTS.

A YEAR LATER MATITYAHU DIES AND JUDAH ASSUMES COMMAND OF THE REBELLION.

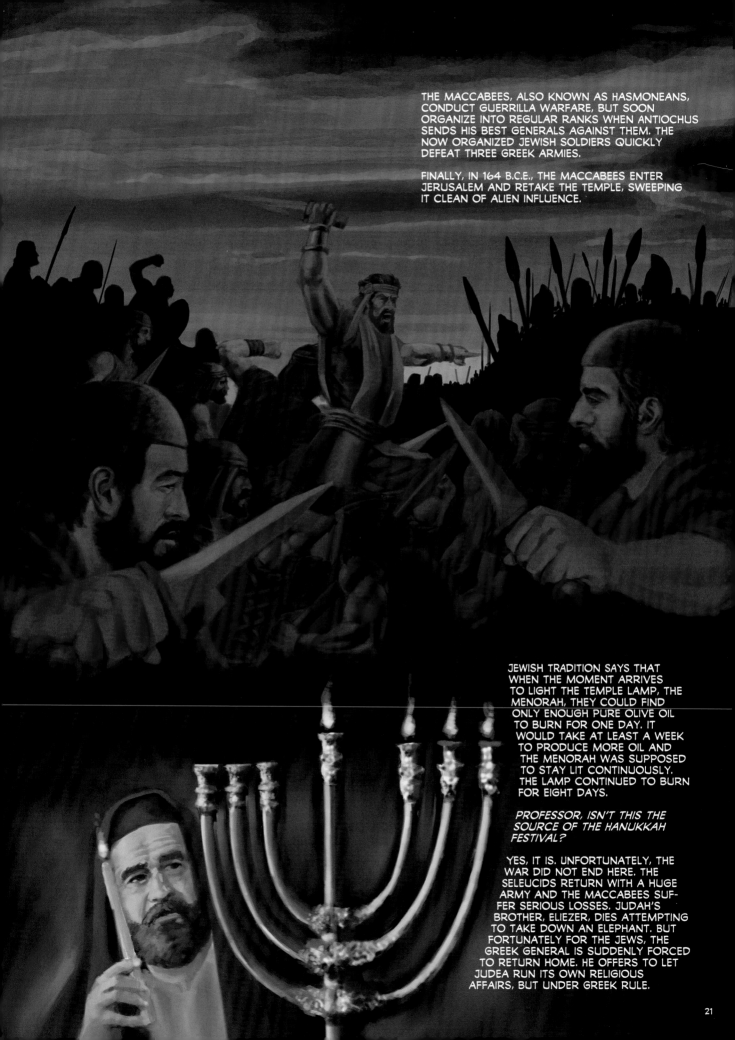

THE MACCABEES, ALSO KNOWN AS HASMONEANS, CONDUCT GUERRILLA WARFARE, BUT SOON ORGANIZE INTO REGULAR RANKS WHEN ANTIOCHUS SENDS HIS BEST GENERALS AGAINST THEM. THE NOW ORGANIZED JEWISH SOLDIERS QUICKLY DEFEAT THREE GREEK ARMIES.

FINALLY, IN 164 B.C.E., THE MACCABEES ENTER JERUSALEM AND RETAKE THE TEMPLE, SWEEPING IT CLEAN OF ALIEN INFLUENCE.

JEWISH TRADITION SAYS THAT WHEN THE MOMENT ARRIVES TO LIGHT THE TEMPLE LAMP, THE MENORAH, THEY COULD FIND ONLY ENOUGH PURE OLIVE OIL TO BURN FOR ONE DAY. IT WOULD TAKE AT LEAST A WEEK TO PRODUCE MORE OIL AND THE MENORAH WAS SUPPOSED TO STAY LIT CONTINUOUSLY. THE LAMP CONTINUED TO BURN FOR EIGHT DAYS.

PROFESSOR, ISN'T THIS THE SOURCE OF THE HANUKKAH FESTIVAL?

YES, IT IS. UNFORTUNATELY, THE WAR DID NOT END HERE. THE SELEUCIDS RETURN WITH A HUGE ARMY AND THE MACCABEES SUFFER SERIOUS LOSSES. JUDAH'S BROTHER, ELIEZER, DIES ATTEMPTING TO TAKE DOWN AN ELEPHANT. BUT FORTUNATELY FOR THE JEWS, THE GREEK GENERAL IS SUDDENLY FORCED TO RETURN HOME. HE OFFERS TO LET JUDEA RUN ITS OWN RELIGIOUS AFFAIRS, BUT UNDER GREEK RULE.

DESCENDANTS OF THE MACCABEES LEAD THE NATION FOR A CENTURY. DURING THIS PERIOD THE COUNTRY'S BORDERS EXPAND INTO AREAS ORIGINALLY HELD BY BIBLICAL ISRAEL. BUT IN A BITTER IRONY, THE HASMONEANS COME TO RESEMBLE GREEK KINGS IN CUSTOMS AND ETHICS. CORRUPTION IS RAMPANT.

JEWISH RELIGIOUS LEADERSHIP DIVIDES INTO THREE MAIN GROUPS: (1) SADDUCEES WHO ARE LARGELY PRIESTS AND ARISTOCRATS; (2) ESSENES WHO CREATE ASCETIC COMMUNITIES LIKE AT QUMRAN, NEAR THE DEAD SEA; AND (3) PHARISEES, THE EARLY RABBINIC SCHOLARS WHO BUILD THE FOUNDATIONS OF POST-BIBLICAL JUDAISM.

THE POPULAR PHARISEES CLASHED WITH THE HASOMEANS, BUT AROUND 80 B.C.E., KING ALEXANDER YANNAI TAKES SHLOMTZION (PEACE OF ZION) AS HIS QUEEN. SHE IS THE SISTER OF A LEADING PHARISEE AND THIS UNION BRINGS TEMPORARY CALM BETWEEN THE TWO SIDES.

WE HAVEN'T HEARD MUCH ABOUT WOMEN LEADERS IN JEWISH HISTORY.

THAT'S TRUE. HOWEVER, IN THIS CASE, BEFORE THE KING DIES IN 76 B.C.E., HE APPOINTS SHLOMTZION TO SUCCEED HIM AS THE FIRST FEMALE RULER OF THE JEWISH PEOPLE. SHE PROVES AN OUTSTANDING POLITICAL EXECUTIVE, AT HOME AND ABROAD.

UPON HER PASSING, SHLOMTZION'S SONS STRUGGLE VIOLENTLY FOR CONTROL OF THE NATION, BUT THIS INTERNAL STRIFE ENDS WHEN A NEW PRESENCE ARRIVES ON THE WORLD SCENE: ROME. IN 63 B.C.E., GENERAL POMPEY SWEEPS THROUGH THE NEAR EAST AND TAKES JERUSALEM FOR ROME. LATER, JULIUS CAESAR RESTORES SOME JEWISH LAND, BUT JUDEA IS A VASSAL STATE.

22

AS ROME TIGHTENS ITS GRIP, ANTIPATER, A DESCENDANT OF EDOMITES WHO CONVERTED TO JUDAISM, IS APPOINTED TO OVERSEE JUDEA. AND IN 40 B.C.E., ROME DECLARES HIS SON, HEROD, "KING OF JUDEA." HEROD IS A BUILDER. DURING HIS 33 YEAR REIGN, HE FOUNDS MANY CITIES AND ESTABLISHES A LINE OF DESERT FORTRESSES, INCLUDING MASADA. HIS MOST IMPRESSIVE ACHIEVEMENT IS GREATLY ENHANCING THE SECOND TEMPLE.

HOWEVER, HEROD IS ALSO A PARANOID TYRANT, MURDERING MANY IN HIS OWN FAMILY. ONE OF HIS SURVIVING SONS, HEROD ANTIPAS, LATER BECOMES GOVERNOR OF THE GALILEE REGION AND ENCOUNTERS THERE A CHARISMATIC, UNSETTLING FIGURE, JESUS.

JESUS EMERGES FROM AMONG THE JEWISH PEOPLE, A MAN WHO, LIKE HIS RABBINIC CONTEMPORARIES, TEACHES ABOUT LOVING GOD AND OTHER PEOPLE:

A gentile came before Hillel and said, "Convert me on the condition that you teach me the entire Torah while I stand on one foot." He converted him; then Hillel said: "What is hateful to you do not do to your fellow. This is the entire Torah, the rest is its explanation. Go and study."
-Talmud Shabbat 31A

DURING HIS JOURNEYS THROUGH THE LAND OF ISRAEL, HE PLANTS SEEDS OF FAITH, BRINGING MANY TO THE GOD OF ABRAHAM. HIS TEACHINGS SET THE STAGE FOR THE EMERGENCE OF A NEW RELIGION, CHRISTIANITY:

"Teacher, which is the greatest commandment in the Law?" Jesus replied: "Love the Lord your God with all your heart and with all your soul and with all your mind. This is the first and greatest commandment. And the second is like it: Love your neighbor as yourself. All the Law and the Prophets hang on these two commandments."
-Matthew 22:37-40

HE DIES BY CRUCIFIXION, A METHOD OF EXECUTION USED FREQUENTLY IN THE LAND OF ISRAEL BY ROME, BUT, FOR CHRISTIANS, JESUS' CROSS OF EXECUTION SOON BECOMES A SYMBOL OF HOPE.

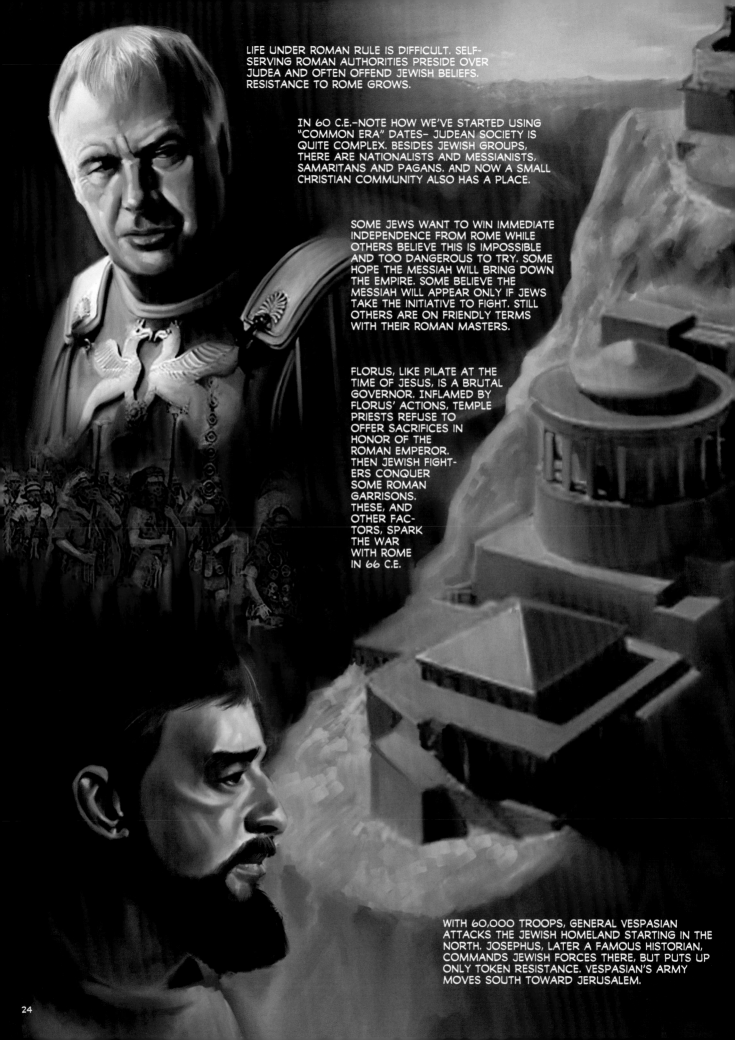

LIFE UNDER ROMAN RULE IS DIFFICULT. SELF-SERVING ROMAN AUTHORITIES PRESIDE OVER JUDEA AND OFTEN OFFEND JEWISH BELIEFS. RESISTANCE TO ROME GROWS.

IN 60 C.E.–NOTE HOW WE'VE STARTED USING "COMMON ERA" DATES– JUDEAN SOCIETY IS QUITE COMPLEX. BESIDES JEWISH GROUPS, THERE ARE NATIONALISTS AND MESSIANISTS, SAMARITANS AND PAGANS. AND NOW A SMALL CHRISTIAN COMMUNITY ALSO HAS A PLACE.

SOME JEWS WANT TO WIN IMMEDIATE INDEPENDENCE FROM ROME WHILE OTHERS BELIEVE THIS IS IMPOSSIBLE AND TOO DANGEROUS TO TRY. SOME HOPE THE MESSIAH WILL BRING DOWN THE EMPIRE. SOME BELIEVE THE MESSIAH WILL APPEAR ONLY IF JEWS TAKE THE INITIATIVE TO FIGHT. STILL OTHERS ARE ON FRIENDLY TERMS WITH THEIR ROMAN MASTERS.

FLORUS, LIKE PILATE AT THE TIME OF JESUS, IS A BRUTAL GOVERNOR. INFLAMED BY FLORUS' ACTIONS, TEMPLE PRIESTS REFUSE TO OFFER SACRIFICES IN HONOR OF THE ROMAN EMPEROR. THEN JEWISH FIGHT-ERS CONQUER SOME ROMAN GARRISONS. THESE, AND OTHER FAC-TORS, SPARK THE WAR WITH ROME IN 66 C.E.

WITH 60,000 TROOPS, GENERAL VESPASIAN ATTACKS THE JEWISH HOMELAND STARTING IN THE NORTH. JOSEPHUS, LATER A FAMOUS HISTORIAN, COMMANDS JEWISH FORCES THERE, BUT PUTS UP ONLY TOKEN RESISTANCE. VESPASIAN'S ARMY MOVES SOUTH TOWARD JERUSALEM.

EVENTUALLY, THROUGH
A COMBINATION OF
DIRECT ATTACK AND
LONG SIEGE, THE
ROMANS PENETRATE
THE CITY. IN 70 C.E.,
KING DAVID'S ANCIENT
CAPITAL FALLS FOR THE
SECOND TIME.

THIS WAR COSTS THE JEWISH PEOPLE DEARLY.
BESIDES HEAVY CASUALTIES FROM THE FIGHTING,
SURVIVORS ARE EXILED, EXECUTED, ENSLAVED
OR SENT TO DIE IN GLADIATORIAL GAMES. THE
TEMPLE IS DESTROYED. AMONG THE REMAINS IS
A PORTION OF THE WESTERN RETAINING WALL.

AS JERUSALEM TEETERS ON THE BRINK OF CAPTURE,
ONE OF THE LEADING PHARISEES, RABBI YOCHANAN
BEN ZAKKAI, SMUGGLES HIMSELF OUT OF THE CITY
AND GAINS ROME'S PERMISSION TO FOUND A
CENTER FOR TORAH STUDY IN YAVNEH, A SMALL
TOWN NEAR THE SEA.

THE MOST MILITANT JEWS MAKE ANOTHER
DECISION. WHEN JERUSALEM IS CONQUERED,
THEY RETREAT TO THE DESERT FORTRESS,
MASADA. IN 73 C.E., AFTER INTENSE FIGHTING,
ALMOST 1000 JEWS END THEIR OWN LIVES
THERE RATHER THAN FALL INTO ROMAN HANDS.

*PROFESSOR, ARE THE JEWS OF
MASADA CONSIDERED HEROES?*

I THINK THE ANSWER DEPENDS ON WHO
YOU ASK. BUT KEEP IN MIND THE DIFFICULT
PROBLEM OF DECIDING WHEN TO FIGHT AND
WHEN TO COMPROMISE.

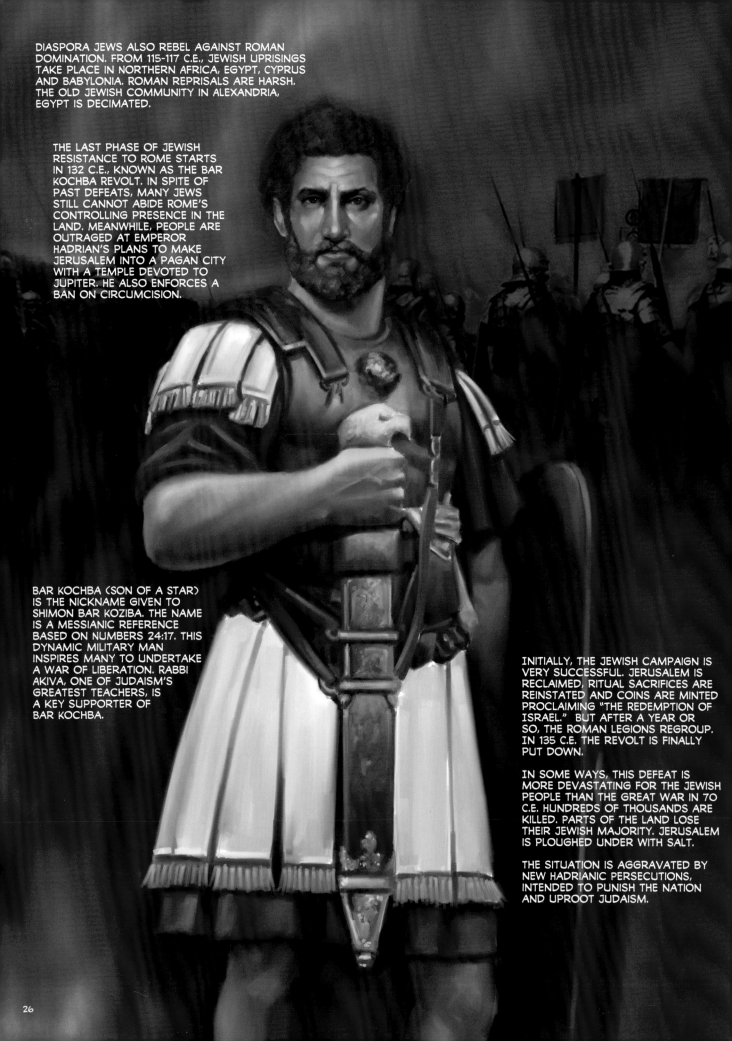

DIASPORA JEWS ALSO REBEL AGAINST ROMAN DOMINATION. FROM 115-117 C.E., JEWISH UPRISINGS TAKE PLACE IN NORTHERN AFRICA, EGYPT, CYPRUS AND BABYLONIA. ROMAN REPRISALS ARE HARSH. THE OLD JEWISH COMMUNITY IN ALEXANDRIA, EGYPT IS DECIMATED.

THE LAST PHASE OF JEWISH RESISTANCE TO ROME STARTS IN 132 C.E., KNOWN AS THE BAR KOCHBA REVOLT. IN SPITE OF PAST DEFEATS, MANY JEWS STILL CANNOT ABIDE ROME'S CONTROLLING PRESENCE IN THE LAND. MEANWHILE, PEOPLE ARE OUTRAGED AT EMPEROR HADRIAN'S PLANS TO MAKE JERUSALEM INTO A PAGAN CITY WITH A TEMPLE DEVOTED TO JUPITER. HE ALSO ENFORCES A BAN ON CIRCUMCISION.

BAR KOCHBA (SON OF A STAR) IS THE NICKNAME GIVEN TO SHIMON BAR KOZIBA. THE NAME IS A MESSIANIC REFERENCE BASED ON NUMBERS 24:17. THIS DYNAMIC MILITARY MAN INSPIRES MANY TO UNDERTAKE A WAR OF LIBERATION. RABBI AKIVA, ONE OF JUDAISM'S GREATEST TEACHERS, IS A KEY SUPPORTER OF BAR KOCHBA.

INITIALLY, THE JEWISH CAMPAIGN IS VERY SUCCESSFUL. JERUSALEM IS RECLAIMED, RITUAL SACRIFICES ARE REINSTATED AND COINS ARE MINTED PROCLAIMING "THE REDEMPTION OF ISRAEL." BUT AFTER A YEAR OR SO, THE ROMAN LEGIONS REGROUP. IN 135 C.E. THE REVOLT IS FINALLY PUT DOWN.

IN SOME WAYS, THIS DEFEAT IS MORE DEVASTATING FOR THE JEWISH PEOPLE THAN THE GREAT WAR IN 70 C.E. HUNDREDS OF THOUSANDS ARE KILLED. PARTS OF THE LAND LOSE THEIR JEWISH MAJORITY. JERUSALEM IS PLOUGHED UNDER WITH SALT.

THE SITUATION IS AGGRAVATED BY NEW HADRIANIC PERSECUTIONS, INTENDED TO PUNISH THE NATION AND UPROOT JUDAISM.

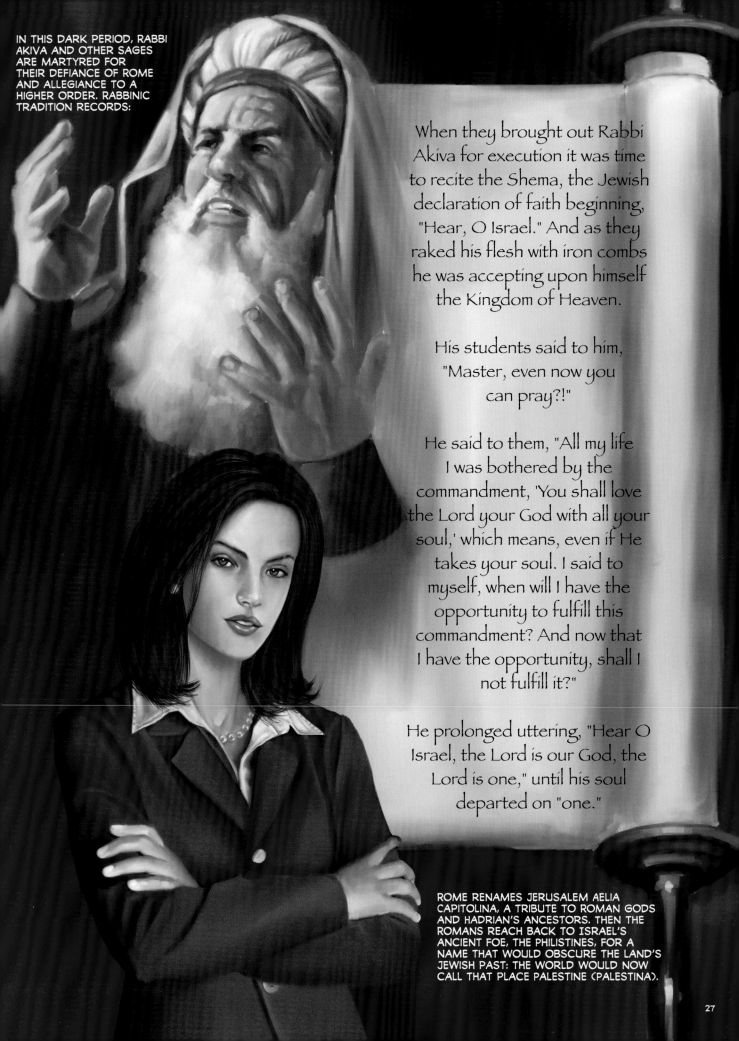

IN THIS DARK PERIOD, RABBI AKIVA AND OTHER SAGES ARE MARTYRED FOR THEIR DEFIANCE OF ROME AND ALLEGIANCE TO A HIGHER ORDER. RABBINIC TRADITION RECORDS:

When they brought out Rabbi Akiva for execution it was time to recite the Shema, the Jewish declaration of faith beginning, "Hear, O Israel." And as they raked his flesh with iron combs he was accepting upon himself the Kingdom of Heaven.

His students said to him, "Master, even now you can pray?!"

He said to them, "All my life I was bothered by the commandment, 'You shall love the Lord your God with all your soul,' which means, even if He takes your soul. I said to myself, when will I have the opportunity to fulfill this commandment? And now that I have the opportunity, shall I not fulfill it?"

He prolonged uttering, "Hear O Israel, the Lord is our God, the Lord is one," until his soul departed on "one."

ROME RENAMES JERUSALEM AELIA CAPITOLINA, A TRIBUTE TO ROMAN GODS AND HADRIAN'S ANCESTORS. THEN THE ROMANS REACH BACK TO ISRAEL'S ANCIENT FOE, THE PHILISTINES, FOR A NAME THAT WOULD OBSCURE THE LAND'S JEWISH PAST: THE WORLD WOULD NOW CALL THAT PLACE PALESTINE (PALESTINA).

THE LOSS OF JERUSALEM LEADS TO A SHIFT IN JEWISH LEADERSHIP. FOR GENERATIONS RABBINIC SCHOLARS HAD PLAYED A ROLE IN NATIONAL AFFAIRS, BUT NOW, WITH NO TEMPLE OR KING, RABBIS BECOME THE DEFINING VOICE OF THE PEOPLE.

ACCORDING TO RABBINIC TRADITION, MOSES RECEIVED TWO TORAHS, ONE WRITTEN (THE FIVE BOOKS OF MOSES), AND THE OTHER ORAL (LAWS AND LEARNING PASSED DOWN FROM TEACHER TO DISCIPLE). BY THE YEAR 200 C.E., A NEED IS FELT TO COMPILE ALL THE ORAL MATERIAL INTO ONE TEXT. THIS SIX-PART CODE, CALLED THE MISHNAH, IS EDITED BY RABBI JUDAH THE PATRIARCH.

Late Talmudic Scholar,
Mesopotamia, c. 400 C.E.

Rabbi Jacob ben Meir,
Germany, c. 1150 C.E.

Early Talmudic Scholar,
Land of Israel, c. 150 C.E.

Rabbi Shlomo ben Isaac, Rashi,
France, c. 1080 C.E.

THE MISHNAH SERVES AS THE STARTING POINT FOR THE RICH LEGAL, ETHICAL AND THEOLOGICAL DISCUSSIONS AND STORIES BROUGHT TOGETHER IN TWO VERSIONS OF THE TALMUD, FIRST IN THE LAND OF ISRAEL AROUND 400 C.E. AND LATER, APPROXIMATELY 500 C.E., IN BABYLON. HUNDREDS OF SCHOLARS, WORKING FOR OVER SIX CENTURIES, CONTRIBUTE TO THESE SACRED TEXTS. THESE SAME RABBIS CREATE THE MIDRASH COMMENTARY WE HAVE MENTIONED.

THE TALMUD ITSELF BECOMES THE CORE OF A GREAT BODY OF JUDAIC LITERATURE DOWN TO THE PRESENT. ON A CONTEMPORARY PAGE OF TALMUD, YOU FIND MATERIAL RANGING OVER A PERIOD OF 1500 YEARS WITH SCHOLARS FROM MANY DIFFERENT COUNTRIES TAKING PART IN AN ONGOING CONVERSATION.

Rabbi Isaac Alfasi,
Egypt, c. 1050 C.E.

THE TOP JEWISH POLITICAL LEADER IN PALESTINE FROM THE LATE SECOND CENTURY C.E. UNTIL THE EARLY FIFTH CENTURY IS THE PATRIARCH. HE ACTS AS THE OFFICIAL LINK BETWEEN RULING ROME AND THE JEWISH PEOPLE.

FOLLOWING THE LOSS OF THE TEMPLE, SYNAGOGUES AND SCHOOLS FOR TORAH STUDY MULTIPLY IN PALESTINE. THE FOCUS OF JEWISH LIFE ALSO BEGINS TO SHIFT GEOGRAPHICALLY IN THE LAND. AFTER JERUSALEM, TOWNS LIKE YAVNEH, BEIT SHEARIM AND TIBERIAS ARE, BY TURNS, HOME TO THE SANHEDRIN, THE PRINCIPAL RABBINIC COURT.

BUT THINGS BEGIN TO CHANGE FOR JEWS IN THE LAND SOON AFTER EMPEROR CONSTANTINE LEGALIZES CHRISTIANITY IN 313 C.E. THIS ACT OPENS THE DOOR FOR SAFE CONVERSIONS TO CHRISTIANITY BY LARGE NUMBERS OF NON-JEWS. CONSTANTINE HIMSELF EITHER CONVERTS OR BECOMES VERY SYMPATHETIC TO THE CHRISTIAN CAUSE. TOWARD THE END OF THE CENTURY, THEODOSIUS I MAKES CHRISTIANITY THE STATE RELIGION.

CHRISTIANS DEVELOP NEW INTEREST IN WHAT THEY CALL "THE HOLY LAND." EMPERORS ORDER THE CONSTRUCTION OF CHURCHES AND MONASTERIES. CHRISTIAN IMMIGRATION TO PALESTINE INCREASES DRAMATICALLY. ROMAN POWER AND CHURCH POLICY JOIN HANDS TO PROHIBIT SOCIAL CONTACT BETWEEN JEWS AND CHRISTIANS. NEAR 430 C.E. ROME ABOLISHES THE POSITION OF PATRIARCH, AND JEWS ARE BANNED FROM JERUSALEM.

BY THIS TIME, A BODY OF HARSH TEACHINGS AGAINST JEWS AND JUDAISM HAS EVOLVED WITHIN THE CHURCH. JEWS ARE PORTRAYED AS BLIND AND DANGEROUS, WHILE THE CHARGE OF KILLING JESUS BECOMES A THEME IN CHRISTIAN PREACHING. OVER THE NEXT TWO CENTURIES, THE SITUATION OF JEWS IN CHRISTIAN REGIMES WORSENS. A FEW ANTI-JEWISH RIOTS AND FORCED CONVERSIONS ARE WITNESSED. JEWS ARE FORBIDDEN TO HOLD PUBLIC OFFICE.

PROBABLY AROUND 600 C.E., CHRISTIANS BECOME A MAJORITY IN PALESTINE. THE JEWISH COMMUNITY THERE PERSISTS, WHILE AT THE SAME TIME JEWS CONTINUE TO SPREAD OUT IN MANY DIRECTIONS. THE PRIMARY CENTER OF DIASPORA JEWISH LIFE BECOMES PERSIAN MESOPOTAMIA, THE REGION JEWS CALLED BABYLON.

IN 603, THE SASSANID PERSIANS ATTACK THE MUCH-REDUCED SUCCESSOR TO THE ROMAN EMPIRE, THE BYZANTINES. IN 614, THE PERSIANS, WHO PRACTICE ZOROASTRIANISM, CONQUER PALESTINE. THE CHRISTIAN BYZANTINES SUCCESSFULLY FIGHT BACK, BUT THESE STRUGGLES ARE SOON OVERSHADOWED BY THE RISE OF A MAJOR NEW PLAYER ON THE HISTORICAL FIELD: ISLAM.

WITH THE APPEARANCE OF MUHAMMAD ON THE ARABIAN PENINSULA NEAR 610, A THIRD RELIGION IS BORN THAT REVERES THE GOD OF ABRAHAM. EMPHASIZING STRICT MONOTHEISM AND A SYSTEM OF RELIGIOUS LAW ADDRESSING ALL ASPECTS OF LIFE, ISLAM HAS SIGNIFICANT SIMILARITIES TO JUDAISM IN RITUAL PRACTICE. THE ISLAMIC RELIGION IS BASED ON THE *QUR'AN* (KORAN), WHICH MUSLIMS BELIEVE TO BE THE WORD OF GOD, AS WELL AS TRADITIONS OF MUHAMMAD'S LIFE.

MUSLIMS MARK TIME FROM THE YEAR MUHAMMAD MOVES TO THE TOWN OF MEDINA IN 622 TO ESCAPE INTENSE OPPOSITION. SOME 10,000 JEWS RESIDE IN MEDINA AND MUHAMMAD HOPES THEY WILL ACCEPT HIS TEACHINGS. WHEN THIS DOES NOT OCCUR, JEWISH CLANS THERE ARE OPPRESSED, EXPELLED OR DESTROYED. MUHAMMAD NOW DIRECTS MUSLIMS TO FACE MECCA IN PRAYER INSTEAD OF JERUSALEM.

THE MUSLIM FAITH GROWS WITH AWESOME SPEED. BY 636, ARAB MUSLIMS CONTROL MUCH OF THE FERTILE CRESCENT, INCLUDING PALESTINE.

THE SEVENTH CENTURY PACT OF UMAR GIVES JEWS IN ISLAMIC LANDS THE STATUS OF *DHIMMI* (PROTECTED). THE PACT ASSIGNS JEWS AND CHRISTIANS CERTAIN RIGHTS, BUT MAKES THEIR STATUS INFERIOR TO MUSLIMS. NEVERTHELESS, JEWS ARE PERMITTED TO LIVE IN JERUSALEM FOR THE FIRST TIME IN GENERATIONS, THOUGH MUSLIM AUTHORITIES TAKE CONTROL OF THE TEMPLE MOUNT WHERE SOLOMON'S TEMPLE STOOD. THE DOME OF THE ROCK IS BUILT THERE IN 691 TO EMPHASIZE THE SUPERIORITY OF ISLAM.

OVER THE NEXT 300 YEARS, JEWISH LEADERS IN PALESTINE SHARE AUTHORITY WITH THEIR BABYLONIAN COUNTERPARTS. THESE ARE THE *GEONIM* (PRIDE OF ISRAEL), THE MOST FAMOUS OF WHOM, SA'ADIAH (882-942), WROTE ON HEBREW GRAMMAR, PRAYER AND JEWISH PHILOSOPHY.

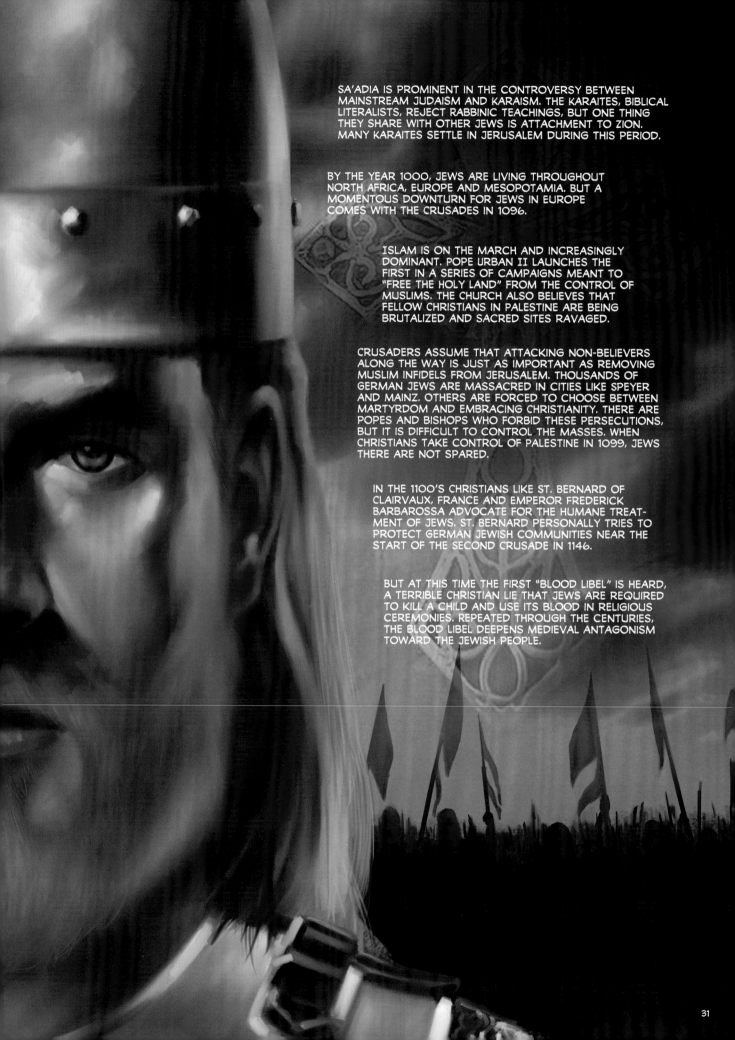

SA'ADIA IS PROMINENT IN THE CONTROVERSY BETWEEN MAINSTREAM JUDAISM AND KARAISM. THE KARAITES, BIBLICAL LITERALISTS, REJECT RABBINIC TEACHINGS, BUT ONE THING THEY SHARE WITH OTHER JEWS IS ATTACHMENT TO ZION. MANY KARAITES SETTLE IN JERUSALEM DURING THIS PERIOD.

BY THE YEAR 1000, JEWS ARE LIVING THROUGHOUT NORTH AFRICA, EUROPE AND MESOPOTAMIA. BUT A MOMENTOUS DOWNTURN FOR JEWS IN EUROPE COMES WITH THE CRUSADES IN 1096.

ISLAM IS ON THE MARCH AND INCREASINGLY DOMINANT. POPE URBAN II LAUNCHES THE FIRST IN A SERIES OF CAMPAIGNS MEANT TO "FREE THE HOLY LAND" FROM THE CONTROL OF MUSLIMS. THE CHURCH ALSO BELIEVES THAT FELLOW CHRISTIANS IN PALESTINE ARE BEING BRUTALIZED AND SACRED SITES RAVAGED.

CRUSADERS ASSUME THAT ATTACKING NON-BELIEVERS ALONG THE WAY IS JUST AS IMPORTANT AS REMOVING MUSLIM INFIDELS FROM JERUSALEM. THOUSANDS OF GERMAN JEWS ARE MASSACRED IN CITIES LIKE SPEYER AND MAINZ. OTHERS ARE FORCED TO CHOOSE BETWEEN MARTYRDOM AND EMBRACING CHRISTIANITY. THERE ARE POPES AND BISHOPS WHO FORBID THESE PERSECUTIONS, BUT IT IS DIFFICULT TO CONTROL THE MASSES. WHEN CHRISTIANS TAKE CONTROL OF PALESTINE IN 1099, JEWS THERE ARE NOT SPARED.

IN THE 1100'S CHRISTIANS LIKE ST. BERNARD OF CLAIRVAUX, FRANCE AND EMPEROR FREDERICK BARBAROSSA ADVOCATE FOR THE HUMANE TREAT-MENT OF JEWS. ST. BERNARD PERSONALLY TRIES TO PROTECT GERMAN JEWISH COMMUNITIES NEAR THE START OF THE SECOND CRUSADE IN 1146.

BUT AT THIS TIME THE FIRST "BLOOD LIBEL" IS HEARD, A TERRIBLE CHRISTIAN LIE THAT JEWS ARE REQUIRED TO KILL A CHILD AND USE ITS BLOOD IN RELIGIOUS CEREMONIES. REPEATED THROUGH THE CENTURIES, THE BLOOD LIBEL DEEPENS MEDIEVAL ANTAGONISM TOWARD THE JEWISH PEOPLE.

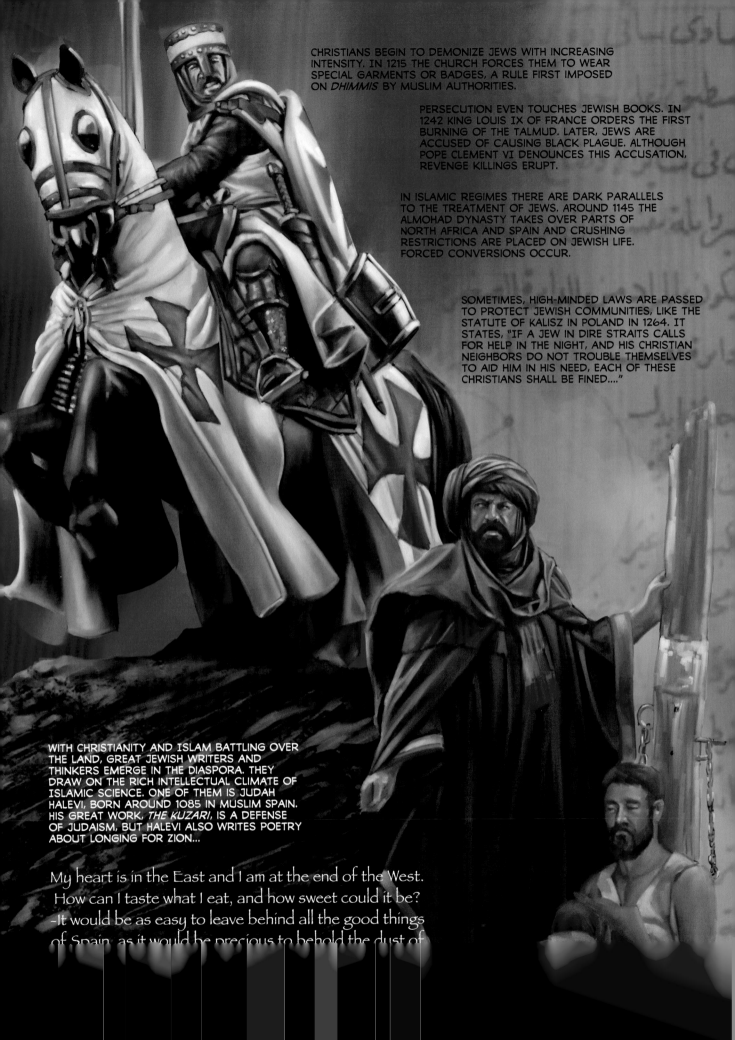

CHRISTIANS BEGIN TO DEMONIZE JEWS WITH INCREASING INTENSITY. IN 1215 THE CHURCH FORCES THEM TO WEAR SPECIAL GARMENTS OR BADGES, A RULE FIRST IMPOSED ON *DHIMMIS* BY MUSLIM AUTHORITIES.

PERSECUTION EVEN TOUCHES JEWISH BOOKS. IN 1242 KING LOUIS IX OF FRANCE ORDERS THE FIRST BURNING OF THE TALMUD. LATER, JEWS ARE ACCUSED OF CAUSING BLACK PLAGUE. ALTHOUGH POPE CLEMENT VI DENOUNCES THIS ACCUSATION, REVENGE KILLINGS ERUPT.

IN ISLAMIC REGIMES THERE ARE DARK PARALLELS TO THE TREATMENT OF JEWS. AROUND 1145 THE ALMOHAD DYNASTY TAKES OVER PARTS OF NORTH AFRICA AND SPAIN AND CRUSHING RESTRICTIONS ARE PLACED ON JEWISH LIFE. FORCED CONVERSIONS OCCUR.

SOMETIMES, HIGH-MINDED LAWS ARE PASSED TO PROTECT JEWISH COMMUNITIES, LIKE THE STATUTE OF KALISZ IN POLAND IN 1264. IT STATES, "IF A JEW IN DIRE STRAITS CALLS FOR HELP IN THE NIGHT, AND HIS CHRISTIAN NEIGHBORS DO NOT TROUBLE THEMSELVES TO AID HIM IN HIS NEED, EACH OF THESE CHRISTIANS SHALL BE FINED...."

WITH CHRISTIANITY AND ISLAM BATTLING OVER THE LAND, GREAT JEWISH WRITERS AND THINKERS EMERGE IN THE DIASPORA. THEY DRAW ON THE RICH INTELLECTUAL CLIMATE OF ISLAMIC SCIENCE. ONE OF THEM IS JUDAH HALEVI, BORN AROUND 1085 IN MUSLIM SPAIN. HIS GREAT WORK, *THE KUZARI*, IS A DEFENSE OF JUDAISM, BUT HALEVI ALSO WRITES POETRY ABOUT LONGING FOR ZION...

My heart is in the East and I am at the end of the West.
How can I taste what I eat, and how sweet could it be?
-It would be as easy to leave behind all the good things
of Spain, as it would be precious to behold the dust of

Rabbi Abraham ibn-Ezra: Spain; 1092-1167. Biblical scholar, Hebrew grammarian, poet, and world traveler.

Rashi (Rabbi Shlomo ben Yitzchaki): Troyes, France; 1040-1105. Preeminent Jewish commentator on Bible and Talmud.

Nachmanides (Rabbi Moses ben Nachman): Spain and Palestine; 1194-1270. interpreter of Bible and Talmud and early sage of Kabbalah. Defends Judaism in a public debate.

THE MOST FAMOUS JEW OF THE MIDDLE AGES IS PROBABLY RABBI MOSES BEN MAIMON (1135-1204), KNOWN AS MAIMONIDES. HE IS A TOWERING FIGURE IN THE FIELDS OF JEWISH LAW AND PHILOSOPHY, AND SERVES AS PHYSICIAN TO MUSLIM RULERS. IN HIS *MISHNEH TORAH*, MAIMONIDES SUMMARIZES ALL OF JEWISH RELIGIOUS PRACTICE, OR *HALACHA*, INCLUDING TRADITIONS ABOUT THE IMPORTANCE OF THE LAND...

MISHNEH TORAH, LAWS OF KINGS 5:9-11

• It is always forbidden to leave the land of Israel to go abroad, except to study Torah, or get married, or to save someone...and then one must return to the land.

• The greatest of the Sages would kiss the borders of the land of Israel [upon arrival there], kiss its stones, and roll in its dirt...

JEWS INCORPORATE THOUGHTS OF THE HOMELAND INTO EVERY CORNER OF LIFE. THEY RECALL ZION WHEN EATING, PRAYING, MOURNING AND CELEBRATING. A SMALL PART OF THE HOUSE IS LEFT UNFINISHED IN MEMORY OF THE JERUSALEM TEMPLE. THE BEST-KNOWN CUSTOM REMINDING JEWS OF THEIR EXILE CONDITION IS BREAKING A GLASS AT THE WEDDING CEREMONY.

Rabbi Moses ben Maimon

BEYOND WORDS AND SYMBOLS, SOME JEWS BEGIN TO MOVE TO PALESTINE. IN 1140 JUDAH HALEVI MAKES *ALIYAH* (ASCENDS) TO THE LAND. STARTING IN 1210, ABOUT 300 RABBIS, LARGELY FROM FRANCE AND ENGLAND, EMIGRATE THERE TOO.

JEWS OF THE MIDDLE AGES KNOW THAT OFTEN THEY ARE NOT WELCOME IN THE SOCIETIES WHERE THEY LIVE. TEACHINGS OF HATRED LEAD TO THE EXPULSION OF JEWS FROM ENGLAND IN 1290 AND AGAIN IN 1322; FROM FRANCE IN 1306 AND 1394. FROM 1450-1520, JEWS ARE DRIVEN OUT OF 90 GERMAN TOWNS. OTHER EXAMPLES INCLUDE LITHUANIA (1495), PORTUGAL (1496), THE SAXONY REGION (1536) AND PARTS OF ITALY (1569-1571).

THE MOST FAMOUS EXPULSION OCCURS FROM SPAIN IN 1492. JEWS ARE UNDER VIOLENT PRESSURE IN SPAIN TO CONVERT TO CHRISTIANITY AND MANY DO SO. BUT SOME "NEW CHRISTIANS" (*CONVERSOS*) RISE TO POSITIONS OF WEALTH AND POWER AND ARE DEEPLY RESENTED.

AT THE SAME TIME, THE CHURCH IS WORRIED ABOUT RELIGIOUS HERESY AND THINKS *CONVERSOS* ARE SECRETLY CLINGING TO JEWISH BELIEFS. TO ROOT OUT "JUDAIZERS," THE OFFICE OF THE INQUISITION EXTRACTS CONFESSIONS THROUGH TORTURE. INQUISITORS SOON BECOME CONVINCED THAT THE ENTIRE JEWISH COMMUNITY ENCOURAGES HERESY, SO THE ONLY SOLUTION IS TO RID THE COUNTRY OF JEWS. SPANISH RULERS CLAIM THE MONEY AND PROPERTY THE JEWS MUST LEAVE BEHIND.

PROFESSOR, I'M A CHRISTIAN, AND I HAVE TO SAY I DON'T RECOGNIZE MY CHRISTIANITY IN THE HISTORY YOU'VE BEEN DESCRIBING. I WOULDN'T CALL PEOPLE WHO COMMIT TORTURE "CHRISTIANS."

I APPRECIATE YOUR COMMENT. FIRST, I BELIEVE MOST RELIGIOUS TRADITIONS HAVE TIMES IN THEIR PAST THAT ARE HARD TO CONFRONT. GOD MAY BE PERFECT, BUT HIS FOLLOWERS ARE NOT. OF COURSE, CHRISTIAN TEACHERS TODAY WOULD AGREE THAT BLOOD LIBELS, INQUISITIONS AND EXPULSIONS DO NOT REPRESENT CHRISTIAN IDEALS. BUT SHOULDN'T WE LEARN FROM WHAT PEOPLE HAVE DONE IN THE NAME OF GOD?

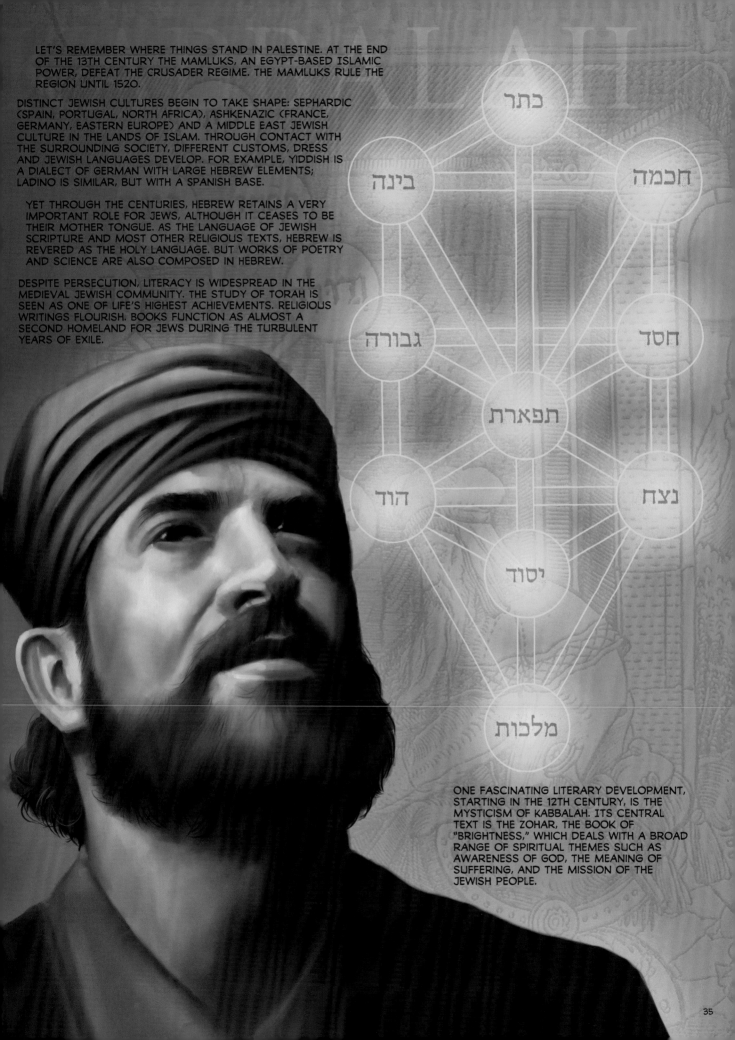

LET'S REMEMBER WHERE THINGS STAND IN PALESTINE. AT THE END OF THE 13TH CENTURY THE MAMLUKS, AN EGYPT-BASED ISLAMIC POWER, DEFEAT THE CRUSADER REGIME. THE MAMLUKS RULE THE REGION UNTIL 1520.

DISTINCT JEWISH CULTURES BEGIN TO TAKE SHAPE: SEPHARDIC (SPAIN, PORTUGAL, NORTH AFRICA), ASHKENAZIC (FRANCE, GERMANY, EASTERN EUROPE) AND A MIDDLE EAST JEWISH CULTURE IN THE LANDS OF ISLAM. THROUGH CONTACT WITH THE SURROUNDING SOCIETY, DIFFERENT CUSTOMS, DRESS AND JEWISH LANGUAGES DEVELOP. FOR EXAMPLE, YIDDISH IS A DIALECT OF GERMAN WITH LARGE HEBREW ELEMENTS; LADINO IS SIMILAR, BUT WITH A SPANISH BASE.

YET THROUGH THE CENTURIES, HEBREW RETAINS A VERY IMPORTANT ROLE FOR JEWS, ALTHOUGH IT CEASES TO BE THEIR MOTHER TONGUE. AS THE LANGUAGE OF JEWISH SCRIPTURE AND MOST OTHER RELIGIOUS TEXTS, HEBREW IS REVERED AS THE HOLY LANGUAGE. BUT WORKS OF POETRY AND SCIENCE ARE ALSO COMPOSED IN HEBREW.

DESPITE PERSECUTION, LITERACY IS WIDESPREAD IN THE MEDIEVAL JEWISH COMMUNITY. THE STUDY OF TORAH IS SEEN AS ONE OF LIFE'S HIGHEST ACHIEVEMENTS. RELIGIOUS WRITINGS FLOURISH. BOOKS FUNCTION AS ALMOST A SECOND HOMELAND FOR JEWS DURING THE TURBULENT YEARS OF EXILE.

כתר

בינה

חכמה

גבורה

חסד

תפארת

הוד

נצח

יסוד

מלכות

ONE FASCINATING LITERARY DEVELOPMENT, STARTING IN THE 12TH CENTURY, IS THE MYSTICISM OF KABBALAH. ITS CENTRAL TEXT IS THE ZOHAR, THE BOOK OF "BRIGHTNESS," WHICH DEALS WITH A BROAD RANGE OF SPIRITUAL THEMES SUCH AS AWARENESS OF GOD, THE MEANING OF SUFFERING, AND THE MISSION OF THE JEWISH PEOPLE.

KABBALAH TAKES ROOT IN SOUTHERN FRANCE AND SPAIN, BUT SPREADS RAPIDLY. JERUSALEM (13TH CENTURY) AND SAFED IN THE GALILEE (16TH CENTURY) BECOME MAJOR SITES OF JEWISH MYSTICAL ACTIVITY.

MAINSTREAM JEWISH LAW IS ALSO BEING STANDARDIZED NOW. AROUND 1555 THE *SHULCHAN ARUCH*, THE SET TABLE, COMBINES SEPHARDI AND ASHKENAZI TRADITIONS TO BECOME AUTHORITATIVE FOR RELIGIOUS PRACTICE.

IN THE 16TH CENTURY CONTROL OF THE LAND PASSES TO THE OTTOMANS. ORIGINATING FROM A SMALL TURKISH PROVINCE, THIS ISLAMIC EMPIRE EVENTUALLY REACHES AS FAR WEST AS VIENNA. SULEIMAN, THE MAGNIFICENT, RULES AT THE HEIGHT OF OTTOMAN POWER, 1520-1566. AFTER CONQUERING PALESTINE, HE BUILDS THE LARGE OUTER WALLS OF JERUSALEM'S OLD CITY, WHICH STILL STAND TODAY.

PROFESSOR, YOU MADE IT SOUND AS IF THE JEWS WERE EXPELLED FROM ALL OF WESTERN EUROPE, BUT I KNOW THEY LIVED IN FRANCE AND ENGLAND FROM THE 18TH CENTURY ON.

YOUR QUESTION IS WELL-TIMED BECAUSE IN THE LATE 1500'S JEWS ARE RE-ADMITTED INTO AREAS FROM WHICH THEY WERE DRIVEN OUT.

WAIT, YOU SAID SOME COUNTRIES WERE FORCING JEWS TO LEAVE THEN.

TRUE. DURING THIS TIME, EUROPEANS HAVE VERY MIXED FEELINGS TOWARD JEWS. CHANGING ATTITUDES ARE OFTEN LINKED TO ECONOMICS. FOR RELIGIOUS REASONS, CHRISTIANS WOULD NOT PERMIT THEMSELVES TO LEND MONEY WITH INTEREST. JEWS ARE FREQUENTLY THE ONLY ONES ALLOWED TO ARRANGE INTEREST-BEARING LOANS. JEWS GET BLAMED FOR TAKING ON THIS IMPORTANT FUNCTION.

HOWEVER, JEWISH MERCHANTS ARE SOMETIMES INVITED BACK TO STIMULATE COMMERCE. THE YIDDISH MEMOIRS OF A BUSINESSWOMAN NAMED GLUECKEL OF HAMELN (B. 1645) DESCRIBE WIDE-SPREAD JEWISH COMMERCIAL ACTIVITY IN EUROPE.

CENTURIES OF OPPRESSION AND LIVING AS OUTSIDERS FEED THE HOPE FOR REDEMPTION AMONG JEWS. THIS HOPE OFTEN CENTERS AROUND THE BIBLICAL IDEA OF A MESSIAH WHO WOULD DELIVER THE PEOPLE FROM ITS SUFFERING AND BRING THEM TO ZION.

UNDER THE RIGHT CONDITIONS, JEWS OCCASIONALLY TURNED TO "FALSE MESSIAHS." SHABBETAI TZVI OF THE OTTOMAN EMPIRE IS THE MOST FAMOUS OF THESE FIGURES FROM THE MIDDLE AGES.

TERRIBLE PERSECUTIONS IN POLAND AND THE UKRAINE, KNOWN AS THE CHMIELNICKI MASSACRES (1648-49), HELP INSPIRE DEVOTION TO CAPTIVATING MEN LIKE TZVI. LATER IN HIS CAREER, HE EMBRACES ISLAM TO ESCAPE EXECUTION.

Shabbetai Tzvi

PROFESSOR, WERE JEWS LITERALLY WAITING FOR THE MESSIAH TO TAKE THEM TO ISRAEL?

WELL, IN THIS PERIOD VAST NUMBERS GET SWEPT UP IN MESSIANIC FERVOR. SOME EVEN SELL THEIR POSSESSIONS, EXPECTING A MIRACULOUS DEPARTURE FOR THE HOMELAND.

ON THE OTHER HAND, OVER THE YEARS, JEWS HAD BECOME QUITE CAUTIOUS OF MESSIANIC CLAIMS. BACK IN THE FIRST CENTURY C.E., RABBI YOCHANAN BEN ZAKKAI TAUGHT: "IF YOU ARE ABOUT TO PLANT A TREE AND YOU HEAR THE MESSIAH HAS COME, *FIRST PLANT THE TREE* AND THEN GO OUT TO GREET HIM."

WITH THE PASSING CENTURIES, JEWS CONTINUE TO
TRAVEL ACROSS THE WORLD. THEY FIRST SETTLE IN
NORTH AMERICA IN 1654. ON THE OTHER SIDE OF
THE GLOBE, JEWISH COMMUNITIES EXIST IN CHINA
AND INDIA FROM AS EARLY AS THE MIDDLE AGES.
JEWS ARRIVE IN LATIN AMERICA IN 1660.

IN THE LATE 17TH CENTURY, A MAJOR CHANGE IN
WESTERN EUROPEAN THOUGHT TAKES SHAPE. THIS
"ENLIGHTENMENT" WILL HAVE A MASSIVE IMPACT
ON JEWISH LIFE AS PHILOSOPHERS TRY TO
REFORM SOCIETY BASED ON REASON, SCIENCE,
PROGRESS, HUMAN RIGHTS, EQUALITY AND
FREEDOM FROM RELIGIOUS CONTROLS.

JEWS ARE A CHALLENGING PROBLEM FOR EUROPEAN
NATIONS TRYING TO BECOME MODERN AND LIBERAL.
NEW STANDARDS OF EQUALITY CLASH WITH VERY OLD
PREJUDICES. IN THE 18TH AND EARLY 19TH CENTURIES,
SOME COUNTRIES, STARTING WITH FRANCE, GRANT
CIVIL RIGHTS TO JEWS, BUT THESE LAWS DO NOT
TRANSFORM LONG-STANDING HOSTILITY.

NAPOLEON, WHO RULES FRANCE AND CONQUERS
MUCH OF EUROPE FROM 1799-1815, EXPORTS
ASPECTS OF FRENCH LIBERTY TO OTHER LANDS.
DURING ONE OF HIS CAMPAIGNS, NAPOLEON
OCCUPIES PART OF PALESTINE, BUT FAILS TO
DEFEAT THE OTTOMANS.

IN EUROPE, THE ISOLATING GHETTO COMMUNITIES WHERE
JEWS WERE REQUIRED TO LIVE BEGIN TO OPEN. JEWS IN
THE MUSLIM WORLD ALSO EXPERIENCE CHANGE. IN 1839,
ABD AL-MAJID, THE SULTAN OF TURKEY, GIVES RIGHTS TO
NON-MUSLIMS IN THE OTTOMAN EMPIRE, BUT OPENNESS
TOWARD JEWS IS SHAKY. ANTI-JEWISH RIOTS OCCUR IN
MOROCCO IN 1877 AND IN ALGERIA 20 YEARS LATER.

JEWS ARE EXPOSED TO MANY NEW INFLUENCES.
TRADITIONAL JUDAISM CEASES TO BE A UNIVERSAL
REALITY FOR JEWISH LIFE. MANY BECOME SECULAR
AND ASSIMILATE TO NON-JEWISH CULTURES. OTHERS
WANT TO REFORM JUDAISM. IN THE 1800'S, GERMANY
IS A CENTER OF RELIGIOUS CHANGE.

*Napoleon
Bonaparte*

ANOTHER POWERFUL INFLUENCE ON JEWS IS NATIONALISM, THE BELIEF THAT ETHNIC COMMUNITIES ARE ENTITLED TO SELF-GOVERNMENT ON THEIR OWN TERRITORY. IN THE 19TH CENTURY, SOME JEWS START TO THINK SERIOUSLY ABOUT RETURNING THE JEWISH PEOPLE TO PALESTINE IN MASS NUMBERS. MODERN ZIONISM IS BORN.

ZIONISM BUILDS ON THE DEEP RELATIONSHIP BETWEEN JEWS AND THEIR HOMELAND, BUT THE MOVEMENT IS ALSO A RESPONSE TO ONGOING ANTI-JEWISH VIOLENCE. THE YEAR 1881 WAS PARTICULARLY BAD, WITH WIDESPREAD ATTACKS ON JEWS IN RUSSIA AND EASTERN EUROPE. ZIONISM WANTS TO PUT JEWISH FATE BACK INTO JEWISH HANDS. AT THIS TIME, MORE THAN 20,000 JEWS LIVE IN PALESTINE, MOST OF THEM IN JERUSALEM AND THE LARGE TOWNS.

Theodor Herzl

SOME RELIGIOUS JEWS OF THE DAY OBJECT TO ZIONIST POLITICS AS REBELLION AGAINST GOD. THEY SEE THE MOVEMENT AS SINFUL BECAUSE THEY BELIEVE ONLY GOD WILL BRING THE PEOPLE TO ZION—AND MOST ZIONIST LEADERS ARE SECULAR.

ONE OF THESE LEADERS IS THEODOR HERZL, AN AUSTRIAN JOURNALIST BORN IN 1860. HERZL IS THE FOUNDING FATHER OF MODERN ZIONISM. HE IS FAMOUS FOR THE MOTTO: IF YOU DESIRE [TO BUILD A JEWISH STATE], IT IS NO MERE DREAM. HERZL'S ROLE IS ESSENTIAL, BUT EARLY ZIONISM COMES IN MANY FORMS WITH MANY LEADERS.

ZION

RELIGIOUS ZIONISM

ALTHOUGH SOME TRADITIONAL JEWS OPPOSE ZIONISM, RABBIS ARE ALSO AMONG THE MOVEMENT'S EARLY ACTIVISTS. IN 1834, RABBI YEHUDA ALKALAI ARGUES THAT A JEWISH RETURN TO THE LAND WOULD HELP BRING THE MESSIAH. IN 1862, RABBI ZVI-HIRSCH KALISCHER WRITES *SEEKING ZION* SUGGESTING SIMILAR IDEAS.

SOCIALIST ZIONISM

MOSES HESS PUBLISHES *ROME AND JERUSALEM* IN 1862. A COLLEAGUE OF MARX, HESS IS PERSUADED BY JEW-HATRED IN GERMANY TO EMBRACE THE CONCEPT OF A JEWISH STATE. LIKE HIM, MANY ZIONIST LEADERS WANT TO FUSE LIVING IN PALESTINE WITH SOCIALIST IDEALS.

CULTURAL ZIONISM

SOME HOPE TO REVITALIZE PALESTINE AS A CENTER OF JEWISH CULTURE. AHAD HA'AM (ONE OF THE PEOPLE), THE PEN NAME OF ASHER GINZBERG (B. 1856), ALONG WITH H.N. BIALIK (B. 1873), THE GREAT HEBREW POET, REPRESENT THIS EFFORT TO CREATE A NEW NATIONAL JEWISH LIFE.

LABOR ZIONISM

A.D. GORDON (B. 1856) PROMOTES HEBREW LABOR, THE IDEA THAT WORKING THE LAND WILL TRANSFORM THE JEWISH PEOPLE. GORDON THINKS OF A RELATIONSHIP WITH NATURE IN SPIRITUAL TERMS: WHEN JEWS REBUILD THE LAND, THE LAND REBUILDS THE JEWS.

POLITICAL ZIONISM

IN 1881, LEON PINSKER, AN ASSIMILATED RUSSIAN JEW, IS ALARMED BY THE OUTBREAK OF POGROMS, OFFICIALLY SANCTIONED VIOLENT ATTACKS AGAINST JEWS. HE CALLS FOR JEWISH SELF-EMANCIPATION. A SIMILAR STORY BEGINS AT THE 1894 TRIAL OF ALFRED DREYFUS, A FRENCH-JEWISH ARMY CAPTAIN FALSELY ACCUSED OF SPYING FOR GERMANY. THEODOR HERZL, COVERS THE TRIAL AS AN AUSTRIAN JOURNALIST. SHOCKED AT THE ANIMOSITY THE TRIAL PROVOKES AGAINST JEWS, HE BEGINS TO CAMPAIGN INTENSIVELY FOR A JEWISH TERRITORY.

ISM

IN 1897, HERZL CONVENES THE FIRST ZIONIST CONGRESS IN BASLE, SWITZERLAND WITH 197 DELEGATES. THEY ADOPT SEVERAL GOALS:

• TO CREATE A HOME FOR THE JEWISH PEOPLE IN PALESTINE, "SECURED BY PUBLIC LAW"
• TO ADVANCE IMMIGRATION TO THE LAND
• TO UNITE WORLD JEWRY BEHIND THIS MOVEMENT
• TO GAIN INTERNATIONAL SUPPORT

ZIONISTS ALSO ADOPT A BLUE AND WHITE FLAG (COLORS OF THE TRADITIONAL JEWISH PRAYER SHAWL), AND A NATIONAL ANTHEM BASED ON A POEM BY NAPHTALI IMBER THAT DRAWS ON EZEKIEL'S VISION OF DEAD BONES RETURNING TO LIFE. GOD USED THIS PROPHETIC VISION TO CHALLENGE THE BITTER COMPLAINTS OF JEWS AT THE TIME OF THE BABYLONIAN EXILE WHO SAID, "OUR HOPE IS LOST." THE ANTHEM IS CALLED HATIKVAH, "THE HOPE":

> As long as deep within the heart a Jewish soul still yearns.
> And toward the far reaches of the East, an eye looks ahead toward Zion.
> Then our hope is not lost, the two thousand year-old hope,
> To be a free people in our land: the land of Zion and Jerusalem.

EARLY ZIONIST CONGRESSES ESTABLISH THE ANGLO-PALESTINE BANK AND JEWISH NATIONAL FUND (JNF) TO DEVELOP INDUSTRIAL AND AGRICULTURAL ACTIVITIES IN THE LAND. ZIONISTS INVEST GREAT RESOURCES TO PURCHASE TERRITORY FROM LANDLORDS, SOME OF WHOM ARE ARAB, WHO OWN TITLE TO LARGE PORTIONS OF PALESTINE. THESE LANDLORDS RESIDE BOTH IN AND OUTSIDE PALESTINE.

REMEMBER, TOO, THAT THE OTTOMAN EMPIRE STILL RULES THE ENTIRE NEAR EAST. THERE ARE NO RECOGNIZED STATES CALLED SYRIA, PALESTINE, LEBANON OR JORDAN AT THIS POINT.

FROM 1899 TO 1901, HERZL TRIES TO GET LEGAL
PERMISSION FROM THE OTTOMAN TURKS FOR
MASS JEWISH SETTLEMENT IN PALESTINE.

WITH GROWING ANTI-JEWISH MEASURES IN EUROPE,
ALTERNATE SITES FOR A JEWISH TERRITORY ARE
BRIEFLY CONSIDERED, INCLUDING EAST AFRICA.
HOWEVER, HISTORICAL AND RELIGIOUS TIES TO THE
HOMELAND PREVAIL WITHIN THE ZIONIST MOVEMENT.

*BUT PROFESSOR, THERE WERE OTHER
PEOPLE ALSO LIVING IN THE LAND. DID
ZIONISTS CONSIDER THE RIGHTS OF
ARABS THERE?*

YOU ARE RAISING A VERY SIGNIFICANT QUESTION
CONCERNING THE MIDDLE EAST CONFLICT. AS I
RESPOND, YOU MAY SEE MORE CLEARLY WHY IT
WAS NECESSARY TO GO SO FAR BACK IN TIME TO
TELL THE JEWISH SIDE OF THIS STORY.

THE ZIONISTS BELIEVE IN THE JUSTICE OF THEIR
CAUSE. JEWISH RIGHTS, ROOTED IN AN ANCIENT
BOND WITH THE LAND, TAKE PRECEDENCE OVER
OTHER CLAIMS. THE ZIONIST GOAL IS ESPECIALLY
PRESSING BECAUSE, AS YOU'VE LEARNED, LIFE IN
THE DIASPORA WAS OFTEN TERRIBLY INHUMANE.

THEREFORE, AN ARAB PRESENCE IN PALESTINE
IS NOT THEIR CHIEF WORRY. ON THE OTHER
HAND, SOME ZIONISTS DO THINK ARABS AND
JEWS CAN SHARE LIFE IN THAT SMALL LAND.
IN THE FIRST YEARS OF THE 20TH CENTURY,
THE TWO COMMUNITIES SOMETIMES WORK
COOPERATIVELY, AND THE ARRIVAL OF
JEWISH PIONEERS STIMULATES THE ECONOMY,
BENEFITING EVERYONE.

BE AWARE, TOO, THAT A LARGE PERCENTAGE
OF THE LAND IS SPARSELY POPULATED AT
THIS TIME. JEWS FREQUENTLY GO TO LIVE IN
UNSETTLED PLACES.

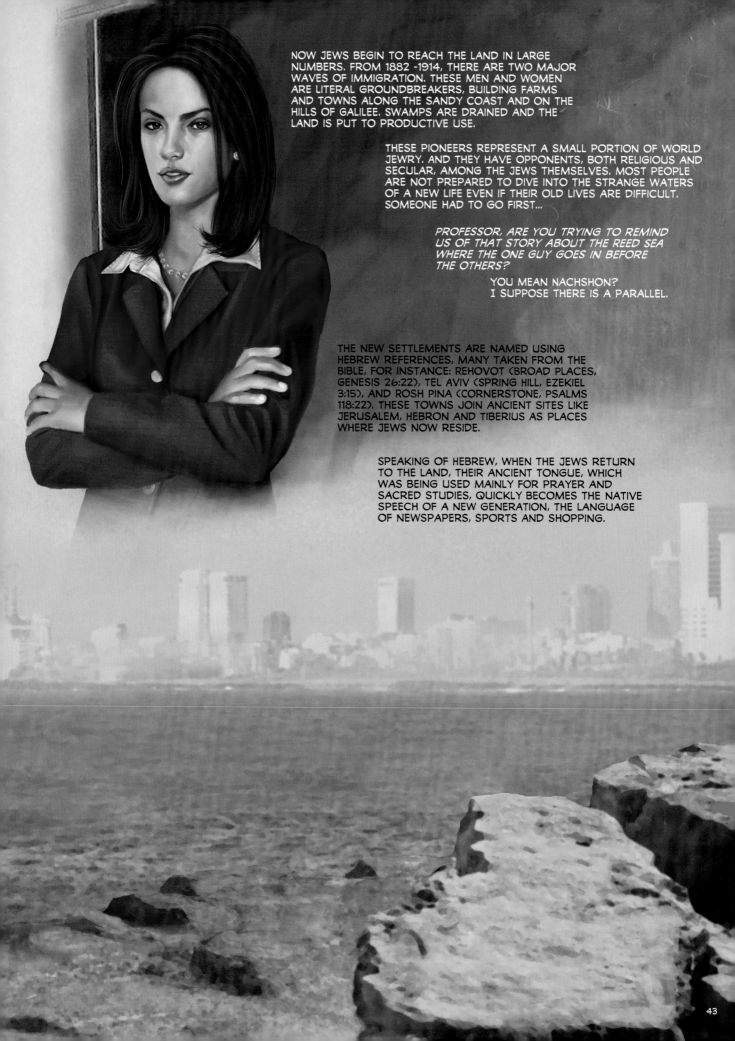

NOW JEWS BEGIN TO REACH THE LAND IN LARGE NUMBERS. FROM 1882 -1914, THERE ARE TWO MAJOR WAVES OF IMMIGRATION. THESE MEN AND WOMEN ARE LITERAL GROUNDBREAKERS, BUILDING FARMS AND TOWNS ALONG THE SANDY COAST AND ON THE HILLS OF GALILEE. SWAMPS ARE DRAINED AND THE LAND IS PUT TO PRODUCTIVE USE.

THESE PIONEERS REPRESENT A SMALL PORTION OF WORLD JEWRY. AND THEY HAVE OPPONENTS, BOTH RELIGIOUS AND SECULAR, AMONG THE JEWS THEMSELVES. MOST PEOPLE ARE NOT PREPARED TO DIVE INTO THE STRANGE WATERS OF A NEW LIFE EVEN IF THEIR OLD LIVES ARE DIFFICULT. SOMEONE HAD TO GO FIRST...

PROFESSOR, ARE YOU TRYING TO REMIND US OF THAT STORY ABOUT THE REED SEA WHERE THE ONE GUY GOES IN BEFORE THE OTHERS?

YOU MEAN NACHSHON? I SUPPOSE THERE IS A PARALLEL.

THE NEW SETTLEMENTS ARE NAMED USING HEBREW REFERENCES, MANY TAKEN FROM THE BIBLE, FOR INSTANCE: REHOVOT (BROAD PLACES, GENESIS 26:22), TEL AVIV (SPRING HILL, EZEKIEL 3:15), AND ROSH PINA (CORNERSTONE, PSALMS 118:22). THESE TOWNS JOIN ANCIENT SITES LIKE JERUSALEM, HEBRON AND TIBERIUS AS PLACES WHERE JEWS NOW RESIDE.

SPEAKING OF HEBREW, WHEN THE JEWS RETURN TO THE LAND, THEIR ANCIENT TONGUE, WHICH WAS BEING USED MAINLY FOR PRAYER AND SACRED STUDIES, QUICKLY BECOMES THE NATIVE SPEECH OF A NEW GENERATION, THE LANGUAGE OF NEWSPAPERS, SPORTS AND SHOPPING.

THE HEBREW LANGUAGE ALSO HAS A BOLD PIONEER, A MAN WHO LEADS THE WAY FOR OTHERS.

YOU MEAN, A "NACHSHON"...

YES, OK, A "NACHSHON"–I SEE YOU'VE GOT THE NAME NOW–THIS NACHSHON WANTS TO RECOVER SPOKEN HEBREW AMONG THE JEWS OF PALESTINE. HIS NAME IS ELIEZER PERELMAN (1858-1922), BUT HE ADOPTS THE HEBREW LAST NAME, BEN-YEHUDAH.

REFUSING TO SPEAK ANYTHING BUT HEBREW, BEN-YEHUDAH FACES AN UPHILL BATTLE TO CONVINCE EVERYONE THAT IT SHOULD BECOME THE NATIONAL LANGUAGE. PALESTINIAN JEWS WERE SPEAKING YIDDISH, ARABIC, FRENCH, RUSSIAN AND OTHER LANGUAGES. BEN-YEHUDAH WRITES A DICTIONARY, OFTEN USING BIBLICAL AND RABBINIC SOURCES, TO CREATE NEW WORDS NEEDED IN THE MODERN ERA.

THE REBIRTH OF SPOKEN HEBREW IS A RICH, ALMOST UNPRECEDENTED STORY. IMAGINE HOW DIFFICULT IT WOULD BE FOR A COUNTRY LIKE ITALY TO START SPEAK-ING LATIN AGAIN! HEBREW IN PALESTINE COMBINED THE OLD WITH THE NEW. MANY OF THE LANGUAGES SPOKEN BY DIASPORA JEWS INFLUENCED ITS VOCABULARY AND STRUCTURE. ARABIC TERMS HAVE BEEN BROUGHT INTO HEBREW USAGE, AS WELL AS MANY ENGLISH ONES.

Eliezer
Ben-Yehuda

ANOTHER IMPORTANT FORM OF EARLY ZIONIST PIONEERING IS THE COLLECTIVE COMMUNITY CALLED KIBBUTZ (GATHERING), AN EXPERIMENT IN ECONOMIC AND SOCIAL EQUALITY. PEOPLE SHARE PROPERTY AND ALL TAKE THEIR TURNS CARRYING OUT THE COMMUNITY'S TASKS. DEGANIA IS THE FIRST KIBBUTZ. FOUNDED IN 1910 BY 12 YOUNG MEN AND WOMEN, IT IS LOCATED ON THE SEA OF GALILEE'S SOUTHERN SHORE.

KIBBUTZIM HAVE ALWAYS MADE UP A VERY SMALL PORTION OF THE LAND'S JEWISH POPULATION, AND THE COLLECTIVE CHARACTER OF THE KIBBUTZ HAS CHANGED GREATLY OVER THE YEARS. NEVERTHELESS, THE KIBBUTZ COMES TO SYMBOLIZE A NATIONAL IDEAL OF DEVOTION TO THE LAND THROUGH HARD WORK AND SELF-SACRIFICE.

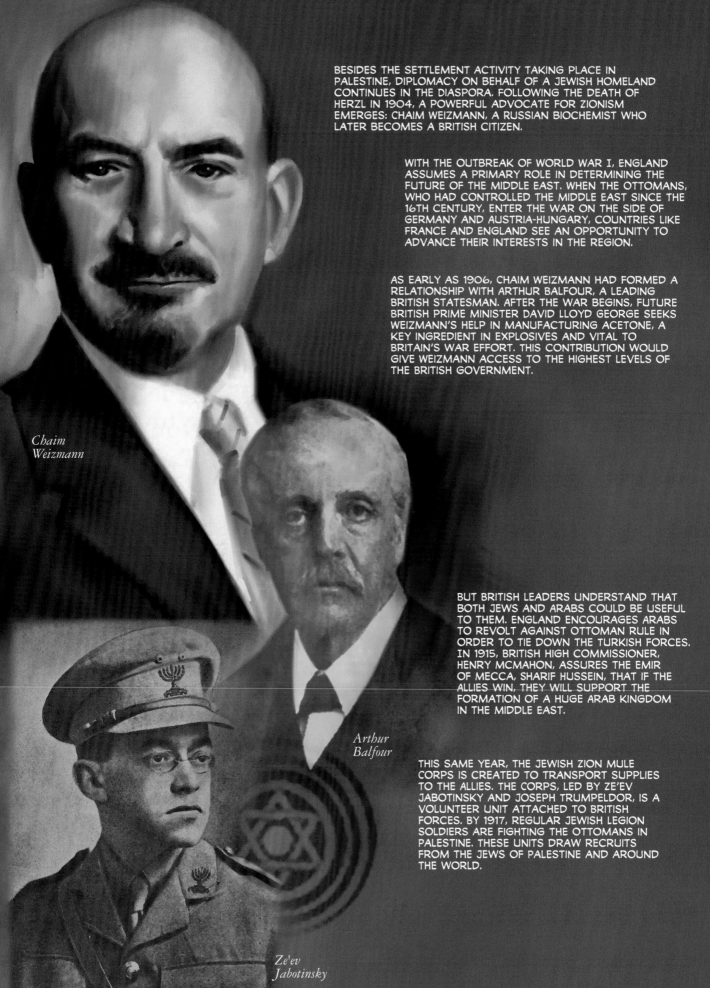

BESIDES THE SETTLEMENT ACTIVITY TAKING PLACE IN PALESTINE, DIPLOMACY ON BEHALF OF A JEWISH HOMELAND CONTINUES IN THE DIASPORA. FOLLOWING THE DEATH OF HERZL IN 1904, A POWERFUL ADVOCATE FOR ZIONISM EMERGES: CHAIM WEIZMANN, A RUSSIAN BIOCHEMIST WHO LATER BECOMES A BRITISH CITIZEN.

WITH THE OUTBREAK OF WORLD WAR I, ENGLAND ASSUMES A PRIMARY ROLE IN DETERMINING THE FUTURE OF THE MIDDLE EAST. WHEN THE OTTOMANS, WHO HAD CONTROLLED THE MIDDLE EAST SINCE THE 16TH CENTURY, ENTER THE WAR ON THE SIDE OF GERMANY AND AUSTRIA-HUNGARY, COUNTRIES LIKE FRANCE AND ENGLAND SEE AN OPPORTUNITY TO ADVANCE THEIR INTERESTS IN THE REGION.

AS EARLY AS 1906, CHAIM WEIZMANN HAD FORMED A RELATIONSHIP WITH ARTHUR BALFOUR, A LEADING BRITISH STATESMAN. AFTER THE WAR BEGINS, FUTURE BRITISH PRIME MINISTER DAVID LLOYD GEORGE SEEKS WEIZMANN'S HELP IN MANUFACTURING ACETONE, A KEY INGREDIENT IN EXPLOSIVES AND VITAL TO BRITAIN'S WAR EFFORT. THIS CONTRIBUTION WOULD GIVE WEIZMANN ACCESS TO THE HIGHEST LEVELS OF THE BRITISH GOVERNMENT.

Chaim Weizmann

BUT BRITISH LEADERS UNDERSTAND THAT BOTH JEWS AND ARABS COULD BE USEFUL TO THEM. ENGLAND ENCOURAGES ARABS TO REVOLT AGAINST OTTOMAN RULE IN ORDER TO TIE DOWN THE TURKISH FORCES. IN 1915, BRITISH HIGH COMMISSIONER, HENRY MCMAHON, ASSURES THE EMIR OF MECCA, SHARIF HUSSEIN, THAT IF THE ALLIES WIN, THEY WILL SUPPORT THE FORMATION OF A HUGE ARAB KINGDOM IN THE MIDDLE EAST.

Arthur Balfour

THIS SAME YEAR, THE JEWISH ZION MULE CORPS IS CREATED TO TRANSPORT SUPPLIES TO THE ALLIES. THE CORPS, LED BY ZE'EV JABOTINSKY AND JOSEPH TRUMPELDOR, IS A VOLUNTEER UNIT ATTACHED TO BRITISH FORCES. BY 1917, REGULAR JEWISH LEGION SOLDIERS ARE FIGHTING THE OTTOMANS IN PALESTINE. THESE UNITS DRAW RECRUITS FROM THE JEWS OF PALESTINE AND AROUND THE WORLD.

Ze'ev Jabotinsky

EVEN BEFORE WWI ENDS, FRANCE, ENGLAND AND RUSSIA'S PLAN TO CONTROL THE MIDDLE EAST, CALLED THE SYKES-PICOT AGREEMENT, LEAVES BRITAIN THE DOMINANT FORCE IN PALESTINE.

THE STAGE IS NOW SET FOR BRITAIN TO ISSUE ONE OF THE KEY DOCUMENTS IN THE HISTORY OF THE YOUNG ZIONIST MOVEMENT, THE BALFOUR DECLARATION:

Lord Edmond de Rothschild

Foreign Office,
November 2nd, 1917.

Dear Lord Rothschild,

I have much pleasure in conveying to you, on behalf of His Majesty's Government, the following declaration of sympathy with Jewish Zionist aspirations which has been submitted to, and approved by, the Cabinet

"His Majesty's Government view with favour the establishment in Palestine of a national home for the Jewish people, and will use their best endeavours to facilitate the achievement of this object, it being clearly understood that nothing shall be done which may prejudice the civil and religious rights of existing non-Jewish communities in Palestine, or the rights and political status enjoyed by Jews in any other country"

I should oe grateful if you would bring this declaration to the knowledge of the Zionist Federation.

Y. in.

SOME OF THE FACTORS THAT LEAD TO BRITAIN'S COMMITMENT ON NOVEMBER 2, 1917 ARE: (1) THE PRESENCE OF TENS OF THOUSANDS OF JEWS IN PALESTINE (2) INTENSIVE ZIONIST LOBBYING (3) JEWISH SERVICE TO THE ALLIES IN WWI (4) BRITAIN'S INTEREST IN HAVING A JUNIOR PARTNER IN THE REGION (5) BRITAIN'S DESIRE TO GET U.S. SUPPORT FOR THE WAR.

WE SHOULD ALSO NOTE THAT MEN LIKE ARTHUR BALFOUR AND DAVID LLOYD GEORGE ARE CHRISTIAN ZIONISTS WHO SEE THE RETURN OF JEWS TO THE LAND AS A FULFILLMENT OF GOD'S PLAN. RELIGIOUS BELIEFS MAKE CERTAIN POLITICIANS MORE OPEN TO THE ZIONIST VISION.

BECAUSE OF BRITISH PLEDGES, BOTH JEWS AND ARABS ARE HOPING FOR IMMEDIATE BENEFITS AT THE CONCLUSION OF WWI. THE NEW LEAGUE OF NATIONS, ESTABLISHED IN 1919, IS GIVEN AUTHORITY TO DEAL WITH THE CHANGES RESULTING FROM THE GREAT WAR.

ZIONISM IS AT A CRITICAL CROSSROADS, ESPECIALLY FOR ITS RELATIONSHIP TO THE ARAB COMMUNITY. AT FIRST THERE ARE SOME ARAB VOICES THAT ACCEPT THE JEWISH COMMUNITY IN PALESTINE, BUT THERE IS ALSO DEEP OPPOSITION TO ZIONISM.

IN 1919, EMIR FEISAL HUSSEIN SIGNS AN AGREEMENT WITH CHAIM WEIZMANN LAYING OUT A VISION FOR ARAB-JEWISH COOPERATION IN THE REGION. THE DOCUMENT DESCRIBES TWO ENTITIES: AN ARAB STATE AND PALESTINE. FEISAL BECOMES KING OF IRAQ AND LATER DENIES KNOWING ABOUT THE AGREEMENT.

SYRIAN ARABS CLAIM THE LAND FOR THEMSELVES. THEY REJECT "THE PRETENSIONS OF THE ZIONISTS TO CREATE A JEWISH COMMONWEALTH IN THE SOUTHERN PART OF SYRIA, KNOWN AS PALESTINE." SOME LOCAL PALESTINIAN ARABS ARE VERY CONCERNED ABOUT JEWISH EXPANSION IN THE LAND.

Emir Feisal Hussein

IN 1922-23, THE LEAGUE OF NATIONS GIVES THE BRITISH A FORMAL MANDATE TO GOVERN PALESTINE AND MAKES THEM "RESPONSIBLE FOR PUTTING INTO EFFECT THE DECLARATION...IN FAVOR OF THE ESTABLISHMENT IN PALESTINE OF A NATIONAL HOME FOR THE JEWISH PEOPLE."

HOWEVER, THE CHARACTER OF THIS NATIONAL HOME REMAINS UNDEFINED. WILL IT BE A FULL JEWISH STATE OR SIMPLY AN ORGANIZED ETHNIC COMMUNITY? WHAT BORDERS WILL IT HAVE? AND HOW WILL THE JEWS OF PALESTINE LIVE WITH THEIR MORE NUMEROUS ARAB NEIGHBORS?

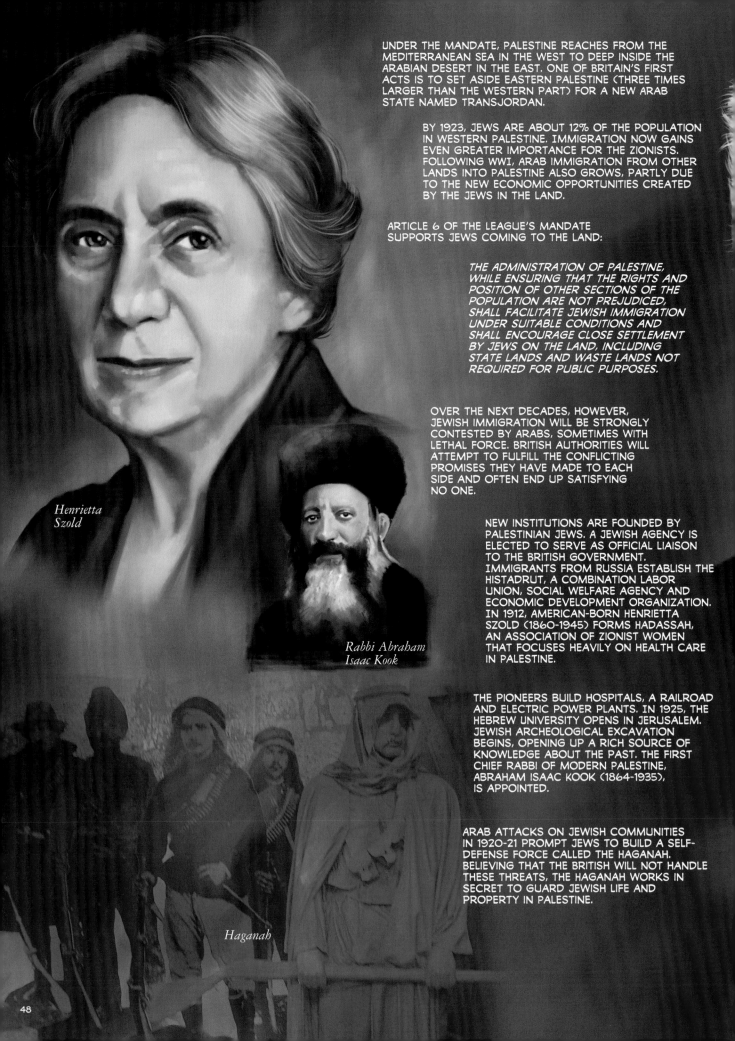

UNDER THE MANDATE, PALESTINE REACHES FROM THE MEDITERRANEAN SEA IN THE WEST TO DEEP INSIDE THE ARABIAN DESERT IN THE EAST. ONE OF BRITAIN'S FIRST ACTS IS TO SET ASIDE EASTERN PALESTINE (THREE TIMES LARGER THAN THE WESTERN PART) FOR A NEW ARAB STATE NAMED TRANSJORDAN.

BY 1923, JEWS ARE ABOUT 12% OF THE POPULATION IN WESTERN PALESTINE. IMMIGRATION NOW GAINS EVEN GREATER IMPORTANCE FOR THE ZIONISTS. FOLLOWING WWI, ARAB IMMIGRATION FROM OTHER LANDS INTO PALESTINE ALSO GROWS, PARTLY DUE TO THE NEW ECONOMIC OPPORTUNITIES CREATED BY THE JEWS IN THE LAND.

ARTICLE 6 OF THE LEAGUE'S MANDATE SUPPORTS JEWS COMING TO THE LAND:

THE ADMINISTRATION OF PALESTINE, WHILE ENSURING THAT THE RIGHTS AND POSITION OF OTHER SECTIONS OF THE POPULATION ARE NOT PREJUDICED, SHALL FACILITATE JEWISH IMMIGRATION UNDER SUITABLE CONDITIONS AND SHALL ENCOURAGE CLOSE SETTLEMENT BY JEWS ON THE LAND, INCLUDING STATE LANDS AND WASTE LANDS NOT REQUIRED FOR PUBLIC PURPOSES.

OVER THE NEXT DECADES, HOWEVER, JEWISH IMMIGRATION WILL BE STRONGLY CONTESTED BY ARABS, SOMETIMES WITH LETHAL FORCE. BRITISH AUTHORITIES WILL ATTEMPT TO FULFILL THE CONFLICTING PROMISES THEY HAVE MADE TO EACH SIDE AND OFTEN END UP SATISFYING NO ONE.

Henrietta Szold

NEW INSTITUTIONS ARE FOUNDED BY PALESTINIAN JEWS. A JEWISH AGENCY IS ELECTED TO SERVE AS OFFICIAL LIAISON TO THE BRITISH GOVERNMENT. IMMIGRANTS FROM RUSSIA ESTABLISH THE HISTADRUT, A COMBINATION LABOR UNION, SOCIAL WELFARE AGENCY AND ECONOMIC DEVELOPMENT ORGANIZATION. IN 1912, AMERICAN-BORN HENRIETTA SZOLD (1860-1945) FORMS HADASSAH, AN ASSOCIATION OF ZIONIST WOMEN THAT FOCUSES HEAVILY ON HEALTH CARE IN PALESTINE.

Rabbi Abraham Isaac Kook

THE PIONEERS BUILD HOSPITALS, A RAILROAD AND ELECTRIC POWER PLANTS. IN 1925, THE HEBREW UNIVERSITY OPENS IN JERUSALEM. JEWISH ARCHEOLOGICAL EXCAVATION BEGINS, OPENING UP A RICH SOURCE OF KNOWLEDGE ABOUT THE PAST. THE FIRST CHIEF RABBI OF MODERN PALESTINE, ABRAHAM ISAAC KOOK (1864-1935), IS APPOINTED.

ARAB ATTACKS ON JEWISH COMMUNITIES IN 1920-21 PROMPT JEWS TO BUILD A SELF-DEFENSE FORCE CALLED THE HAGANAH. BELIEVING THAT THE BRITISH WILL NOT HANDLE THESE THREATS, THE HAGANAH WORKS IN SECRET TO GUARD JEWISH LIFE AND PROPERTY IN PALESTINE.

Haganah

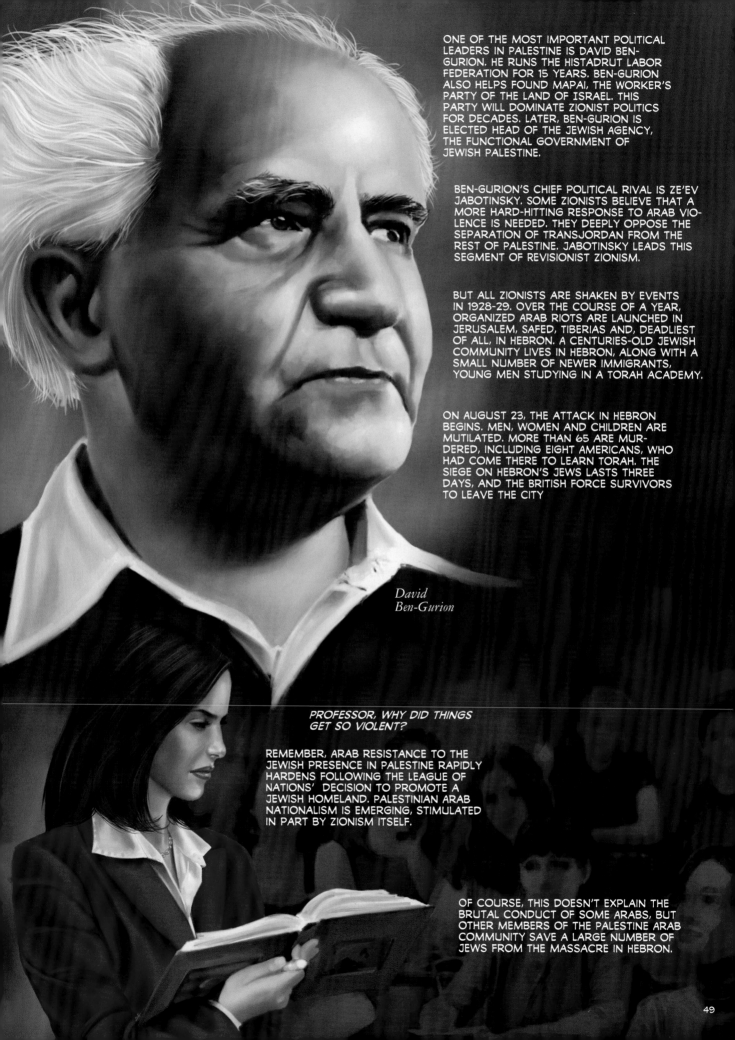

ONE OF THE MOST IMPORTANT POLITICAL LEADERS IN PALESTINE IS DAVID BEN-GURION. HE RUNS THE HISTADRUT LABOR FEDERATION FOR 15 YEARS. BEN-GURION ALSO HELPS FOUND MAPAI, THE WORKER'S PARTY OF THE LAND OF ISRAEL. THIS PARTY WILL DOMINATE ZIONIST POLITICS FOR DECADES. LATER, BEN-GURION IS ELECTED HEAD OF THE JEWISH AGENCY, THE FUNCTIONAL GOVERNMENT OF JEWISH PALESTINE.

BEN-GURION'S CHIEF POLITICAL RIVAL IS ZE'EV JABOTINSKY. SOME ZIONISTS BELIEVE THAT A MORE HARD-HITTING RESPONSE TO ARAB VIOLENCE IS NEEDED. THEY DEEPLY OPPOSE THE SEPARATION OF TRANSJORDAN FROM THE REST OF PALESTINE. JABOTINSKY LEADS THIS SEGMENT OF REVISIONIST ZIONISM.

BUT ALL ZIONISTS ARE SHAKEN BY EVENTS IN 1928-29. OVER THE COURSE OF A YEAR, ORGANIZED ARAB RIOTS ARE LAUNCHED IN JERUSALEM, SAFED, TIBERIAS AND, DEADLIEST OF ALL, IN HEBRON. A CENTURIES-OLD JEWISH COMMUNITY LIVES IN HEBRON, ALONG WITH A SMALL NUMBER OF NEWER IMMIGRANTS, YOUNG MEN STUDYING IN A TORAH ACADEMY.

ON AUGUST 23, THE ATTACK IN HEBRON BEGINS. MEN, WOMEN AND CHILDREN ARE MUTILATED. MORE THAN 65 ARE MURDERED, INCLUDING EIGHT AMERICANS, WHO HAD COME THERE TO LEARN TORAH. THE SIEGE ON HEBRON'S JEWS LASTS THREE DAYS, AND THE BRITISH FORCE SURVIVORS TO LEAVE THE CITY

David Ben-Gurion

PROFESSOR, WHY DID THINGS GET SO VIOLENT?

REMEMBER, ARAB RESISTANCE TO THE JEWISH PRESENCE IN PALESTINE RAPIDLY HARDENS FOLLOWING THE LEAGUE OF NATIONS' DECISION TO PROMOTE A JEWISH HOMELAND. PALESTINIAN ARAB NATIONALISM IS EMERGING, STIMULATED IN PART BY ZIONISM ITSELF.

OF COURSE, THIS DOESN'T EXPLAIN THE BRUTAL CONDUCT OF SOME ARABS, BUT OTHER MEMBERS OF THE PALESTINE ARAB COMMUNITY SAVE A LARGE NUMBER OF JEWS FROM THE MASSACRE IN HEBRON.

49

*Haj Amin
Al-Husseini*

Adolf Hitler

BUT ANOTHER FACTOR IS RELEVANT TO ARAB VIOLENCE IN PALESTINE: RELIGIOUS BIGOTRY PROVOKES ANTI-JEWISH ACTION.

HERBERT SAMUEL, THE BRITISH COMMISSIONER OVERSEEING PALESTINE, APPOINTS HAJ AMIN AL-HUSSEINI AS GRAND MUFTI, SUPREME ISLAMIC AUTHORITY. AL-HUSSEINI PLAYS A LARGE ROLE IN INCITING VIOLENCE AGAINST JEWS. NOT UNLIKE THE OLD BLOOD LIBELS, IN ORDER TO AROUSE HATRED, HE FALSELY ASSERTS THAT JEWS HAVE HARMED MUSLIMS AND THEIR HOLY PLACES.

ARAB VIOLENCE ALSO AFFECTS BRITISH POLICY, AND JUST AS THERE ARE ENGLISH SYMPATHETIC TO ZIONISM, SOME FAVOR THE ARABS. THE SHAW COMMISSION, SET UP AFTER HEBRON, RECOMMENDS LIMITING JEWISH IMMIGRATION AND LAND ACQUISITION IN PALESTINE. JEWS VIGOROUSLY OPPOSE THIS AND NO IMMEDIATE POLICY CHANGE RESULTS.

*Orde Charles
Wingate*

OTHER DEVELOPMENTS IN EUROPE WILL SOON IMPACT THE MIDDLE EAST. IN 1933, ADOLF HITLER IS ELECTED TO LEAD GERMANY.

IN 1936, A WIDESPREAD ARAB STRIKE PROTESTING INCREASED JEWISH PRESENCE IN ZION TURNS INTO AN ARMED REVOLT AGAINST BRITISH RULE AND THE ZIONIST PROJECT. JEWISH COMMUNITIES ARE ASSAULTED AND HAGANAH DEFENSE UNITS RESPOND ACCORDINGLY. AT THIS TIME, ORDE CHARLES WINGATE, A BRITISH ARMY OFFICER SERVING IN PALESTINE, SETS A DRAMATIC EXAMPLE OF CHRISTIAN PRO-ZIONIST FEELING. WINGATE TRAINS JEWS—OFTEN AGAINST HIS ORDERS—TO DEVELOP MILITARY SQUADS TO COMBAT ARAB TERROR. JEWS NAME WINGATE "THE FRIEND."

NEW BRITISH COMMISSIONS ARE SET UP TO STUDY THE PROBLEM OF PALESTINE. THE IDEA IS RAISED, FOR THE FIRST TIME, TO PARTITION THE LAND INTO ARAB AND JEWISH SECTIONS.

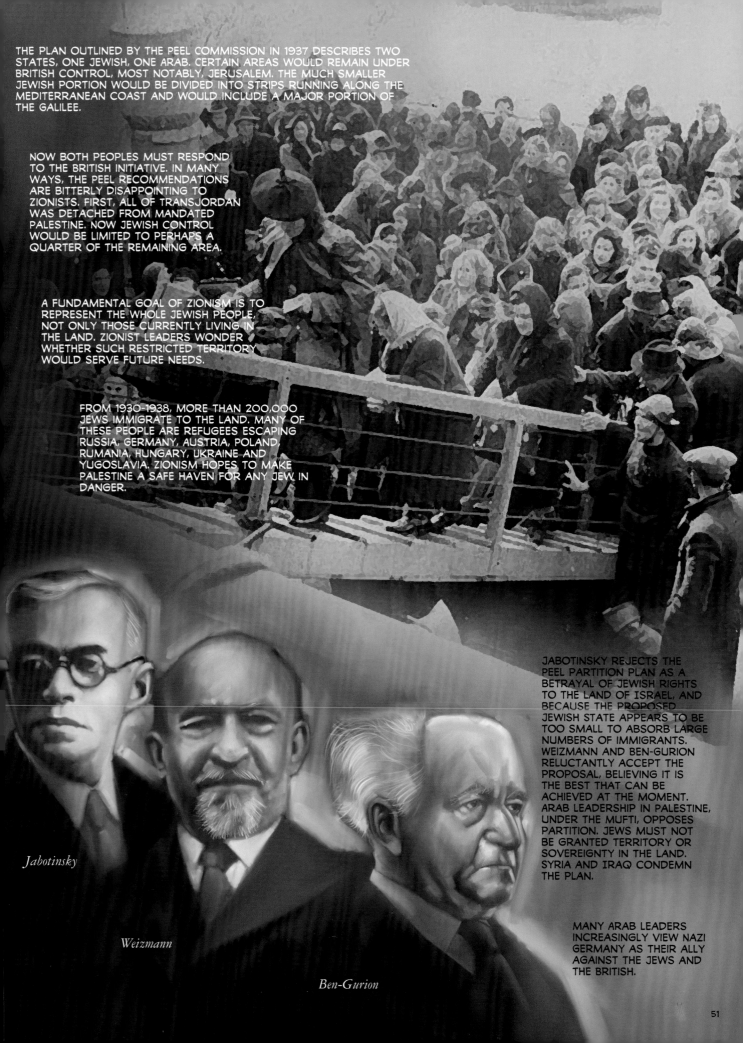

THE PLAN OUTLINED BY THE PEEL COMMISSION IN 1937 DESCRIBES TWO STATES, ONE JEWISH, ONE ARAB. CERTAIN AREAS WOULD REMAIN UNDER BRITISH CONTROL, MOST NOTABLY, JERUSALEM. THE MUCH SMALLER JEWISH PORTION WOULD BE DIVIDED INTO STRIPS RUNNING ALONG THE MEDITERRANEAN COAST AND WOULD INCLUDE A MAJOR PORTION OF THE GALILEE.

NOW BOTH PEOPLES MUST RESPOND TO THE BRITISH INITIATIVE. IN MANY WAYS, THE PEEL RECOMMENDATIONS ARE BITTERLY DISAPPOINTING TO ZIONISTS. FIRST, ALL OF TRANSJORDAN WAS DETACHED FROM MANDATED PALESTINE. NOW JEWISH CONTROL WOULD BE LIMITED TO PERHAPS A QUARTER OF THE REMAINING AREA.

A FUNDAMENTAL GOAL OF ZIONISM IS TO REPRESENT THE WHOLE JEWISH PEOPLE, NOT ONLY THOSE CURRENTLY LIVING IN THE LAND. ZIONIST LEADERS WONDER WHETHER SUCH RESTRICTED TERRITORY WOULD SERVE FUTURE NEEDS.

FROM 1930-1938, MORE THAN 200,000 JEWS IMMIGRATE TO THE LAND. MANY OF THESE PEOPLE ARE REFUGEES ESCAPING RUSSIA, GERMANY, AUSTRIA, POLAND, RUMANIA, HUNGARY, UKRAINE AND YUGOSLAVIA. ZIONISM HOPES TO MAKE PALESTINE A SAFE HAVEN FOR ANY JEW IN DANGER.

Jabotinsky

Weizmann

Ben-Gurion

JABOTINSKY REJECTS THE PEEL PARTITION PLAN AS A BETRAYAL OF JEWISH RIGHTS TO THE LAND OF ISRAEL, AND BECAUSE THE PROPOSED JEWISH STATE APPEARS TO BE TOO SMALL TO ABSORB LARGE NUMBERS OF IMMIGRANTS. WEIZMANN AND BEN-GURION RELUCTANTLY ACCEPT THE PROPOSAL, BELIEVING IT IS THE BEST THAT CAN BE ACHIEVED AT THE MOMENT. ARAB LEADERSHIP IN PALESTINE, UNDER THE MUFTI, OPPOSES PARTITION. JEWS MUST NOT BE GRANTED TERRITORY OR SOVEREIGNTY IN THE LAND. SYRIA AND IRAQ CONDEMN THE PLAN.

MANY ARAB LEADERS INCREASINGLY VIEW NAZI GERMANY AS THEIR ALLY AGAINST THE JEWS AND THE BRITISH.

SHOAH: THE HOLOCAUST

FOLLOWING PEEL, THE ARAB REVOLT WHICH BEGAN IN 1936 TURNS EVEN MORE VIOLENT. WOODHEAD, THE NEXT BRITISH COMMISSION ON PALESTINE, CONCLUDES THAT REAL PARTITION IS NOT POSSIBLE.

BY SPRING 1939, LONDON IS IN FULL RETREAT FROM SUPPORTING AN INDEPENDENT JEWISH STATE. BRITAIN ISSUES A NEW POLICY STATEMENT (A WHITE PAPER) LIMITING JEWISH IMMIGRATION TO 75,000 OVER FIVE YEARS AND THEN NO MORE WITHOUT ARAB CONSENT. JEWISH LAND PURCHASES WOULD BE LIMITED. THE BALFOUR CONCEPT OF A JEWISH NATIONAL HOME WOULD BECOME PART OF A BI-NATIONAL STATE OF PALESTINE.

JEWS SEE THE WHITE PAPER AS AN ASSAULT ON THE ZIONIST DREAM, COMING AT THE WORST POSSIBLE TIME. NOW THERE ARE SOME ISOLATED JEWISH RIOTS DIRECTED AGAINST THE BRITISH. BUT PALESTINIAN ARABS ALSO REJECT THE NEW PROPOSAL SINCE IT DOES NOT IMMEDIATELY TURN PALESTINE INTO AN ARAB STATE.

PROFESSOR, BY "WORST POSSIBLE TIME" YOU MEAN BECAUSE THE NAZIS ARE IN POWER AND WWII IS ABOUT TO START, RIGHT?

YES. IN 1935 THE NAZIS IMPLEMENT THE NUREMBERG LAWS THAT FORMALLY STRIP GERMAN JEWS OF THEIR CITIZENSHIP AND RIGHTS. THEIR SITUATION SOON WORSENS. IN NOVEMBER 1938, HITLER UNLEASHES THE KRISTALLNACHT POGROM. NAZI STORMTROOPERS RAVAGE JEWISH COMMUNITIES IN GERMANY AND AUSTRIA, MURDERING MORE THAN 100 JEWS, SENDING SOME 30,000 TO CONCENTRATION CAMPS AND DESTROYING HUNDREDS OF SYNAGOGUES AND JEWISH BUSINESSES.

MOST NATIONS TAKE NO STEPS TO EASE THE EMER- GENCY DEVELOPING IN GERMANY AND AUSTRIA. IN 1938, AN INTERNATIONAL CONFERENCE IS CALLED AT EVIAN, FRANCE TO FACE THE PROBLEM OF JEWS TRYING TO FLEE HITLER'S REGIME. ONLY DENMARK, HOLLAND AND THE TINY DOMINICAN REPUBLIC ARE WILLING TO CHANGE IMMIGRATION RULES TO HELP JEWS.

IN 1939, A GROUP OF REFUGEE ADVOCATES – CHRISTIANS AS WELL AS JEWS – PUSH TO ADMIT ANOTHER 20,000 GERMAN-JEWISH CHILDREN INTO AMERICA. IMMEDIATELY, 4,000 FAMILIES OFFER TO HOUSE THE CHILDREN, BUT DUE TO BOTH CONGRESSIONAL AND PRESIDENTIAL OPPOSITION TO A CHANGE IN THE IMMIGRATION QUOTA, THE EFFORT FAILS.

IN MAY 1939, THE S.S. ST. LOUIS, CARRYING 930 GERMAN REFUGEES, IS TURNED AWAY FROM THE PORT OF HAVANA AFTER BOTH THE U.S. AND CUBA REFUSE THEM ENTRY. THE SHIP'S SAD RETURN TO EUROPE SYMBOLIZES THE FREE WORLD'S FAILURE TO TAKE MEANINGFUL HUMANITARIAN ACTION TO RESCUE JEWS FROM HITLER.

BUT GERMANY IS DEVELOPING OTHER SOLUTIONS TO THE PROBLEM OF WHERE TO PUT JEWS.

IN STAGES, GERMAN JEWS ARE SYSTEMATICALLY ISOLATED AND TERRORIZED. THE NAZIS EXPLOIT OLD CHRISTIAN IMAGES ABOUT THE JEWISH PEOPLE AND THEY PROMOTE NEW LANGUAGE OF JEW-HATRED, LABELING JEWS A SICK, VERMIN-LIKE RACE. MANY OTHER GROUPS ARE ALSO TARGETED FOR DESTRUCTION LIKE GYPSIES, HOMOSEXUALS, JEHOVAH'S WITNESSES AND THE DISABLED.

EVENTUALLY, COMBINING THE CRUELEST CONCEIVABLE TORTURES WITH METICULOUS BUREAUCRATIC EFFICIENCY, THE NAZIS DEDICATE THEMSELVES TO AN ALL-OUT EFFORT TO END THE EXISTENCE OF THE JEWISH PEOPLE.

THE YEARS 1939-1945 PROVE THAT SOME EARLY ZIONIST THINKERS WERE MORE CORRECT THAN THEY COULD IMAGINE. JEWS OF EUROPE ARE LIVING ON BORROWED TIME. A JEWISH HOMELAND IS A LIFE OR DEATH NEED.

THE NAZIS HAVE COLLABORATORS AND RESISTORS. UNFORTUNATELY, THE FORMER GREATLY OUTNUMBER THE LATTER. BUT THOUSANDS OF ORDINARY PEOPLE DO RISK ALL TO SAVE FELLOW HUMAN BEINGS. SOME RESCUERS ARE INSPIRED BY CHRISTIAN FAITH AND SOME BY SIMPLE HUMAN KINDNESS. MANY ARE KILLED FOR GIVING AID AND COMFORT TO JEWS.

MOST JEWS WHO WILL BE GASSED, SHOT, STARVED OR WORKED TO DEATH UNDER HITLER ARE DECEIVED ABOUT THE FATE AWAITING THEM OR OVERWHELMED BY THE BRUTALITY OF THE NAZI MACHINE. BUT JEWISH RESISTANCE DEVELOPS, BOTH PHYSICAL AND SPIRITUAL RESISTANCE.

THE NAZI CAMPAIGN IS DIRECTED AGAINST THE JEWISH SPIRIT AS WELL AS JEWISH LIVES. HITLER'S GERMANY INTENDS TO STRIP JEWS OF EVERY SHRED OF DIGNITY BEFORE DELIVERING THEM TO A GRUESOME DEATH. RELIGIOUS PRACTICES, FROM PRAYER TO HOLIDAYS TO JEWISH DRESS TO TORAH STUDY, ARE PUNISHABLE BY EXECUTION. YET MANY OBSERVE THESE PRACTICES IN THE GHETTOS AND DEATH CAMPS. SOME PERISH WHILE RECITING THE *SHEMA*. CAPTIVE JEWS PERFORM MUSIC AND THEATER, TEACH HEBREW LANGUAGE CLASSES AND PUBLISH NEWSPAPERS.

SMALL JEWISH REVOLTS OCCUR THROUGHOUT THE WAR. THE MOST WELL-KNOWN RESISTANCE BEGINS ON APRIL 19, 1943. HOURS BEFORE PASSOVER, JEWS STAND AGAINST THE NAZI ATTEMPT TO LIQUIDATE THE SURVIVING 60,000 IN THE WARSAW, POLAND GHETTO. 700 MEN AND WOMEN LED BY MORDECAI ANIELEWICZ BATTLE WITH PISTOLS, A FEW RIFLES AND MOLOTOV COCKTAILS. JEWISH RESISTANCE HOLDS OUT FOR NEARLY A MONTH UNTIL THE GERMANS BURN THE GHETTO TO THE GROUND.

IRONICALLY, ON THE DAY THE UPRISING BEGINS, ALLIED POWERS HOLD A CONFERENCE IN BERMUDA TO DISCUSS HELPING JEWISH REFUGEES, BUT NO ACTION IS TAKEN.

JEWS IN PALESTINE SUPPORT THE ALLIED DRIVE TO DEFEAT HITLER. ZIONIST LEADERS SEEK PERMISSION TO FORM JEWISH ARMY UNITS ALLIED WITH BRITAIN. FOR SEVERAL YEARS, LONDON REFUSES, FEARING TO PROVOKE MORE ARAB UNREST OR INCUR BURDENS OF GRATITUDE TOWARD JEWS. AN OFFICIAL JEWISH BRIGADE IS ESTABLISHED TOWARD THE WAR'S END.

Mordecai Anielewicz

IN THE MEANTIME, THOUSANDS OF PALESTINIAN JEWS JOIN THE BRITISH WAR EFFORT AS INDIVIDUAL SOLDIERS. SPECIAL TEAMS OF HAGANAH FIGHTERS CALLED STRIKE FORCES (PALMACH) ARE ALSO FORMED IN PALESTINE IN RESPONSE TO THE GROWING NAZI THREAT IN THE MIDDLE EAST. IN VARIOUS WAYS, THE PRESSURES OF WWII HELP DEVELOP JEWISH MILITARY COMPETENCE IN THE LAND.

BY 1942, ZIONIST LEADERSHIP MUST FACE THE POSSIBILITY THAT THE NAZIS COULD DRIVE THROUGH SOUTHERN RUSSIA, LINK UP WITH ROMMEL'S AFRIKA CORPS AND HAVE ACCESS TO ARAB OIL. THE MUFTI, NOW LIVING IN GERMANY, COLLABORATES WITH THE NAZIS, ORGANIZES A MUSLIM DIVISION OF THE SS AND HELPS DEFEAT A PRO- POSED PRISONER EXCHANGE WITH THE ALLIES THAT WOULD HAVE SAVED 5,000 JEWISH CHILDREN FROM THE GAS CHAMBERS.

TO PROTECT PALESTINE'S JEWS, THE HAGANAH BEGINS TO DEVELOP THE CARMEL PLAN. IF THE NAZIS INVADE, THE COASTAL HIGHLANDS AROUND HAIFA WOULD BECOME A STRONGHOLD FOR ALL PALESTINIAN JEWS. FROM THERE, THEY COULD LAUNCH GUERILLA COUNTERATTACKS TO HOLD OFF THE ENEMY UNTIL ALLIED AID ARRIVED. SINCE THE NAZIS WERE STOPPED BEFORE INVADING PALESTINE, THE PLAN WAS NEVER IMPLEMENTED.

Erwin Rommel

PALESTINE'S JEWS MAKE ANOTHER CONTRI-
BUTION TO THE ALLIED CAUSE. 240 YOUNG
PEOPLE WHO CAME TO THE LAND FROM
EUROPE VOLUNTEER TO GO BACK TO THEIR
NAZI-CONTROLLED BIRTHPLACES TO GATHER
MILITARY INTELLIGENCE AND SUPPORT
LOCAL RESISTANCE. TRAINED BY THE
BRITISH, 33 OF THE VOLUNTEERS ARE SENT.
SEVEN ARE CAUGHT, TORTURED AND EXE-
CUTED, INCLUDING TWO WOMEN, CHAVIVA
REIK AND CHANA SZENES.

GROWING UP, SZENES KEPT A DIARY
AND WROTE POEMS AND A PLAY. ON
JULY 17, 1939, WHILE STILL LIVING IN
HUNGARY, SHE WROTE:

*Today is my birthday, and I am
eighteen. One idea occupies me
continually -the Land of Israel. There is
one place on earth in which we are not
refugees, not emigrants, but where we
are returning home -the Land of Israel.*

Chana Szenes

LESS THAN A YEAR LATER, SZENES MAKES
ALIYAH. SHE BEGINS TO KEEP HER DIARY IN
HEBREW. IN 1943, SZENES IS RECRUITED
FOR THE DANGEROUS MISSION, AFTER
PARACHUTING INTO EUROPE, AT AGE 23,
SHE COMPOSES ONE OF HER LAST POEMS:

*Happy is the match that
burned and lit flames.
Happy is the flame that blazed
in the secret places of the heart.
Happy are the hearts that
knew how to cease with honor.
Happy is the match that
burned and lit flames.*

Chaviva Reik

*PROFESSOR, DO WE KNOW
WHERE SHE'S BURIED?*

YES. IN 1950 HER REMAINS WERE MOVED FROM
HUNGARY TO JERUSALEM. IN FACT, ON OUR TRIP
TO THE REGION WE WILL VISIT HER GRAVE AT
MOUNT HERZL NATIONAL CEMETERY.

DURING THE NAZI ERA, THE ALLIES WERE LARGELY INDIFFERENT TO THE
JEWISH REFUGEE PROBLEM. INDEED, IT WAS EASIER FOR JEWS OF
PALESTINE TO GET INTO EUROPE THAN FOR EUROPE'S JEWS TO REACH
PALESTINE. TO FULFILL ITS WHITE PAPER, BRITAIN CLAMPS DOWN ON
ATTEMPTS TO BRING DOOMED JEWS TO PALESTINE, BUT THOSE LIVING IN
PALESTINE HAVE OTHER IDEAS.

ארגון צבאי לאומי

REFUGEES ARE SMUGGLED INTO THE AREA BY LAND AND SEA, BUT THE WAR EFFORT ALSO FORCES ZIONISTS TO COOPERATE WITH LONDON. EVEN THE IRGUN, FOUNDED IN THE 1930'S AS A MORE HARD-LINE, REVISIONIST MOVEMENT, AGREES TO SUPPORT BRITAIN. THIS DECISION LEADS A SMALL, MILITANT FACTION CALLED LECHI TO SPLIT OFF FROM THE IRGUN IN 1940.

AS THE WAR WINDS DOWN, THE FRICTION BETWEEN ENGLAND AND THE JEWS COMES TO A HEAD. FOR MOST ZIONISTS, BRITAIN HAS BETRAYED THE BALFOUR DECLARATION AND ITS MANDATE DUTIES. THE BRITISH ARE BLOCKING LIFE-SAVING IMMIGRATION.

IN 1944, THE IRGUN LED BY MENACHEM BEGIN, DECLARES A REVOLT AGAINST ENGLISH RULE. THEY ATTACK THE BRITISH MILITARY, POLICE AND CIVIL ADMINISTRATION. THOUGH NO SERIOUS MATCH FOR THE BRITISH, THE IRGUN'S GOAL IS TO DRIVE THEM OUT OF PALESTINE. RELATIONS BETWEEN THE IRGUN AND THE JEWISH AGENCY GO UP AND DOWN. WHILE SHARING FIERCE OPPOSITION TO BRITAIN'S POLICIES, JEWISH GROUPS OFTEN DIFFER ON TACTICS.

Menachem Begin

IRGUN ZWAÏ ... EREZ JISRAËL
ORGANISATION MILIT... JUIVE D'EREZ JISRAËL
JEWISH NATIONAL M... TION OF EREZ JISRAËL

LATER THAT YEAR, THE LECHI FACTION ASSASSINATES A HIGH-RANKING BRITISH OFFICIAL IN CAIRO.

WHAT IS THE REACTION TO THAT?

THE ZIONIST ESTABLISHMENT IS SHOCKED AND EXPOSED TO WORLDWIDE CRITICISM. BEN-GURION, AS HEAD OF THE JEWISH AGENCY, LAUNCHES A CAMPAIGN TO TURN LECHI AND IRGUN MEMBERS OVER TO BRITISH POLICE.

BUT "OPEN SEASON," AS IT WAS CALLED, ON MILITANT JEWISH GROUPS BY OTHER JEWS IS SHORT-LIVED. WHEN WWII ENDS, ZIONISTS UNITE IN THEIR EFFORTS TO RESIST THE BRITISH ON IMMIGRATION. ONE OUT OF EVERY THREE JEWS IN THE WORLD HAD BEEN MURDERED, INCLUDING MORE THAN A MILLION CHILDREN. NOW HUNDREDS OF THOUSANDS ARE IN DISPLACED-PERSONS CAMPS, OR ELSEWHERE, AWAITING RESETTLEMENT. MANY HOPE TO COME TO PALESTINE.

A JOINT BRITISH-AMERICAN COMMITTEE RECOMMENDS BRINGING 100,000 JEWS TO THE LAND IMMEDIATELY, BUT THE BRITISH GOVERNMENT REJECTS THIS. BRITISH SHIPS CONTINUE BLOCKADING THE COAST. CAPTURED REFUGEES ARE OFTEN TAKEN TO CYPRUS. PASSENGERS ON ONE SHIP, THE *BEAUHARNAIS*, DISPLAY A BANNER DECLARING, "WE SURVIVED HITLER. DEATH IS NO STRANGER TO US. NOTHING CAN KEEP US FROM OUR JEWISH HOMELAND."

BEGINNING IN OCTOBER 1945, JEWS OF PALESTINE STRIKE OUT AT BRITISH OPERATIONS. THEY ATTACK A LARGE DETENTION CAMP, DESTROY RAILWAYS AND RADAR INSTALLATIONS AND BOMB PATROL BOATS AND BRIDGES.

ON JUNE 29, 1946, THE BRITISH RETALIATE. COMBING JEWISH PALESTINE STREET BY STREET, 2,700 ARE ARRESTED, INCLUDING IMPORTANT ZIONIST LEADERS.

THE MOST INFAMOUS EPISODE OF THIS PERIOD IS THE IRGUN BOMBING OF THE KING DAVID HOTEL, SITE OF A BRITISH ARMY HEADQUARTERS IN JERUSALEM ON JULY 22, 1946. NINETY-ONE PEOPLE ARE LEFT DEAD, BRITISH, ARABS AND JEWS. THE IRGUN CLAIMS A WARNING WAS DELIVERED BY TELEPHONE 25 MINUTES BEFORE THE EXPLOSION. OTHERS DENY THE CALL OCCURRED, OR THAT IT ARRIVED IN TIME.

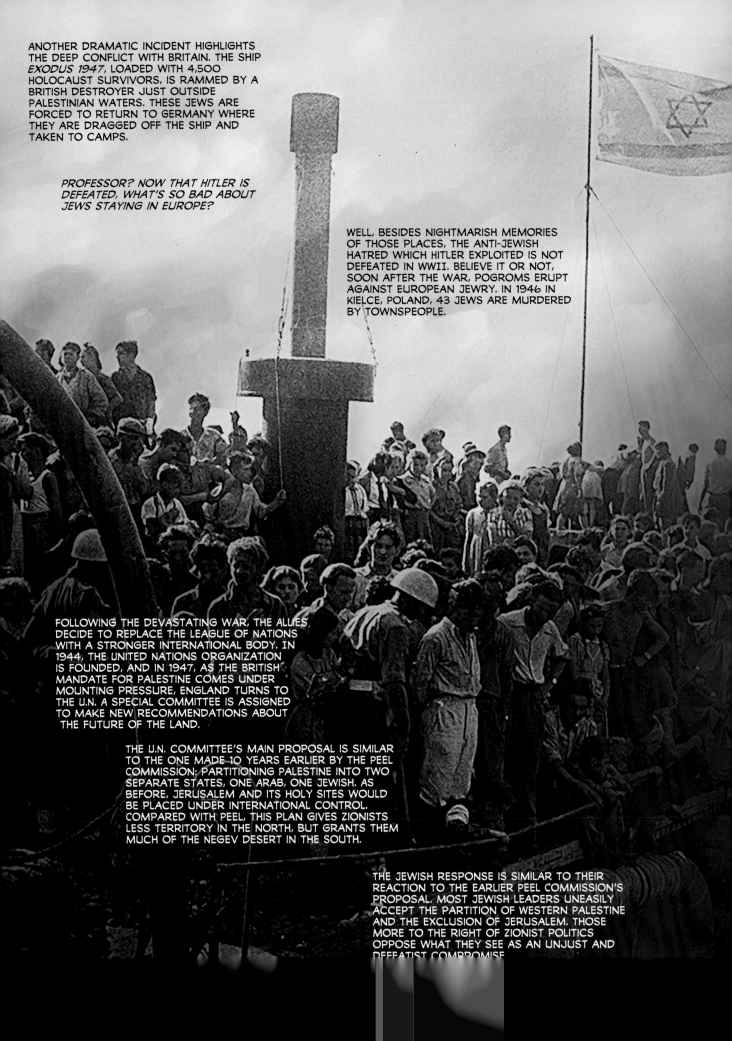

ANOTHER DRAMATIC INCIDENT HIGHLIGHTS THE DEEP CONFLICT WITH BRITAIN. THE SHIP *EXODUS 1947*, LOADED WITH 4,500 HOLOCAUST SURVIVORS, IS RAMMED BY A BRITISH DESTROYER JUST OUTSIDE PALESTINIAN WATERS. THESE JEWS ARE FORCED TO RETURN TO GERMANY WHERE THEY ARE DRAGGED OFF THE SHIP AND TAKEN TO CAMPS.

PROFESSOR? NOW THAT HITLER IS DEFEATED, WHAT'S SO BAD ABOUT JEWS STAYING IN EUROPE?

WELL, BESIDES NIGHTMARISH MEMORIES OF THOSE PLACES, THE ANTI-JEWISH HATRED WHICH HITLER EXPLOITED IS NOT DEFEATED IN WWII. BELIEVE IT OR NOT, SOON AFTER THE WAR, POGROMS ERUPT AGAINST EUROPEAN JEWRY. IN 1946 IN KIELCE, POLAND, 43 JEWS ARE MURDERED BY TOWNSPEOPLE.

FOLLOWING THE DEVASTATING WAR, THE ALLIES DECIDE TO REPLACE THE LEAGUE OF NATIONS WITH A STRONGER INTERNATIONAL BODY. IN 1944, THE UNITED NATIONS ORGANIZATION IS FOUNDED, AND IN 1947, AS THE BRITISH MANDATE FOR PALESTINE COMES UNDER MOUNTING PRESSURE, ENGLAND TURNS TO THE U.N. A SPECIAL COMMITTEE IS ASSIGNED TO MAKE NEW RECOMMENDATIONS ABOUT THE FUTURE OF THE LAND.

THE U.N. COMMITTEE'S MAIN PROPOSAL IS SIMILAR TO THE ONE MADE 10 YEARS EARLIER BY THE PEEL COMMISSION: PARTITIONING PALESTINE INTO TWO SEPARATE STATES, ONE ARAB, ONE JEWISH. AS BEFORE, JERUSALEM AND ITS HOLY SITES WOULD BE PLACED UNDER INTERNATIONAL CONTROL. COMPARED WITH PEEL, THIS PLAN GIVES ZIONISTS LESS TERRITORY IN THE NORTH, BUT GRANTS THEM MUCH OF THE NEGEV DESERT IN THE SOUTH.

THE JEWISH RESPONSE IS SIMILAR TO THEIR REACTION TO THE EARLIER PEEL COMMISSION'S PROPOSAL. MOST JEWISH LEADERS UNEASILY ACCEPT THE PARTITION OF WESTERN PALESTINE AND THE EXCLUSION OF JERUSALEM. THOSE MORE TO THE RIGHT OF ZIONIST POLITICS OPPOSE WHAT THEY SEE AS AN UNJUST AND DEFEATIST COMPROMISE.

ARABS IN AND BEYOND PALESTINE RECOIL
FROM THE PARTITION BELIEVING THE LAND
IS THEIRS. ARAB SPOKESMEN SUGGEST THAT
PARTITION IS A STEPPING-STONE FOR
ZIONISTS TO DOMINATE ALL OF PALESTINE.
THEY ALSO CLAIM THE JEWISH PRESENCE
HARMS ARAB NATIONAL CULTURE.

SO AN INTENSE DIPLOMATIC STRUGGLE
BEGINS FOR THE VOTES OF U.N. MEMBERS
WHO WILL DECIDE WHETHER TO ENDORSE
THE PARTITION PLAN, END THE BRITISH
MANDATE, AND ESTABLISH THESE NEW
STATES. TWO-THIRDS OF THE MEMBERSHIP
IS REQUIRED FOR PASSAGE.

THE ARGUMENTS JEWISH LEADERS MAKE IN FAVOR OF
PARTITION INCLUDE: (1) THE HISTORIC CONNECTION OF
JEWS TO THE LAND; (2) THE BALFOUR DECLARATION AND
THE BRITISH MANDATE; (3) THE JEWISH POPULATION THERE,
NOW NUMBERING MORE THAN 600,000; (4) WORK DONE
BY JEWS TO DEVELOP PALESTINE; (5) JEWISH SUFFERING IN
THE DIASPORA AND THE URGENT NEED TO PROVIDE A
HOME FOR REFUGEES; (6) THE IMPOSSIBILITY OF JEWISH
PALESTINIANS LIVING FREELY UNDER ARAB RULE.

BOTH THE UNITED STATES AND THE SOVIET UNION
SUPPORT PARTITION. PRESIDENT TRUMAN REJECTS
THE U.S. STATE DEPARTMENT'S RECOMMENDATIONS
AND LOBBIES FOR ISRAEL'S CREATION. SOME
COUNTRIES, LIKE FRANCE, ARE UNDECIDED.

THE U.N. VOTE IS HELD ON NOVEMBER 29, 1947. JEWS
IN PALESTINE AND AROUND THE WORLD HUDDLE NEAR
RADIOS TO HEAR THE LIVE BROADCAST FROM NEW
YORK CITY AS THE NATIONS ARE POLLED. THE RESULTS:
33 IN FAVOR OF PARTITION, 13 AGAINST, 10 ABSTAIN.
THE INTERNATIONAL COMMUNITY HAS AUTHORIZED THE
FORMATION OF A SOVEREIGN JEWISH STATE.

In Favor:
Australia, Belgium, Bolivia, Brazil,
Byelorussian SSR, Canada, Costa Rica,
Czechoslovakia, Denmark, Dominican
Republic, Ecuador, France, Guatemala,
Haiti, Iceland, Liberia, Luxembourg,
Netherlands, New Zealand, Nicaragua,
Norway, Panama, Paraguay, Peru,
Philippines, Poland, Sweden, Ukrainian
SSR, Union of South Africa, USSR, USA,
Uruguay, Venezuela

Against:
Afghanistan, Cuba, Egypt, Greece, India,
Iran, Iraq, Lebanon, Pakistan, Saudi Arabia,
Syria, Turkey, Yemen

Abstaining:
Argentina, Chile, China, Columbia, El
Salvador, Ethiopia, Honduras, Mexico,
United Kingdom, Yugoslavia

JEWISH CELEBRATION IS DAMPENED BY ARAB REACTIONS. THE GOVERNMENT OF SAUDI ARABIA REJECTS THE RESOLUTION AND "RESERVES TO ITSELF THE FULL RIGHT TO ACT FREELY IN WHATEVER WAY IT DEEMS FIT, IN ACCORDANCE WITH THE PRINCIPLES OF RIGHT AND JUSTICE."

THE NEXT DAY LOCAL ARABS BEGIN TO ATTACK THE JEWISH POPULATION OF PALESTINE. FIRST, THE VIOLENCE STRIKES SMALLER TARGETS LIKE BUSES AND SHOPS. LATER, JEWISH SETTLEMENTS ARE HIT. HAGANAH, IRGUN AND LECHI SOLDIERS RESPOND, USUALLY WITH DEFENSIVE ACTION, BUT INNOCENT ARABS ARE ALSO KILLED IN SOME JEWISH REPRISALS.

ARAB ASSAULTS ON JEWS ARE NOT CONFINED TO PALESTINE. IN RESPONSE TO U.N. RESOLUTION 181, HUNDREDS OF SYRIAN JEWS WITNESS THEIR HOMES AND SYNAGOGUES DESTROYED. MOBS IN LIBYA KILL MORE THAN 130.

IN THE WEEKS TO COME, THOUSANDS OF ARAB FIGHTERS CROSS INTO PALESTINE FROM SURROUNDING LANDS TO JOIN THE BATTLE. THE BRITISH DO LITTLE TO STOP THIS INFLUX OR THE ATTACKS ON JEWS. IN FACT, FORTRESSES AND STOCKADES ARE HANDED OVER TO ARAB FORCES. BRITISH SOLDIERS CONTINUE TO ARREST JEWISH IMMIGRANTS.

THE BRITISH DO NOT COOPERATE WITH IMPLEMENTING PARTITION. EVENTUALLY RAILROADS STOP OPERATING AND MAIL IS NOT DELIVERED BECAUSE NO ARRANGEMENT IS MADE TO TRANSITION SUCH SERVICES.

THROUGH THE WINTER OF 1947-1948, HAGANAH UNITS, WITH LIMITED WEAPONRY, CONDUCT A STRONG DEFENSE. BY MARCH 1948, THE WAR INTENSIFIES.

ARAB FORCES BEGIN TO SHACKLE JEWISH TRANSPORTATION, DESTROY SUPPLY LINES AND ISOLATE JERUSALEM. THE VIOLENCE, ALONG WITH PRESSURE FROM OIL-RICH ARAB GOVERNMENTS, CAUSES SOME AMERICAN LEADERS TO WITHDRAW SUPPORT FOR PARTITION. THE U.S. IMPOSES AN ARMS EMBARGO, BUT THE SOVIET UNION ALLOWS JEWS TO PURCHASE DESPERATELY NEEDED ARMS THROUGH CZECHOSLOVAKIA.

BEN-GURION AND OTHER ZIONIST LEADERS DECIDE THAT THE ONLY WAY TO SAVE THE SITUATION IS THROUGH A BOLD COUNTER-OFFENSIVE DESIGNED TO CAPTURE ARAB TOWNS AND ELIMINATE ENEMY BASES. THIS CAMPAIGN INCLUDES A PLAN TO OPEN THE ROAD TO JERUSALEM. THE PLAN IS NAMED OPERATION NACHSHON.

NOW JEWS MAKE SERIOUS GAINS. ARAB RESIDENTS, ESPECIALLY THOSE FROM THE UPPER-CLASSES, OFTEN ABANDON AREAS THAT JEWS HAVE WON, PERHAPS BASED ON CALLS FROM THEIR LEADERS. BUT SOME ARABS MAY HAVE BEEN EXPELLED FROM VILLAGES CONSIDERED VITAL TO ZIONIST INTERESTS.

ONE OF THE MOST CONTROVERSIAL ACTS DURING THIS WAR OCCURS AT THE BATTLE FOR DEIR YASIN, A VILLAGE NEAR JERUSALEM USED AS A STAGING AREA BY ARAB FORCES. MEN FROM IRGUN AND LECHI SLAY BETWEEN 100 AND 250 ARABS, INCLUDING WOMEN, CHILDREN AND ELDERLY MEN. THE NUMBER OF DEAD, AND ALMOST EVERYTHING ELSE ABOUT THE EVENT, HAS BEEN DISPUTED EVER SINCE.

FOUR DAYS LATER ARAB FIGHTERS KILL SCORES OF DOCTORS, NURSES AND THEIR PATIENTS TRAVELING IN A CONVOY TO A JERUSALEM HOSPITAL.

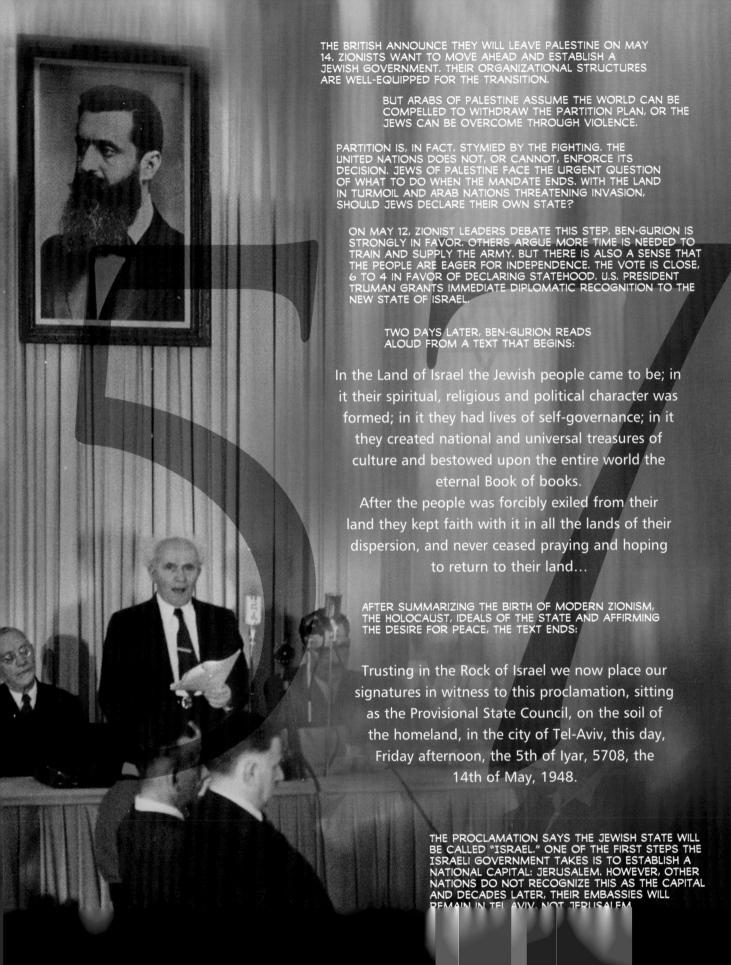

THE BRITISH ANNOUNCE THEY WILL LEAVE PALESTINE ON MAY 14. ZIONISTS WANT TO MOVE AHEAD AND ESTABLISH A JEWISH GOVERNMENT. THEIR ORGANIZATIONAL STRUCTURES ARE WELL-EQUIPPED FOR THE TRANSITION.

BUT ARABS OF PALESTINE ASSUME THE WORLD CAN BE COMPELLED TO WITHDRAW THE PARTITION PLAN, OR THE JEWS CAN BE OVERCOME THROUGH VIOLENCE.

PARTITION IS, IN FACT, STYMIED BY THE FIGHTING. THE UNITED NATIONS DOES NOT, OR CANNOT, ENFORCE ITS DECISION. JEWS OF PALESTINE FACE THE URGENT QUESTION OF WHAT TO DO WHEN THE MANDATE ENDS. WITH THE LAND IN TURMOIL AND ARAB NATIONS THREATENING INVASION, SHOULD JEWS DECLARE THEIR OWN STATE?

ON MAY 12, ZIONIST LEADERS DEBATE THIS STEP. BEN-GURION IS STRONGLY IN FAVOR. OTHERS ARGUE MORE TIME IS NEEDED TO TRAIN AND SUPPLY THE ARMY. BUT THERE IS ALSO A SENSE THAT THE PEOPLE ARE EAGER FOR INDEPENDENCE. THE VOTE IS CLOSE, 6 TO 4 IN FAVOR OF DECLARING STATEHOOD. U.S. PRESIDENT TRUMAN GRANTS IMMEDIATE DIPLOMATIC RECOGNITION TO THE NEW STATE OF ISRAEL.

TWO DAYS LATER, BEN-GURION READS ALOUD FROM A TEXT THAT BEGINS:

In the Land of Israel the Jewish people came to be; in it their spiritual, religious and political character was formed; in it they had lives of self-governance; in it they created national and universal treasures of culture and bestowed upon the entire world the eternal Book of books.
After the people was forcibly exiled from their land they kept faith with it in all the lands of their dispersion, and never ceased praying and hoping to return to their land…

AFTER SUMMARIZING THE BIRTH OF MODERN ZIONISM, THE HOLOCAUST, IDEALS OF THE STATE AND AFFIRMING THE DESIRE FOR PEACE, THE TEXT ENDS:

Trusting in the Rock of Israel we now place our signatures in witness to this proclamation, sitting as the Provisional State Council, on the soil of the homeland, in the city of Tel-Aviv, this day, Friday afternoon, the 5th of Iyar, 5708, the 14th of May, 1948.

THE PROCLAMATION SAYS THE JEWISH STATE WILL BE CALLED "ISRAEL." ONE OF THE FIRST STEPS THE ISRAELI GOVERNMENT TAKES IS TO ESTABLISH A NATIONAL CAPITAL: JERUSALEM. HOWEVER, OTHER NATIONS DO NOT RECOGNIZE THIS AS THE CAPITAL AND DECADES LATER, THEIR EMBASSIES WILL REMAIN IN TEL AVIV, NOT JERUSALEM.

LEBANON

SYRIA

MEDITERRANEAN SEA

IRAQ

HOURS AFTER DECLARING INDEPENDENCE, ISRAEL IS
ATTACKED BY EGYPT, LEBANON, SYRIA, TRANSJORDAN
AND IRAQ, JOINING PALESTINIAN ARABS ALREADY IN
CONFLICT WITH THE JEWS. THOUGH NOT UNITED IN
OBJECTIVES OR TACTICS, THESE GROUPS POSE A
GRAVE THREAT TO THE ZIONIST ACHIEVEMENT.

ISRAEL

ISRAEL CONSOLIDATES ITS MILITARY. OFFICIALLY,
HAGANAH, IRGUN AND LECHI BECOME A SINGLE DEFENSE
FORCE. BUT THIS NEXT PHASE OF THE WAR IS DIFFICULT
FOR THE JEWISH STATE. ARAB ARMIES TAKE CONTROL
OF LAND DESIGNATED FOR ISRAEL BY THE U.N. PARTITION
PLAN. TRANSJORDANIAN TROOPS EXPEL JEWS FROM THE
OLD CITY OF JERUSALEM.

TRANSJORDAN

WHEN THE FIRST TRUCE IS ARRANGED ON JUNE 11, 1948,
SUPPLIES ON BOTH SIDES ARE REPLENISHED. THOUSANDS
OF JEWISH AND NON-JEWISH VOLUNTEERS ARRIVE FROM
AROUND THE WORLD TO FIGHT FOR ISRAEL INCLUDING
MANY AMERICAN JEWISH PILOTS.

EGYPT

MEMBERS OF THE IRGUN GO TO FRANCE TO BRING
BACK MEN AND ARMS. THEY NAME THEIR TRANSPORT
VESSEL THE *ALTALENA*, A PEN NAME OF THE LATE
JABOTINSKY. WHEN THE SHIP RETURNS, BEN-GURION
LEARNS THE IRGUN PLANS TO KEEP SOME WEAPONS
FOR ITSELF. HE FEELS SUCH A CHALLENGE TO ISRAEL'S
NEW CENTRAL GOVERNMENT WOULD BE DISASTROUS.
AFTER DAYS OF TENSION, BEN-GURION ORDERS THE
ALTALENA FIRED UPON AND IT IS SUNK WITH THE ARMS
ON BOARD.

ARABS RESUME HOSTILITIES ON JULY 8, BUT THIS
TIME THE WAR GOES BETTER FOR ISRAEL. BY
DECEMBER, ISRAEL HAS WON ABOUT 20% MORE
TERRITORY THAN WAS ORIGINALLY GRANTED, BUT
TRANSJORDAN RETAINS CONTROL OF THE JEWISH
QUARTER OF THE OLD CITY OF JERUSALEM AND
OCCUPIES WHAT BEGINS TO BE CALLED THE WEST
BANK OF THE JORDAN RIVER, AND EGYPT CONTROLS
THE GAZA STRIP IN THE SOUTH.

THROUGH 1949, ARMISTICE AGREEMENTS ARE SIGNED
BETWEEN ISRAEL AND ITS FOREIGN ATTACKERS. THESE
ARE MEANT TO BE REPLACED BY PEACE TREATIES, BUT
THIS FAILS TO OCCUR.

NEVERTHELESS, THE JEWS OF PALESTINE ARE NOW ISRAELIS AND THE STATE OF ISRAEL IS A FACT. IN MARCH 1949, ISRAEL IS APPROVED FOR MEMBERSHIP IN THE U.N.

PROFESSOR, WHAT ABOUT THE PALESTINIAN ARABS? WHAT HAPPENED TO THEIR STATE? YOU STARTED TELLING US ABOUT THE ONES WHO LEFT OR WERE EXPELLED, BUT THERE'S A LOT MORE TO IT, RIGHT?

FIRST OF ALL, PALESTINIAN ARABS WHO STAY BECOME ISRAELI CITIZENS. HOWEVER AS I'VE SAID, THE PALESTINIAN LEADERS REJECTED PARTITION, SO ON A PRACTICAL LEVEL, THEY DID NOT PREPARE FOR STATEHOOD. DURING THE WAR, WHILE DEFENDING THEMSELVES, ISRAELIS GAIN MORE TERRITORY. NEIGHBORING ARABS TAKE OVER LAND ASSIGNED TO THEIR PALESTINIAN BROTHERS AND SISTERS. EGYPT AND TRANSJORDAN COULD NOW ESTABLISH A PALESTINIAN STATE IF THEY CHOOSE.

IT IS DIFFICULT TO DETERMINE ALL THE CAUSES OF THE ARAB REFUGEE PROBLEM, BUT FEAR OF THE FIGHTING AND UNWILL-INGNESS TO LIVE IN A JEWISH STATE ARE PROBABLY THE MAIN ONES. SOME BELIEVE ARAB LEADERS ENCOURAGED PEOPLE TO CLEAR OUT OF THEIR HOMES WITH THE PROMISE OF RETURNING AFTER ISRAEL'S DEFEAT. SOME BELIEVE JEWISH LEADERS EVICTED PALESTINIAN ARABS.

ARAB SPOKESMEN, FOR THEIR PART, WERE ANNOUNCING THEIR INTENTION TO CONDUCT A "WAR OF EXTERMINATION" AND TO BRING ABOUT "THE ELIMINATION OF THE JEWISH STATE." DURING THE WAR, ARABS CAPTURED THE VILLAGE OF K'FAR ETZION AND MANY JEWS WHO HAD SURRENDERED WERE MASSACRED.

HUNDREDS OF THOUSANDS OF ARABS END UP FLEEING. MOST GO TO THE WEST BANK CONTROLLED BY JORDAN AND TO JORDAN ITSELF. A LARGE NUMBER GO TO THE GAZA STRIP UNDER EGYPT. OTHERS MAKE THEIR WAY TO LEBANON OR SYRIA. IN THESE ARAB COUNTRIES, LARGE NUMBERS OF PALESTINIANS ARE PLACED IN OPPRESSIVE CAMPS.

AS ISRAEL TURNS FROM ITS WAR OF INDEPENDENCE, THE COUNTRY FACES MANY CHALLENGES: TO DEVELOP ITS GOV-ERNMENT; TO PROMOTE CULTURAL, TECHNOLOGICAL AND ECONOMIC PROGRESS; TO ABSORB MASSES OF NEW IMMI-GRANTS; TO EXPLORE THE ROLE OF JUDAISM WITHIN A DEM-OCRATIC STATE; TO DEAL WITH CONTINUED PHYSICAL THREATS AND TO SEARCH FOR PEACE.

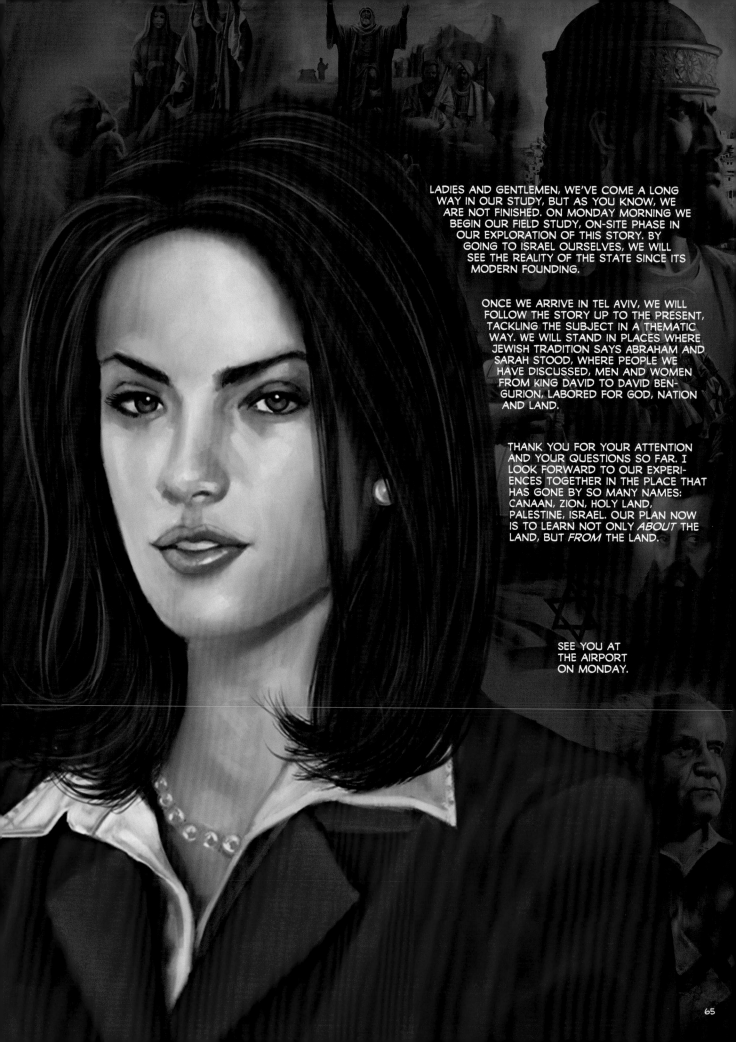

LADIES AND GENTLEMEN, WE'VE COME A LONG WAY IN OUR STUDY, BUT AS YOU KNOW, WE ARE NOT FINISHED. ON MONDAY MORNING WE BEGIN OUR FIELD STUDY, ON-SITE PHASE IN OUR EXPLORATION OF THIS STORY. BY GOING TO ISRAEL OURSELVES, WE WILL SEE THE REALITY OF THE STATE SINCE ITS MODERN FOUNDING.

ONCE WE ARRIVE IN TEL AVIV, WE WILL FOLLOW THE STORY UP TO THE PRESENT, TACKLING THE SUBJECT IN A THEMATIC WAY. WE WILL STAND IN PLACES WHERE JEWISH TRADITION SAYS ABRAHAM AND SARAH STOOD, WHERE PEOPLE WE HAVE DISCUSSED, MEN AND WOMEN FROM KING DAVID TO DAVID BEN-GURION, LABORED FOR GOD, NATION AND LAND.

THANK YOU FOR YOUR ATTENTION AND YOUR QUESTIONS SO FAR. I LOOK FORWARD TO OUR EXPERI-ENCES TOGETHER IN THE PLACE THAT HAS GONE BY SO MANY NAMES: CANAAN, ZION, HOLY LAND, PALESTINE, ISRAEL. OUR PLAN NOW IS TO LEARN NOT ONLY *ABOUT* THE LAND, BUT *FROM* THE LAND.

SEE YOU AT
THE AIRPORT
ON MONDAY.

TICKETS ARE MATCHED TO PASSPORTS AND I.D.S ARE RUN THROUGH INTERPOL, FBI, ISRAELI AND OTHER INTELLIGENCE DATABASES. CARRY-ON LUGGAGE IS PASSED THROUGH A DECOMPRESSION CHAMBER TO SCREEN FOR EXPLOSIVES TRIGGERED BY AIR-PRESSURE.

PLAINCLOTHES OFFICERS TRAVEL ON EACH FLIGHT. PILOTS, ALL WITH ISRAELI MILITARY BACKGROUND, AND FLIGHT CREW ARE CERTIFIED IN HAND-TO-HAND COMBAT.

REINFORCED STEEL FLOORS INSULATE THE PASSENGER CABIN FROM POSSIBLE CARGO-HOLD BLASTS. COCKPIT DOORS ARE SEALED BEFORE PASSENGERS BOARD AND AREN'T OPENED AGAIN UNTIL ALL PASSENGERS HAVE DISEMBARKED.

Welcome to Israel ישראל

EL AL HAS DAILY FLIGHTS TO OVER FIFTY DESTINATIONS. THEIR ELABORATE SECURITY ARRANGEMENTS COST THE AIRLINE NEARLY $90 MILLION A YEAR, BUT MOST PEOPLE WHO FLY EL AL HAVE A GREATER FEELING OF SAFETY.

PROFESSOR, WHY IS THERE A SPECIAL LINE FOR NEW IMMIGRANTS?

REMEMBER, ISRAEL IS A COUNTRY BUILT UP BY NEW IMMIGRANTS AND PRIORITY IS GIVEN TO THOSE ARRIVING TO HELP BUILD THE NATION. THERE IS STILL A SENSE HERE THAT ALL IMMIGRANTS ARE PIONEERS.

THE JEWISH AGENCY FOR ISRAEL (JAFI), SUPPORTED BY ISRAEL AND WORLD JEWRY, BECOMES RESPONSIBLE FOR IMMIGRATION AND ABSORPTION.

IN 1948, ISRAEL'S POPULATION IS 806,000, INCLUDING MORE THAN 600,000 JEWS. WITH THE END OF WWII AND THE DECLARATION OF ISRAELI INDEPENDENCE, MORE WOULD SOON BE COMING. FROM 1948-1958, MORE THAN 900,000 IMMIGRANTS ARRIVE: 40% FROM WESTERN COUNTRIES, 60% FROM THE EAST.

IMMIGRATION & RESCUE

THE FOUNDING OF ISRAEL IS LIKE A MAGNET FOR JEWS ACROSS THE WORLD. WITH THE HOPE OF FREEDOM AND THE DESIRE TO BECOME PART OF THE OLD-NEW ZIONIST STORY, THEY COME FROM MANY CORNERS OF THE WORLD, INCLUDING SUCH FAR-FLUNG JEWISH COMMUNITIES AS COCHIN, INDIA.

239,000 HOLOCAUST SURVIVORS REACH ISRAEL FROM DISPLACED PERSONS CAMPS IN 1949. IN MANY ARAB COUNTRIES, WHERE JEWS HAD LIVED FOR TENS OF GENERATIONS, THEY ARE EXPELLED WITH LITTLE BUT THE CLOTHES ON THEIR BACKS BECAUSE OF INCREASING ARAB HOSTILITY.

Vietnamese refugees rescued by Israel

DURING THE EARLY YEARS AS A STATE, ISRAEL ABSORBS:

50,553 JEWS FROM YEMEN
129,290 JEWS FROM IRAQ
17,482 JEWS FROM IRAN
4,500 JEWS FROM SYRIA
6,000 JEWS FROM LEBANON
89,525 JEWS FROM EGYPT
33,217 JEWS FROM TURKEY
35,000 JEWS FROM LIBYA
35,946 JEWS FROM MOROCCO AND TUNISIA
14,000 JEWS FROM ALGERIA

BY THE END OF THE 20TH CENTURY, MORE THAN 700,000 JEWS FROM MIDDLE EAST COUNTRIES EMIGRATE TO ISRAEL AND HUNDREDS OF THOUSANDS MORE COME FROM EASTERN EUROPE.

Avital and Natan Sharansky thank President Reagan for securing his freedom.

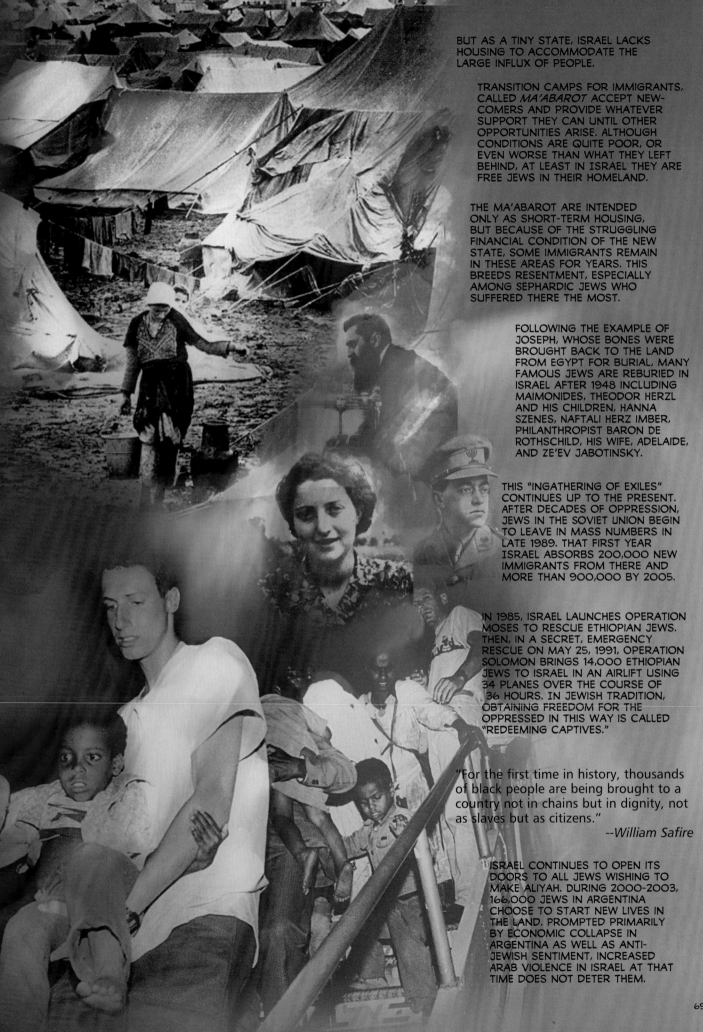

BUT AS A TINY STATE, ISRAEL LACKS HOUSING TO ACCOMMODATE THE LARGE INFLUX OF PEOPLE.

TRANSITION CAMPS FOR IMMIGRANTS, CALLED *MA'ABAROT* ACCEPT NEW-COMERS AND PROVIDE WHATEVER SUPPORT THEY CAN UNTIL OTHER OPPORTUNITIES ARISE. ALTHOUGH CONDITIONS ARE QUITE POOR, OR EVEN WORSE THAN WHAT THEY LEFT BEHIND, AT LEAST IN ISRAEL THEY ARE FREE JEWS IN THEIR HOMELAND.

THE MA'ABAROT ARE INTENDED ONLY AS SHORT-TERM HOUSING, BUT BECAUSE OF THE STRUGGLING FINANCIAL CONDITION OF THE NEW STATE, SOME IMMIGRANTS REMAIN IN THESE AREAS FOR YEARS. THIS BREEDS RESENTMENT, ESPECIALLY AMONG SEPHARDIC JEWS WHO SUFFERED THERE THE MOST.

FOLLOWING THE EXAMPLE OF JOSEPH, WHOSE BONES WERE BROUGHT BACK TO THE LAND FROM EGYPT FOR BURIAL, MANY FAMOUS JEWS ARE REBURIED IN ISRAEL AFTER 1948 INCLUDING MAIMONIDES, THEODOR HERZL AND HIS CHILDREN, HANNA SZENES, NAFTALI HERZ IMBER, PHILANTHROPIST BARON DE ROTHSCHILD, HIS WIFE, ADELAIDE, AND ZE'EV JABOTINSKY.

THIS "INGATHERING OF EXILES" CONTINUES UP TO THE PRESENT. AFTER DECADES OF OPPRESSION, JEWS IN THE SOVIET UNION BEGIN TO LEAVE IN MASS NUMBERS IN LATE 1989. THAT FIRST YEAR ISRAEL ABSORBS 200,000 NEW IMMIGRANTS FROM THERE AND MORE THAN 900,000 BY 2005.

IN 1985, ISRAEL LAUNCHES OPERATION MOSES TO RESCUE ETHIOPIAN JEWS. THEN, IN A SECRET, EMERGENCY RESCUE ON MAY 25, 1991, OPERATION SOLOMON BRINGS 14,000 ETHIOPIAN JEWS TO ISRAEL IN AN AIRLIFT USING 34 PLANES OVER THE COURSE OF 36 HOURS. IN JEWISH TRADITION, OBTAINING FREEDOM FOR THE OPPRESSED IN THIS WAY IS CALLED "REDEEMING CAPTIVES."

"For the first time in history, thousands of black people are being brought to a country not in chains but in dignity, not as slaves but as citizens."

--William Safire

ISRAEL CONTINUES TO OPEN ITS DOORS TO ALL JEWS WISHING TO MAKE ALIYAH. DURING 2000-2003, 166,000 JEWS IN ARGENTINA CHOOSE TO START NEW LIVES IN THE LAND. PROMPTED PRIMARILY BY ECONOMIC COLLAPSE IN ARGENTINA AS WELL AS ANTI-JEWISH SENTIMENT, INCREASED ARAB VIOLENCE IN ISRAEL AT THAT TIME DOES NOT DETER THEM.

THE CONDITION OF THE EARLY STATE

THE EARLY STATE OF ISRAEL FACES MAJOR CHALLENGES INCLUDING TEACHING A NEW TONGUE, HEBREW, TO THE NEW CITIZENS. ALMOST IMMEDIATELY, 600,000 MEN, WOMEN AND CHILDREN NEED TO BE ACCLIMATED INTO ISRAELI SOCIETY. THOUSANDS ARE TRAINED TO ASSIST THEM AS TEACHERS AND TUTORS.

BECAUSE OF THE DEMAND ON THE NEW COUNTRY'S RESOURCES, AUSTERITY IS THE WATCHWORD FOR ISRAELIS THROUGHOUT THE 1950'S. RATIONING IS THE NORM. MEAT IS IN SHORTER SUPPLY THAN OTHER FOODS. CLOTHING, TEXTILES, GAS AND ELECTRICITY ARE NOT CONSISTENTLY AVAILABLE; SOMETIMES SUPPLIES RUN OUT.

RATIONING

PEOPLE ARE LIMITED TO ONE LIGHT BULB PER ROOM, 60 WATTS EACH. ELECTRICAL APPLIANCES, INCLUDING STOVES, ARE NOT PERMITTED DURING THE HOURS OF 4:30 P.M. TO 8:00 P.M.

FOUNDING A NEW COUNTRY IS DIFFICULT; MAINTAINING IT PROVES EVEN HARDER AND VERY EXPENSIVE. THE COST OF IMMIGRANT ABSORPTION AND MILITARY DEFENSE IS TREMENDOUS, BUT THE FLEDGLING STATE IS NOT ALONE.

EVEN BEFORE STATEHOOD, CHARITABLE DONATIONS FROM PHILANTHROPISTS LIKE SIR MOSES MONTEFIORE (1784-1885) AND BARON EDMOND DE ROTHSCHILD (1845-1934) ARE A VITAL FUNDING SOURCE FOR JEWISH PALESTINE.

HUMANITARIAN SUPPORT

AFTER 1948, SUBSTANTIAL HUMANITARIAN SUPPORT CONTINUES TO COME FROM INDIVIDUAL DONATIONS ORGANIZED THROUGH NON-PROFIT INSTITUTIONS INCLUDING JEWISH FEDERATIONS, THE JEWISH NATIONAL FUND AND ISRAEL BONDS. GERMAN HOLOCAUST REPARATIONS, U.S. LOANS AND OTHER GUARANTEES ALSO ENABLE ISRAEL TO UPDATE ELECTRICAL PLANTS, IRRIGATION PROJECTS, RAILROADS AND PORTS.

SINCE ISRAEL'S FOUNDING, JEWISH FEDERATIONS IN THE U.S. AND CANADA, PART OF THE UNITED JEWISH COMMUNITIES, HAVE CONTRIBUTED BILLIONS OF DOLLARS TOWARD ISRAEL'S SOCIAL NEEDS THROUGH THE JEWISH AGENCY FOR ISRAEL. THESE FUNDS SUPPORT IMMIGRATION AND ABSORPTION, EDUCATION, HEALTH SERVICES AND EMERGENCY RESPONSE TO THE TERRORISM ISRAELIS ENDURE.

FROM PROVIDING SUMMER CAMPS FOR CHILDREN WHO ARE VICTIMS OF ATTACKS, TO REBUILDING HOMES AND BUSINESSES, THIS SUPPORT HAS BEEN ESSENTIAL TO THE ISRAELI PEOPLE.

THIS SUPPORT STEMS FROM PEOPLE'S RECOGNITION OF THEIR CONNECTION TO ISRAEL. IN 1999, FEDERATIONS, PARTNERING WITH THE STATE OF ISRAEL AND A GROUP OF PHILANTHROPISTS, ESTABLISH BIRTHRIGHT, A MAJOR NEW VENTURE TO BRING JEWISH YOUNG ADULTS, AGES 18-26 WHO HAVE NEVER BEEN TO ISRAEL, ON AN EDUCATIONAL EXPERIENCE IN THE LAND. BY 2006, MORE THAN 100,000 YOUNG JEWS FROM AROUND THE WORLD VISIT ISRAEL THROUGH THIS PROGRAM, STRENGTHENING THEIR PERSONAL IDENTITY AND INTENSIFIED CONNECTION WITH ISRAEL.

THE JEWISH NATIONAL FUND (JNF) IS ESTABLISHED IN 1901 TO PURCHASE AND DEVELOP LAND IN PALESTINE. DURING ITS HISTORY, JNF HAS PLANTED MORE THAN 240 MILLION TREES (ISRAEL HAS THE ONLY TERRITORY IN THE WORLD WHICH ENDED THE 20TH CENTURY POSSESSING MORE TREES THAN IT STARTED WITH), BUILT MORE THAN 180 DAMS AND RESERVOIRS, DEVELOPED 250,000 ACRES OF LAND AND CREATED MORE THAN 1,000 PARKS THROUGHOUT ISRAEL.

ISRAEL BONDS HELD BY INDIVIDUALS AS WELL AS CORPORATIONS, SUCH AS BANKS, LABOR UNIONS AND INSTITUTIONAL INVESTORS OUTSIDE ISRAEL, ARE A VITAL FUNDING SOURCE FOR THE STATE. BEGINNING IN 2008, ISRAEL BONDS WILL BE RESPONSIBLE FOR SECURING 50% OF ISRAEL'S OVERSEAS BORROWING, APPROXIMATELY $1.5 BILLION ANNUALLY.

THE U.S. GOVERNMENT HAS BEEN A CONSISTENT AND CRUCIAL SUPPORTER OF THE STATE OF ISRAEL, BEGINNING IN 1949. SINCE THEN, THE U.S. HAS PROVIDED NEARLY $100 BILLION IN GRANTS AND LOANS. SOME ARGUE THAT INVESTMENT IN ISRAEL MAKES FINANCIAL AND POLITICAL SENSE FOR THE U.S. SINCE ISRAEL IS THE SOLE ESTABLISHED DEMOCRACY IN THE MIDDLE EAST AND HAS VOTED WITH THE U.S. AT THE UNITED NATIONS MORE THAN ANY OTHER COUNTRY. ISRAEL SPENDS A SIGNIFICANT PERCENTAGE OF ITS U.S. AID ON AMERICAN PRODUCTS FOR USE BACK HOME.

LOBBYING GROUPS LIKE AIPAC (AMERICAN ISRAEL PUBLIC AFFAIRS COMMITTEE) SUPPORT ISRAEL BY ADVOCATING FOR FOREIGN AID LEGISLATION AND FOR FUNDING OF JOINT U.S.-ISRAEL STRATEGIC EFFORTS. AIPAC PROFESSIONALS AND MEMBERS ARE AMERICANS OF ALL RELIGIOUS PERSUASIONS WHO MEET WITH CONGRESSMEN, JOURNALISTS AND VOTERS TO PROMOTE A STRONG U.S.-ISRAEL RELATIONSHIP.

DONATIONS AND TRIPS TO ISRAEL BY AMERICAN CHRISTIANS HAVE ALSO BEEN A SIGNIFICANT SOURCE OF MONETARY AND MORAL SUPPORT. AND MILLIONS OF DOLLARS ARE GIVEN DIRECTLY TO ISRAEL FOR SPECIFIC PROJECTS. "FRIENDS OF..." GROUPS HELP FUND HOSPITALS, UNIVERSITIES AND OTHER INSTITUTIONS.

OF COURSE, AVERAGE ISRAELIS BEAR A HUGE SHARE OF THE FINANCIAL COST OF RUNNING THEIR COUNTRY. THE AVERAGE TAX BURDEN FOR CITIZENS THERE IS 39% AND CAN BE AS HIGH AS 50% OF THEIR INCOME.

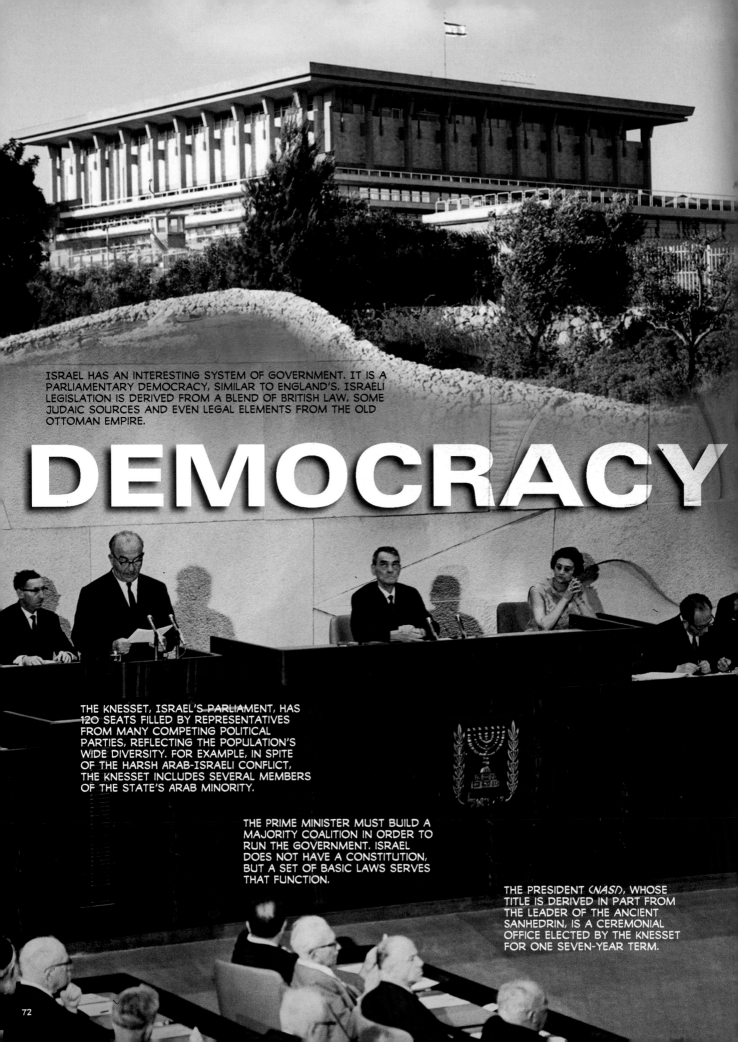

ISRAEL HAS AN INTERESTING SYSTEM OF GOVERNMENT. IT IS A PARLIAMENTARY DEMOCRACY, SIMILAR TO ENGLAND'S. ISRAELI LEGISLATION IS DERIVED FROM A BLEND OF BRITISH LAW, SOME JUDAIC SOURCES AND EVEN LEGAL ELEMENTS FROM THE OLD OTTOMAN EMPIRE.

DEMOCRACY

THE KNESSET, ISRAEL'S PARLIAMENT, HAS 120 SEATS FILLED BY REPRESENTATIVES FROM MANY COMPETING POLITICAL PARTIES, REFLECTING THE POPULATION'S WIDE DIVERSITY. FOR EXAMPLE, IN SPITE OF THE HARSH ARAB-ISRAELI CONFLICT, THE KNESSET INCLUDES SEVERAL MEMBERS OF THE STATE'S ARAB MINORITY.

THE PRIME MINISTER MUST BUILD A MAJORITY COALITION IN ORDER TO RUN THE GOVERNMENT. ISRAEL DOES NOT HAVE A CONSTITUTION, BUT A SET OF BASIC LAWS SERVES THAT FUNCTION.

THE PRESIDENT (NASI), WHOSE TITLE IS DERIVED IN PART FROM THE LEADER OF THE ANCIENT SANHEDRIN, IS A CEREMONIAL OFFICE ELECTED BY THE KNESSET FOR ONE SEVEN-YEAR TERM.

LAWS UNIQUE TO ISRAEL

THREE KEY LAWS ARE PASSED AT THE STATE OF ISRAEL'S BIRTH THAT ADDRESS THE NEEDS OF THE JEWISH PEOPLE, ESPECIALLY AFTER THE DEVASTATION OF THE *SHOAH*, THE HOLOCAUST.

LAW OF RETURN: 1950

EVERY JEW AUTOMATICALLY HAS THE RIGHT TO RETURN TO ISRAEL AS AN *OLEH* (IMMIGRANT). THIS LAW GUARANTEES ASSISTANCE TO NEW IMMIGRANTS AND HELPS EASE THE ABSORPTION PROCESS.

THE LAW OF PUNISHMENT OF NAZIS AND THEIR COLLABORATORS: 1950

CRIMES AGAINST THE JEWISH PEOPLE WILL BE PROSECUTED, WHEREVER AND WHENEVER COMMITTED.

THE HOLOCAUST IS ALSO RECOGNIZED WITH AN OFFICIAL DAY TO MOURN AND HONOR THOSE SUBJECTED TO THE ONSLAUGHT, HOLOCAUST AND HEROISM DAY. ALONG WITH OTHER COMMEMORATIVE EVENTS, TWO MINUTES OF COMPLETE SILENCE ARE OBSERVED EVERY-WHERE ACROSS THE LAND. DRIVERS ON CITY STREETS, YOUNG PEOPLE PLAYING AT HOME, ALL STOP AND COME TO ATTENTION AS SIRENS BLARE. FOR THE DAY, PLACES OF ENTERTAINMENT MUST CLOSE.

THE LAW OF REPARATIONS: 1952

AN AGREEMENT REACHED BETWEEN ISRAEL AND THE FEDERAL REPUBLIC OF GERMANY UNDER WHICH WEST GERMANY WOULD BEGIN TO CONFRONT THEIR RESPONSIBILITY FOR THE NAZI HORROR, INCLUDING THE MASSIVE LOOTING OF JEWISH ASSETS, BY TRANSFERRING FUNDS TO THE NEW JEWISH STATE.

THIS MONEY ALLOWS THE GOVERNMENT TO BUILD THE INFRASTRUCTURE OF THE STATE, INCLUDING MODERN ELECTRICAL PLANTS, AGRICULTURAL IRRIGATION, RAILROADS, EXPANDED PORTS AND ESTABLISHING A STEAMSHIP LINE AND MERCHANT FLEET.

REPRESENTATIVES OF ISRAEL IN THE HAGUE INSIST THAT "NO INDEMNITY, HOWEVER LARGE, CAN MAKE GOOD THE LOSS OF HUMAN LIFE OR CULTURAL VALUES OR ATONE FOR THE SUFFERING OF MEN, WOMEN AND CHILDREN PUT TO DEATH."

MANY ISRAELIS ARE OFFENDED BY THE IDEA THAT ACCEPTING CASH MIGHT SOMEHOW DIMINISH CULPABILITY. BUT BEN-GURION FEELS STRONGLY THAT THESE REPARATIONS ARE VITAL FOR FUNDING THE NEW STATE.

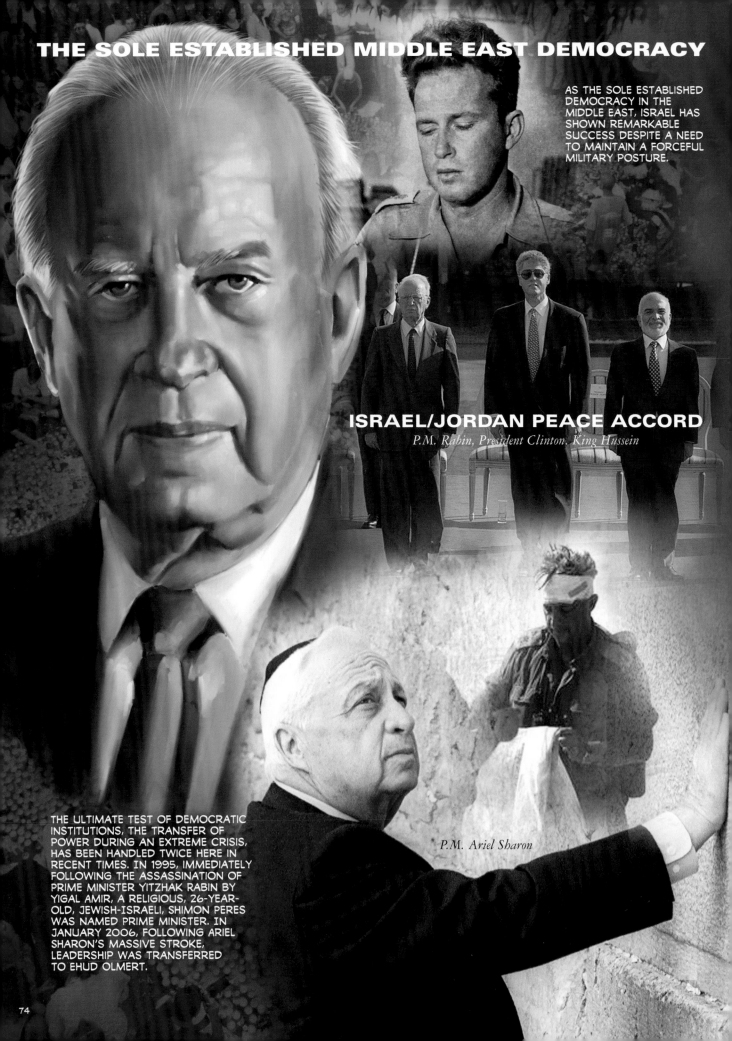

THE SOLE ESTABLISHED MIDDLE EAST DEMOCRACY

AS THE SOLE ESTABLISHED DEMOCRACY IN THE MIDDLE EAST, ISRAEL HAS SHOWN REMARKABLE SUCCESS DESPITE A NEED TO MAINTAIN A FORCEFUL MILITARY POSTURE.

ISRAEL/JORDAN PEACE ACCORD
P.M. Rabin, President Clinton, King Hussein

P.M. Ariel Sharon

THE ULTIMATE TEST OF DEMOCRATIC INSTITUTIONS, THE TRANSFER OF POWER DURING AN EXTREME CRISIS, HAS BEEN HANDLED TWICE HERE IN RECENT TIMES. IN 1995, IMMEDIATELY FOLLOWING THE ASSASSINATION OF PRIME MINISTER YITZHAK RABIN BY YIGAL AMIR, A RELIGIOUS, 26-YEAR-OLD, JEWISH-ISRAELI, SHIMON PERES WAS NAMED PRIME MINISTER. IN JANUARY 2006, FOLLOWING ARIEL SHARON'S MASSIVE STROKE, LEADERSHIP WAS TRANSFERRED TO EHUD OLMERT.

Pres. Hosni Mubarak

P.M. Shimon Peres

P.M. Benjamin Netanyahu

Pres. Bill Clinton

P.M. Ehud Olmert

P.M. Yitzhak Shamir

ALLY OF U.S. AND THE WEST

CURRENTLY, MORE THAN 160 COUNTRIES HAVE DIPLOMATIC RELATIONS WITH ISRAEL. THE STATE OF ISRAEL IS AN ALLY OF THE WESTERN COMMUNITY, BUT TRADES WITH MANY COUNTRIES THROUGHOUT THE WORLD. HOWEVER, SINCE ITS CREATION IN 1948, ISRAEL HAS FACED INTERNATIONAL ARAB BOYCOTTS. THE BOYCOTT HAS EXTENDED TO ISSUES OF CULTURAL EXCHANGE AND ACADEMIC FREEDOM.

SECURITY COUNCIL RESOLUTION 3379 AND "ZIONISM IS RACISM"

IN NOVEMBER 1975, IN THE WAKE OF ISRAEL'S MILITARY SUCCESSES AGAINST ARAB FORCES IN 1967 AND 1973, THE LARGE ANTI-ISRAEL BLOC AT THE U.N. MANAGES TO PASS A RESOLUTION EQUATING ZIONISM WITH RACISM. THE RESOLUTION, BIASED AS IT WAS, IS NOT OVERTURNED UNTIL 16 YEARS LATER.

ISRAEL AS A U.S. ALLY

ALIGNING THEMSELVES WITH THE U.S. AGAINST THE SOVIET UNION IN THE COLD WAR, ISRAEL IS DESIGNATED A MAJOR, NON-NATO ALLY BY U.S. PRESIDENT REAGAN IN THE 1980'S.

THE U.S. AND ISRAEL: A MOMENT OF TENSION

WHILE BOTH ISRAEL AND THE U.S. HAVE BENEFITED FROM SHARED POLITICAL, ECONOMIC AND CULTURAL TIES, THEIR RELATIONSHIP HAS BEEN TESTED AT TIMES. IN 1985, AMERICAN MILITARY ANALYST JONATHAN POLLARD WAS ARRESTED AND CONVICTED OF PASSING CONFIDENTIAL U.S. INFORMATION ON ARAB MILITARY READINESS TO ISRAEL. POLLARD IS SERVING A LIFE SENTENCE IN A U.S. PRISON.

EDUCATION

AS WE LOOK OUT UPON HEBREW UNIVERSITY HERE IN JERUSALEM, I WOULD LIKE TO PRESENT DR. MOLEDET, A SPECIALIST ON ISRAEL'S EDUCATION SYSTEM.

THANK YOU, PROFESSOR AND WELCOME TO YOU ALL. BECAUSE THERE HAS ALWAYS BEEN AN EMPHASIS ON STUDY IN JUDAISM, JEWS HAVE HISTORICALLY HAD A HIGH LITERACY RATE. IN THE SAME SPIRIT, EDUCATION WAS CONSIDERED A CENTRAL COMPONENT IN BUILDING THE JEWISH STATE.

WITH EDUCATION A HIGH PRIORITY, UNIVERSI-TIES AND INSTITUTIONS OF RESEARCH WERE FOUNDED EVEN BEFORE THE STATE ITSELF EXISTED: HEBREW UNIVERSITY (1925), TECHNION (1924) AND THE WEIZMANN INSTITUTE (1934). SINCE THE 1950'S, FIVE MORE HAVE BEEN ESTABLISHED: BEN-GURION, TEL AVIV, BAR-ILAN, THE UNIVERSITY OF HAIFA, AND THE OPEN UNIVERSITY OF ISRAEL.

ISRAEL HAS ALWAYS BEEN A SOURCE OF INNOVATION IN JEWISH RELIGIOUS EDUCATION AS WELL. ONE IMPORTANT EXAMPLE IS NEHAMA LEIBOWITZ (1905-1997), AN ISRAELI PIONEER IN ADVANCING THE STUDY OF THE WEEKLY TORAH PORTION.

HER METHOD OF PROVIDING GUIDED QUESTIONS BASED ON JEWISH COMMENTARIES, ANCIENT AND MODERN, IS USED THROUGHOUT THE WORLD. ISRAEL HAS BECOME THE CENTER OF JUDAIC LEARNING TODAY. VIRTUALLY EVERY JEWISH DENOMINATION HAS STARTED A MAJOR EDUCATIONAL PROGRAM IN THIS LAND.

BASIC EDUCATION IS FREE AND COMPULSORY UNTIL STUDENTS ARE 18 YEARS OLD. UNDER THE MINISTRY OF EDUCATION, THERE ARE FOUR DIFFERENT KINDS OF ELEMENTARY AND MIDDLE SCHOOLS IN ISRAEL: THE STATE EDUCATION SYSTEM, THE STATE RELIGIOUS SYSTEM, INDEPENDENT RELIGIOUS, AND INDEPENDENT SCHOOLS. SUBJECTS MANDATED BY THE MINISTRY OF EDUCATION ARE SCIENCES, MATHEMATICS, ART, PHYSICAL EDUCATION AND JEWISH STUDIES, PRIMARILY HEBREW BIBLE AND JEWISH HISTORY.

THE ARABS OF ISRAEL ALSO HAVE THEIR OWN EDUCATIONAL CURRICULUM DESIGNED FOR THEIR LINGUISTIC AND SPECIFIC CULTURAL NEEDS. ARAB EDUCATION IS ALSO SUPERVISED BY ISRAEL'S MINISTRY OF EDUCATION.

AFTER HIGH SCHOOL, YOUNG ISRAELI MEN AND WOMEN ENTER THE ARMY, MEN FOR NEARLY THREE YEARS AND WOMEN FOR A MINIMUM OF TWO. THE COMMON EXPERIENCE OF MILITARY SERVICE IN DEFENSE OF THE STATE IS A GREAT UNIFYING FORCE IN ISRAELI SOCIETY. ALTHOUGH SOME ORTHODOX JEWS DO NOT SERVE IN THE ARMED FORCES, MANY DO AND THERE IS AN ALTERNATIVE THAT COMBINES TORAH STUDY WITH MILITARY SERVICE.

SOME ORTHODOX WOMEN OPT FOR AN ALTERNATE TYPE OF NATIONAL SERVICE. BECAUSE OF THE CONFLICT WITH ARAB NATIONS, ISRAEL EXEMPTS ITS ARAB CITIZENS FROM ARMY SERVICE. HOWEVER, THE DRUZE COMMUNITY IN ISRAEL, A RELIGIOUS OFFSHOOT OF ISLAM, AND ISRAELI BEDOUIN HAVE SERVED WITH DISTINCTION IN THE ISRAELI MILITARY.

ISRAELI DEFENSE FORCES

THE ISRAEL DEFENSE FORCES (IDF), IS A CITIZEN-ARMY AUTHORIZED BY ISRAEL'S DEMOCRATICALLY ELECTED GOVERNMENT. ONE NOTABLE FEATURE OF MODERN JEWISH HISTORY IS HOW, IN A SHORT TIME, ISRAEL WENT FROM HAVING LITTLE MILITARY EXPERIENCE AS A PEOPLE TO DEVELOPING AN IMPRESSIVE FIGHTING FORCE.

GIVEN ISRAEL'S SMALL SIZE AND LIMITED STRATEGIC DEPTH, THE IDF HAD TO BECOME A MODERN, TECHNOLOGICALLY-ENHANCED MILITARY DESIGNED TO QUICKLY BRING THE BATTLE TO THE TERRITORY OF THE ENEMY.

ISRAEL LIVES IN ONE OF THE MOST UNREMITTINGLY HOSTILE, HEAVILY ARMED AND UNSTABLE REGIONS OF THE WORLD WHERE ACTS OF VIOLENCE AGAINST ITS PEOPLE ARE COMMONPLACE. FOR THIS REASON, MEN IN COMBAT UNITS REMAIN IN THE ARMY RESERVE UNTIL THE AGE OF 40, AND CAN BE CALLED TO ACTIVE DUTY FOR UP TO ONE MONTH A YEAR.

TOHAR HA-NESHEK

TOHAR HANESHEK, (PURITY OF ARMS) IS A MILITARY ETHIC IN ISRAEL REQUIRING SOLDIERS TO PRESERVE THE DIGNITY OF HUMAN LIFE WHEREVER POSSIBLE AND TO MAKE EVERY EFFORT TO LIMIT ENEMY CIVILIAN CASUALTIES.

THIS ARMY OF FELLOW CITIZENS LIVES BY THE PRINCIPLE, "NO SOLDIER LEFT BEHIND." ISRAEL HAS SHOWN A WILLINGNESS TO EXCHANGE HUNDREDS OF CAPTURED ADVERSARIES FOR INDIVIDUAL ISRAELI SOLDIERS. HOWEVER, AT THE BEGINNING OF 2007, IDF MEMBERS RON ARAD, ZACHARY BAUMEL, ZVI FELDMAN, EHUD GOLDWASSER, GUY HEVER, YEHUDA KATZ, ELDAD REGEV AND GILAD SHALIT ARE MISSING OR HELD CAPTIVE AND REMAIN IN THE PUBLIC CONSCIOUSNESS.

IDF'S CAMPAIGNS INCLUDE BOTH OVERT AND COVERT OPERATIONS. LET'S LOOK AT SOME OF THE RICH HISTORY OF THIS MILITARY FORCE, INCLUDING ITS SUCCESSES AND SHORTCOMINGS.

UNIT 101/202

UNIT 101/202

FROM 1948-1952, THE IDF COALESCES INTO A SINGLE FIGHTING FORCE. THEN IN 1953, THE IDF CREATES UNIT 101, WHICH LATER IS INCORPORATED INTO THE 202ND PARACHUTE BRIGADE. THIS ELITE COMMANDO STRIKE FORCE MEETS THE CONSTANT THREATS FROM EGYPTIAN, JORDANIAN AND SYRIAN MILITARIES, AS WELL AS PALESTINIAN GUERILLAS. COMMANDED BY ARIEL "ARIK" SHARON, UNIT 101 STAGES OPERATIONS THAT MAKE CLEAR THE COST OF CONFRONTING ISRAEL WILL BE UNAFFORDABLY HIGH.

IN JULY 1956, IN RESPONSE TO BLOCKED FINANCING FOR THE ASWAN DAM BY THE BRITISH, FRENCH AND AMERICANS, EGYPT'S PRESIDENT NASSER NATIONALIZES THE BRITISH AND FRENCH-OWNED SUEZ CANAL AND BLOCKS THE RED SEA STRAITS OF TIRAN FROM ISRAELI SHIPPING. THE EGYPTIANS ALSO PURCHASE LARGE STOCKS OF MODERN WEAPONS FROM THE SOVIET UNION, THREATENING TO DRASTICALLY ALTER THE BALANCE OF POWER BETWEEN ISRAEL AND THE ARAB WORLD.

OPERATION KADESH

THE IDF'S RESPONSE IS OPERATION KADESH. BEGINNING WITH A PARATROOP DROP INTO THE NARROW SINAI MOUNTAINS' MITLA PASS, THE IDF INVADES AND HOLDS MOST OF THE SINAI PENINSULA. IDF, FRENCH AND BRITISH FORCES TAKE CONTROL OF THE SUEZ CANAL. THE FIGHTING IS COMMANDED BY CHIEF OF STAFF MOSHE DAYAN, LATER DEFENSE MINISTER IN THE 1967 AND 1973 CONFLICTS.

IN 1957, UNDER PRESSURE FROM THE U.S. AND THE SOVIET UNION, OCCUPYING ISRAELI FORCES WITHDRAW FROM THE SINAI AND THE CANAL, LEAVING A MULTI-NATIONAL POLICE FORCE.

COORDINATING WITH THE IDF ARE THE ISRAELI INTELLIGENCE AGENCIES, THE MOSSAD, AMAN AND SHABAK. MOSSAD IS RESPONSIBLE FOR FOREIGN INTELLIGENCE, COUNTER-TERRORISM, COVERT ACTION AND PARAMILITARY OPERATIONS. AMAN IS MILITARY INTELLIGENCE AND SHABAK (KNOWN OUTSIDE ISRAEL AS SHIN-BET) HANDLES INTERNAL SECURITY.

THE MOSSAD'S MOST FAMOUS PUBLIC EXPLOIT IS THE CAPTURE AND SECRET EXTRADITION OF FUGITIVE NAZI WAR CRIMINAL ADOLF EICHMANN FROM BUENOS AIRES, ARGENTINA. EICHMANN, ARCHITECT OF THE INFAMOUS FINAL SOLUTION, THE MURDER OF EUROPEAN JEWRY, IS TRIED IN ISRAEL AND HANGED ON MAY 31, 1962.

EICHMANN IS THE ONLY PERSON IN ISRAEL'S HISTORY TO RECEIVE THE DEATH PENALTY. THE ISRAELIS DISPERSE HIS ASHES IN THE MEDITERRANEAN SEA, FAR FROM ISRAEL, TO AVOID HAVING HIS REMAINS BECOME A SHRINE TO NAZI SUPPORTERS OR TAINT THE HOLY LAND.

ISRAEL'S MOST FAMOUS SPY IS ELI COHEN, AN EGYPTIAN-BORN JEW RECRUITED INTO ISRAELI INTELLIGENCE IN 1960. UNDER COVER AS A RICH SYRIAN, COHEN MOVED TO ARGENTINA IN 1961, EMBEDDING HIMSELF IN THE SYRIAN EMIGRE COMMUNITY.

MOVING TO DAMASCUS THE FOLLOWING YEAR, COHEN HAD ACCESS TO TOP-LEVEL SYRIAN MILITARY SECRETS AND SUPPLIED CRITICAL INFORMATION TO ISRAEL UNTIL HE WAS CAUGHT DURING A RADIO TRANSMISSION. AFTER A SHOW TRIAL, SYRIA HANGED HIM AND STILL RETAINS POSSESSION OF HIS BODY.

Adolf Eichmann

INTELLIGENCE AND SECURITY BECOME EVEN MORE CRUCIAL AFTER MAY 27, 1964, WHEN THE PALESTINE LIBERATION ORGANIZATION (PLO) IS FORMED. THE DESTRUCTION OF ISRAEL IS FUNDAMENTAL TO THE PLO CHARTER. FATAH, THE LARGEST RESISTANCE GROUP WITHIN THE PLO ORGANIZATIONAL UMBRELLA UNDER YASSIR ARAFAT, LAUNCHES THEIR FIRST TERRORIST ATTACK, AGAINST ISRAEL'S NATIONAL WATER CARRIER, IN JANUARY 1965.

PLO

ARAFAT BECOMES HEAD OF THE PLO IN 1968. THE ORGANIZATION WILL BE RESPONSIBLE FOR THOUSANDS OF TERRORIST ATTACKS IN ISRAEL AND AGAINST ISRAELI CITIZENS AND JEWS AROUND THE WORLD.

Eli Cohen

THE SIX-DAY WAR

THE TRANSMISSION OF SYRIAN SECRETS BY ELI COHEN HELPS ISRAEL PREPARE FOR ITS NEXT CONFLICT, JUNE 5-12, 1967, THE SIX-DAY WAR.

ON MAY 22, 1967 EGYPT IMPOSES A BLOCKADE ON THE STRAITS OF TIRAN, AN ACT OF WAR THAT CUTS OFF ISRAELI SHIPPING.

EGYPT MASSES MORE THAN 100,000 TROOPS AND 900 TANKS IN THE SINAI; SYRIA MOBILIZES 75,000 TROOPS AND 400 TANKS ON ISRAEL'S NORTHERN BORDER; AND DESPITE ISRAEL'S REQUESTS TO KING HUSSEIN OF JORDAN TO MAINTAIN NEUTRALITY, 32,000 JORDANIAN TROOPS AND MORE THAN 200 TANKS ARE MARSHALED.

EGYPT EVICTS THE U.N. POLICE FORCE FROM THE SINAI. IN THE WAKE OF NASSER'S PROMISES TO EXTERMINATE THE "ZIONIST ENTITY," ISRAELIS DIG TRENCHES IN THEIR YARDS TO SLOW ANY INVASION.

LESS THAN 10 MILES WIDE AT ITS NARROWEST POINT, ISRAEL IS IN DANGER OF BEING CUT IN HALF. IN A DARING MOVE THAT LEAVES THE COUNTRY WITH A SKELETAL AIR DEFENSE FORCE, ISRAEL LAUNCHES PRE-EMPTIVE AIR STRIKES ON THE MASSED EGYPTIAN ARMIES AND THEIR AIR FORCES.

CATCHING THE EGYPTIAN AIR FORCE UNPREPARED ON THE GROUND WITH SOME PILOTS AT BREAKFAST, THEIR AIR THREAT IS DESTROYED. BY AFTERNOON, THE SYRIAN AND IRAQI AIR FORCES ARE SIMILARLY NEUTRALIZED.

JORDANIAN ARTILLERY SHELLS JERUSALEM, PROMPTING ISRAELI RETALIATION. ON JUNE 7, 1967, ISRAEL LIBERATES THE OLD CITY. FOR THE FIRST TIME IN NEARLY 2,000 YEARS, JEWS CONTROL THE TEMPLE MOUNT AND THE WESTERN WALL. ALMOST IMMEDIATELY, HOWEVER, THEY RETURN CONTROL OF THE MUSLIM HOLY PLACES ON THE TEMPLE MOUNT TO THE MUSLIM RELIGIOUS AUTHORITIES (WAKF).

PROFESSOR, THAT'S A SURPRISING GESTURE ON ISRAEL'S PART, ISN'T IT?

PERHAPS IT ALSO INDICATES HOW SERIOUS ISRAEL WAS ABOUT TRYING TO MAKE PEACE.

BY THE TIME A CEASE-FIRE IS DECLARED ON JUNE 12, 1967, ISRAEL OCCUPIES MORE THAN TWICE ITS ORIGINAL SIZE IN CAPTURED TERRITORY, INCLUDING AREAS THAT WERE HOME TO HUNDREDS OF THOUSANDS OF ARABS. MANY OF THE CHALLENGES FACING ISRAEL TODAY ARE CONSEQUENCES OF THE SIX-DAY WAR.

STINGING FROM THEIR DEFEAT, ARAB NATIONS MEET IN KHARTOUM, SUDAN IN AUGUST 1967 AND ESTABLISH THE "THREE NO'S" POLICY. NO RECOGNITION OF ISRAEL; NO NEGOTIATION WITH ISRAEL; NO PEACE WITH ISRAEL.

U.N. RESOLUTION 242

ON NOVEMBER 22, 1967, THE UNITED NATIONS PASSES RESOLUTION 242 CALLING FOR "A JUST AND DURABLE PEACE" WHICH RECOGNIZES EVERY "STATE IN THE AREA AND THEIR RIGHT TO LIVE IN PEACE WITHIN SECURE AND RECOGNIZED BOUNDARIES FREE FROM THREATS OR ACTS OF FORCE."

IT ALSO CALLS FOR THE "WITHDRAWAL OF ISRAELI ARMED FORCES FROM TERRITORIES OCCUPIED IN THE RECENT WAR." THE RESOLUTION'S WORDING IS NOT "ALL" TERRITORIES, OR EVEN "THE" TERRITORIES, BUT SIMPLY "TERRITORIES," LEAVING ROOM FOR DIFFERENT INTERPRETATIONS BY ALL CONCERNED.

BEGINNING IN 1967, ISRAEL BUILDS A NETWORK OF SETTLEMENTS IN THE WEST BANK AND GAZA STRIP, WHICH WILL BECOME CONTROVERSIAL. THESE COMMUNITIES PLAY A DEFENSIVE ROLE FOR ISRAEL PROPER, OFFER INEXPENSIVE HOUSING, PERMIT SOME FAMILIES TO RETURN TO PLACES THAT WERE OVER-RUN IN 1948 SUCH AS THE K'FAR ETZION AREA AND, FOR SOME RELIGIOUS JEWS, CONTRIBUTE TOWARD RESTORING THE LAND TO ITS ANCIENT BORDERS.

WAR OF ATTRITION

FROM MARCH 1969-AUGUST 1970, ISRAELI AND EGYPTIAN TROOPS SKIRMISH FROM OPPOSITE BANKS OF THE SUEZ CANAL WITH CASUALTIES ON BOTH SIDES.

AFTER INITIAL SUCCESS BY THE ISRAELI AIR FORCE, EGYPT INTRODUCES SOVIET ANTI-AIRCRAFT MISSILES. A STALEMATE ENSUES.

DURING THE CONFLICT, ISRAEL CONDUCTS LIGHTNING RAIDS, CAPTURING EGYPT'S GREEN ISLAND STRONGHOLD AND PERFORMS A SPECTACULAR PARATROOP RAID ON THE FORTIFIED ISLAND OF SHADWAN. LATER, THE IDF DESTROYS FIVE EGYPTIAN MIG-21S FLOWN BY SOVIET PILOTS.

MILITARY TESTING GROUNDS

THE COLD WAR SUPERPOWERS USE THE ARAB-ISRAELI CONFLICT TO TEST WEAPONS, TECHNOLOGY AND TACTICS. BY THIS TIME, THE SOVIET UNION IS POURING RESOURCES TOWARD THE ARAB CAUSE IN AN EFFORT TO UNDERMINE THE JEWISH STATE. ON DECEMBER 26, 1969, DURING A RAID AGAINST THE EGYPTIAN RA'S A'ARAB BASE, THE IDF CAPTURES AND CARRIES AWAY THE MOST ADVANCED SOVIET RADAR SYSTEM OF THE DAY.

CHERBOURG MISSILE BOATS

A FRENCH ARMS EMBARGO PREVENTS DELIVERY OF FIVE MISSILE BOATS. ISRAELI NAVY CREWS, TRAINING IN FRANCE TO OPERATE THE NEW SHIPS, DEFY THE EMBARGO AND STEAM OUT OF CHERBOURG PORT ON DECEMBER 24, 1969.

FOUR YEARS LATER, DURING THE YOM KIPPUR WAR, THESE FAST-ACTION BOATS, WITH THEIR CUTTING-EDGE MISSILE TECHNOLOGIES, PLAY A SIGNIFICANT OFFENSIVE ROLE IN DAMAGING ENEMY NAVAL OPERATIONS.

ISRAEL ALSO BUILDS UP A SMALL SUBMARINE FLEET. ISRAEL WILL LOSE ONE SUBMARINE, THE *DAKAR*, AND ITS 69 CREWMEN, ON ITS MAIDEN VOYAGE ON JANUARY 25, 1968.

IN 1968, TO GAIN PUBLICITY, PALESTINIAN TERRORISTS BEGIN HIJACKING PLANES. THEIR MAIN TARGET, ISRAEL'S NATIONAL AIRLINE EL AL, DEVELOPS STRONG ANTI-TERRORIST PROCEDURES.

ALSO IN RETALIATION, IDF PARATROOPERS SEIZE BEIRUT INTERNATIONAL AIRPORT AND, WITHOUT INJURY TO ANY PASSENGERS, BLOW UP 14 AIRLINERS ON THE GROUND BELONGING TO ARAB NATIONS WHO SUPPORT THE PLO. THIS SENDS A CLEAR MESSAGE TO ARAB GOVERNMENTS THAT SUPPORT FOR HIJACKING WILL NOT BE TOLERATED.

IN MAY 1972, AN ELITE UNIT LED BY LT. COL. EHUD BARAK, (LATER PRIME MINISTER) DRESSED AS AIRPORT TECHNICIANS, SAVE 100 PASSENGERS AND CREW ON A BELGIAN SABENA AIRLINER THAT HAD BEEN HIJACKED TO ISRAEL'S LOD AIRPORT (LATER RENAMED BEN-GURION).

ISRAEL IS NOT ALONE IN BATTLING THE PLO. IN SEPTEMBER 1970, KING HUSSEIN, DISTURBED BY THE PLO "STATE WITHIN A STATE" THAT ESTABLISHED ITSELF IN JORDAN, ATTACKS THE PALESTINIAN GROUP. 8,000 PALESTINIAN FIGHTERS DIE. SYRIAN FORCES INVADING JORDAN IN SUPPORT OF THE PLO ARE REPELLED. ARAFAT SHIFTS HEADQUARTERS TO POLITICALLY WEAK LEBANON.

TERRORISM

CIVILIAN TARGETS

THE PLO AND OTHER PALESTINIAN ARAB GROUPS NOW TAKE THE GUERILLA WAR TO "SOFT TARGETS": SCHOOLS, BUSES, KIBBUTZIM AND PUBLIC GATHERING PLACES.

KIRYAT SHMONA-APRIL 11, 1974

APARTMENT COMPLEX ATTACKED. SIXTEEN CIVILIANS, MOSTLY WOMEN AND CHILDREN, AND TWO SOLDIERS KILLED.

MA'ALOT-MAY 15, 1974

TERRORISTS TAKE 105 STUDENTS AND 10 TEACHERS HOSTAGE AFTER MURDERING A FAMILY INCLUDING A FOUR-YEAR-OLD CHILD. AFTER EFFORTS AT NEGOTIATION, A RESCUE ATTEMPT ENDS BADLY. 21 CHILDREN AND THREE ADULTS ARE LEFT DEAD, 68 WOUNDED.

SAVOY HOTEL-MARCH 3, 1975

GUNMEN TAKE DOZENS OF HOSTAGES. A RESCUE OPERATION, THOUGH SUCCESSFUL OVERALL, COSTS THE LIVES OF THREE SOLDIERS AND EIGHT HOSTAGES ARE INJURED. THIS SURPRISE ATTACK BY SEA LEAVES ISRAELIS FEELING THAT TERROR CAN STRIKE ANYWHERE.

COASTAL ROAD MASSACRE-MARCH 11, 1978

ELEVEN FATAH PALESTINIANS COMMANDEER TWO BUSES HEADED FROM HAIFA TO TEL AVIV. THIRTY-FIVE ISRAELIS ARE MURDERED, INCLUDING MANY CHILDREN. MANY BYSTANDERS ARE INJURED. THIS ATTACK LEADS ISRAEL TO LAUNCH AN INVASION AGAINST PLO BASES IN SOUTHERN LEBANON, UP TO THE LITANI RIVER. ISRAEL LATER WITHDRAWS ITS TROOPS IN EXCHANGE FOR UNITED NATIONS TROOPS WHO FAIL TO PREVENT THE PLO FROM REBUILDING ITS BASES IN THE AREA.

MOSHAV AVIVIM-MAY 22, 1970

ATTACK ON A SCHOOL BUS CARRYING 35 STUDENTS, AGES 6 TO 9. TWELVE ARE MURDERED, 9 INJURED.

KIBBUTZ MISGAV-AM APRIL 7, 1980

PENETRATING THE LEBANESE BORDER FENCE, FIVE TERRORISTS TAKE OVER A CHILDREN'S NURSERY. AN IDF SOLDIER, ONE ADULT AND A THREE-YEAR-OLD KILLED.

ON SEPTEMBER 5, 1972, BLACK SEPTEMBER, A PALESTINIAN TERROR SQUAD, MURDERS 11 ISRAELI ATHLETES AT THE SUMMER OLYMPIC GAMES IN MUNICH, GERMANY.

CONTRIBUTING TO THE DEATHS, SECURITY IN THE OLYMPIC VILLAGE IS MINIMAL AND THE GERMAN POLICE MAKE A CLUMSY RESCUE ATTEMPT. SOME OF THE KILLERS ARE CAPTURED, BUT SOON AFTER RELEASED IN A HOSTAGE EXCHANGE.

THE GAMES ARE SUSPENDED FOR ONE DAY FOLLOWING THE MASSACRE. THE SURVIVING ISRAELI ATHLETES RETURN HOME IN MOURNING.

THE MUNICH GAMES MASSACRE

WRATH OF GOD

PROFESSOR, THERE WAS ISRAELI RETRIBUTION FOR THESE MURDERS, RIGHT?

YES, PRIME MINISTER, GOLDA MEIR ORDERS THE MOSSAD TO HUNT DOWN KNOWN PERPETRATORS. THIS OPERATION IS CALLED "WRATH OF GOD." BY 1979, MOSSAD UNITS HAD ASSASSINATED SEVERAL PALESTINIANS INVOLVED IN THE ATTACK.

UNFORTUNATELY, MISTAKES OCCUR AS WELL. IN THE LILLEHAMMER AFFAIR OF JULY 1973, SIX ISRAELI OPERATIVES ARE ARRESTED FOR THE MURDER OF AN INNOCENT MOROCCAN WAITER WHO WAS MISTAKEN FOR A PLANNER OF MUNICH.

Golda Meir

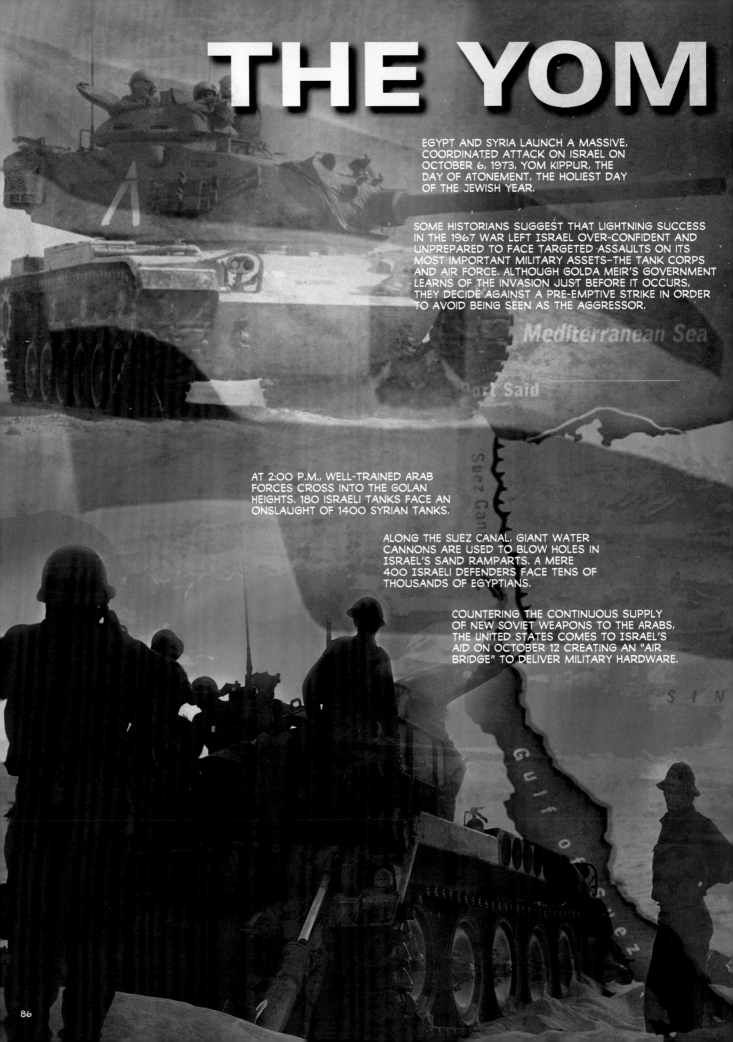

THE YOM

EGYPT AND SYRIA LAUNCH A MASSIVE, COORDINATED ATTACK ON ISRAEL ON OCTOBER 6, 1973, YOM KIPPUR, THE DAY OF ATONEMENT, THE HOLIEST DAY OF THE JEWISH YEAR.

SOME HISTORIANS SUGGEST THAT LIGHTNING SUCCESS IN THE 1967 WAR LEFT ISRAEL OVER-CONFIDENT AND UNPREPARED TO FACE TARGETED ASSAULTS ON ITS MOST IMPORTANT MILITARY ASSETS–THE TANK CORPS AND AIR FORCE. ALTHOUGH GOLDA MEIR'S GOVERNMENT LEARNS OF THE INVASION JUST BEFORE IT OCCURS, THEY DECIDE AGAINST A PRE-EMPTIVE STRIKE IN ORDER TO AVOID BEING SEEN AS THE AGGRESSOR.

AT 2:00 P.M., WELL-TRAINED ARAB FORCES CROSS INTO THE GOLAN HEIGHTS. 180 ISRAELI TANKS FACE AN ONSLAUGHT OF 1400 SYRIAN TANKS.

ALONG THE SUEZ CANAL, GIANT WATER CANNONS ARE USED TO BLOW HOLES IN ISRAEL'S SAND RAMPARTS. A MERE 400 ISRAELI DEFENDERS FACE TENS OF THOUSANDS OF EGYPTIANS.

COUNTERING THE CONTINUOUS SUPPLY OF NEW SOVIET WEAPONS TO THE ARABS, THE UNITED STATES COMES TO ISRAEL'S AID ON OCTOBER 12 CREATING AN "AIR BRIDGE" TO DELIVER MILITARY HARDWARE.

KIPPUR WAR

AT THE BRINK OF BEING OVERRUN ON TWO FRONTS, ISRAELI TROOPS FINALLY BREAK THE ARAB ADVANCE. THE SYRIAN INVASION THROUGH THE GOLAN HEIGHTS IS VALIANTLY STOPPED BY THE ARMORED SEVENTH BRIGADE AND BADLY BLOODIED BARAK BRIGADE. IN THE SOUTH, MAJOR GENERAL ARIEL SHARON DETERMINES THAT A SEAM SEPARATES THE EGYPTIAN 2ND AND 3RD ARMIES, A VULNERABILITY WHICH THE IDF USES TO PENETRATE AND DECIMATE EGYPTIAN ANTI-AIR-CRAFT, TANK UNITS AND SUPPLY CONVOYS. THE EGYPTIAN AND SYRIAN ARMIES ARE SHATTERED, ALONG WITH SMALLER IRAQI UNITS AND A NOMINAL JORDANIAN FORCE.

EGYPT'S SOVIET BACKERS DEMAND A CEASE-FIRE. THE UNITED STATES ALSO SUPPORTS A CEASE-FIRE, AND PRESSURES ISRAEL TO RELEASE THE ENCIRCLED EGYPTIAN THIRD ARMY, TO REFRAIN FROM APPROACHING DAMASCUS, AND TO WITHDRAW FROM TERRITORY CAPTURED ON THE EGYPTIAN AND SYRIAN FRONTS.

IN SPITE OF THE OVERWHELMING SIZE AND PREPAREDNESS OF ENEMY FORCES, ISRAEL MANAGES A REMARKABLE MILITARY RECOVERY THROUGH A COMBINATION OF FACTORS: PRIOR TRAINING, INNOVATIVE TACTICS, CIVILIAN RESERVISTS, INDIVIDUAL DISPLAYS OF HEROISM AND ADVANCED TECHNOLOGY. HOWEVER, THEIR PERSONNEL LOSSES–2,522–ARE THREE TIMES THAT OF THE SIX-DAY WAR. ARAB CASUALTIES ARE NEVER CONFIRMED, BUT WERE SIGNIFICANT.

THERE IS FALLOUT FROM THE WAR ON BOTH SIDES. IN ISRAEL, THE AGRANAT COMMISSION INVESTIGATES THE WAR'S FAILURES IN INTELLIGENCE AND DEFENSIVE STRATEGIES. THE HIGHLY CRITICAL REPORT BRINGS DOWN GOLDA MEIR'S GOVERNMENT. ISRAELI CIVILIANS ARE SHOCKED BY THE WAR'S CASUALTIES AND THEIR ECONOMY SUFFERS TERRIBLY DUE TO INCREASED CIVILIAN RESERVE DUTY AND THE NEED TO REBUILD THE MILITARY.

EGYPT'S INITIAL SUCCESS IN THE WAR HELPS RESTORE SOME PERCEPTION OF ARAB MILITARY DIGNITY AND PROBABLY MAKES IT EASIER FOR EGYPTIAN PRESIDENT ANWAR SADAT TO COME TO JERUSALEM JUST A FEW YEARS LATER.

ENTEBBE
OPERATION THUNDERBOLT

IN 1976, TERRORISTS HIJACK AN AIR FRANCE JET TO UGANDA. JEWISH PASSENGERS ARE SEPARATED FROM NON-JEWS.

AIR FRANCE CAPTAIN MICHEL BACOS DECLARES TO THE TERRORISTS THAT ALL PASSENGERS ARE HIS RESPONSIBILITY AND HE WILL NOT LEAVE THE JEWS. THE ENTIRE FLIGHT CREW FOLLOWS SUIT.

ISRAEL LAUNCHES OPERATION THUNDERBOLT TO RESCUE THE HOSTAGES.

ON JULY 3, 1976, ISRAELI TRANSPORTS TRAVERSE THE 2,500 MILES TO UGANDA AND LAND ELITE UNITS AT ENTEBBE AIRPORT. SOLDIERS STORM THE AIRPORT AND CUT DOWN THE HIJACKERS. THREE HOSTAGES AND ONE ISRAELI SOLDIER ARE KILLED. LATER, IN RETALIATION, ELDERLY HOSTAGE DORA BLOCH IS EXECUTED AT A UGANDAN HOSPITAL.

THE RESCUE IS RENAMED OPERATION YONATAN TO HONOR LT. COL. YONATAN NETANYAHU, THE FALLEN GROUND LEADER OF THE MISSION. THE SUCCESSFUL MISSION, CELEBRATED IN ISRAEL AND AROUND THE WORLD, DEMONSTRATES THAT ISRAEL CAN AND WILL DEFEND THE JEWISH PEOPLE ANYWHERE.

Yonatan Netanyahu

REGIONAL INSTABILITY
IRAN'S ISLAMIC REVOLUTION

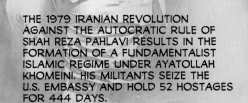

THE 1979 IRANIAN REVOLUTION AGAINST THE AUTOCRATIC RULE OF SHAH REZA PAHLAVI RESULTS IN THE FORMATION OF A FUNDAMENTALIST ISLAMIC REGIME UNDER AYATOLLAH KHOMEINI. HIS MILITANTS SEIZE THE U.S. EMBASSY AND HOLD 52 HOSTAGES FOR 444 DAYS.

THE ECONOMIC AND MILITARY IMPACT OF THE REVOLUTION ON ISRAEL WILL BE CONSIDERABLE. IRAN HAD BEEN ISRAEL'S CLOSEST ALLY IN THE REGION, AND OVER TIME, IRAN'S ANCIENT AND LARGE JEWISH COMMUNITY LOSES BUSINESSES AND PERSONAL FREEDOMS, AND MANY ARE FORCED TO FLEE. THE IRANIAN REVOLUTION BECOMES A FOUNTAIN OF ISLAMIC FUNDAMENTALISM AND BRINGS RADICAL ISLAMIC FORCES IN CONFLICT WITH ISRAEL, THE WEST AND MODERATE ARAB REGIMES.

OPERATION OPERA—THE ATTACK ON OSIRAK

TO PREVENT IRAQ'S SADDAM HUSSEIN FROM DEVELOPING NUCLEAR WEAPONS, IN 1981 THE ISRAELI AIR FORCE SENDS A SQUAD OF F-15 AND F-16 FIGHTERS TO DESTROY THE FRENCH-BUILT NUCLEAR REACTOR IN OSIRAK, IRAQ.

TO LIMIT IRAQI LOSSES, ISRAEL DESTROYS THE REACTOR BEFORE IT GOES LIVE AND AT A TIME WHEN FEW WORKERS ARE ON DUTY. AFTERWARD, PRIME MINISTER BEGIN DECLARES THAT DEADLY ADVERSARIES OF THE JEWISH STATE WILL NOT BE ALLOWED TO ACQUIRE WEAPONS OF MASS DESTRUCTION.

THE FINAL RAIDER THAT DAY WAS ILAN RAMON, LATER ISRAEL'S FIRST ASTRONAUT AND A CASUALTY OF THE FEBRUARY 2003 COLUMBIA SPACE SHUTTLE TRAGEDY. COL. RAMON WAS FROM A FAMILY OF AUSCHWITZ DEATH CAMP SURVIVORS. MANY FEEL HIS CAREER IS AN EXAMPLE OF THE HOPE, DETERMINATION AND INNOVATION THAT DEFINE ISRAEL.

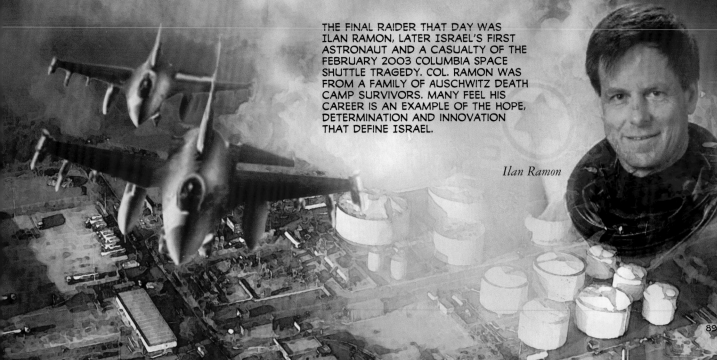

Ilan Ramon

FROM 1975-1990, LEBANON IS ENGAGED IN CIVIL WAR,
PITTING LEBANESE CHRISTIANS AGAINST THOUSANDS
OF PLO FORCES ALIGNED WITH SYRIAN-BACKED
LEBANESE MUSLIMS.

THIS PERIOD IS VERY DIFFICULT FOR THE
LEBANESE PEOPLE AND DOES ENORMOUS
DAMAGE TO THE PHYSICAL INFRASTRUCTURE
OF THE COUNTRY.

AFTER YEARS OF KATYUSHA ROCKET ATTACKS FROM
LEBANON ON NORTHERN ISRAEL BY THE PLO AND THE
SHOOTING OF ISRAEL'S AMBASSADOR TO BRITAIN, ON
JUNE 6, 1982, THE IDF POURS INTO LEBANON BY AIR,
LAND AND SEA LAUNCHING OPERATION PEACE FOR
THE GALILEE. SYRIA ENTERS THE CONFLICT ON JUNE 8
AND ISRAEL DESTROYS NEARLY 100 SYRIAN AIRCRAFT
AND THEIR SOVIET-SUPPLIED MOBILE ANTI-AIRCRAFT
MISSILE SYSTEMS.

THE IDF STRIKES NORTH OF THE LITANI RIVER. THEY
BESIEGE TERRORIST-HELD WEST BEIRUT, SEND ARMS
AND TRAINING TO LEBANESE CHRISTIANS AND OPEN
THE NORTHERN BORDER FOR THEM TO WORK IN ISRAEL.

WAR IN LEBANON I

LEBANESE CIVIL WAR

AN AGREEMENT IS REACHED BETWEEN ISRAEL
AND THE INTERNATIONAL COMMUNITY TO
EXPEL PLO FORCES REMAINING FROM THE
FIGHTING IN BEIRUT TO SURROUNDING NATIONS
ON AUGUST 21, 1982.

YASSIR ARAFAT RELOCATES HIS HEADQUARTERS
TO TUNIS, TUNISIA. THE AGREEMENT AND CEASE-
FIRE IS MAINTAINED BY AMERICAN, ITALIAN AND
FRENCH PEACEKEEPING FORCES.

LEBANESE PRESIDENT AND ISRAELI ALLY, BASHIR JEMAYAL,
IS MURDERED BY A SYRIAN CAR-BOMB ON SEPTEMBER 14,
1982. ON SEPTEMBER 16TH, CHRISTIAN PHALANGIST
FORCES ENTER THE SABRA AND SHATILLA PALESTINIAN
REFUGEE CAMPS AND KILL HUNDREDS OF MUSLIM
LEBANESE, YOUNG AND OLD. ALTHOUGH NO ISRAELI
FORCES ARE DIRECTLY INVOLVED IN THE SLAUGHTER,
400,000 ISRAELIS RALLY TO DEMAND AN INQUIRY.

THE KAHAN COMMISSION FINDS DEFENSE MINISTER ARIEL SHARON, CHIEF OF STAFF RAFAEL EITAN AND INTELLIGENCE CHIEF YEHOSHUA SAGUY INDIRECTLY RESPONSIBLE FOR THE PHALANGIST MASSACRE ON THE GROUNDS THAT THE IDF WAS IN THE AREA SURROUNDING THE CAMPS AND SHOULD HAVE DONE MORE TO PREVENT IT OR INTERVENE.

HEZBOLLAH

THE WAR CONTINUES TO BE BLOODY AND A STEADY FLOW OF ISRAELI CASUALTIES CONTINUES. ISRAELI OPPOSITION GROWS AGAINST THE WAR LED BY MEMBERS OF THE "PEACE NOW" MOVEMENT AND "SOLDIERS AGAINST SILENCE."

IN 1984, THE ISRAELI GOVERNMENT ALSO CONFRONTS ITS OWN JEWISH UNDERGROUND MOVEMENT AND ARRESTS DOZENS OF YOUNG ISRAELIS IN THE WEST BANK FOR ANTI-ARAB INCIDENTS.

BY 1985, ISRAEL DRAWS BACK TO A SECURITY ZONE IN PARTNERSHIP WITH THE CHRISTIAN SOUTH LEBANESE ARMY. ALTHOUGH THERE IS SPORADIC FIGHTING IN AND AROUND THE ZONE, THERE ARE PERIODS OF QUIET ON ISRAEL'S NORTHERN BORDER. ISRAEL'S FINAL WITHDRAWAL FROM LEBANON TO INTERNATIONALLY-RECOGNIZED BORDERS TAKES PLACE IN 2000.

ALSO DURING THIS WAR, WE SEE THE FORMATION OF A NEW TERRORIST ENTITY, HEZBOLLAH, A FUNDAMENTALIST GROUP RESPONSIBLE FOR THE BOMBING OF THE AMERICAN MARINE BARRACKS IN LEBANON IN OCTOBER 1983 KILLING 150 MARINES.

Yassir Arafat

PLO

ON DECEMBER 9, 1987 A PROLONGED PALESTINIAN
UPRISING CALLED IN ARABIC *INTIFADA* (SHAKING OFF)
BREAKS OUT. TENS OF THOUSANDS OF PALESTINIANS
RIOT TO PROTEST THE ISRAELI CONTROL OVER GAZA
AND THE WEST BANK.

INTIFADA

APPARENTLY IGNITED BY A CAR ACCIDENT INVOLVING
AN ISRAELI TRUCK AND PALESTINIAN CIVILIANS, THE
ATTACKS BEGIN WITH ROCK-THROWING AND PETROL
BOMBS AGAINST ISRAELI SOLDIERS AND CIVILIANS.

THE INTIFADA GIVES RISE TO RADICAL YOUNG ACTIVISTS
WHO GREW UP IN REFUGEE CAMPS. RIOTERS ALSO
INTEND TO BRING PRESSURE ON THEIR OWN LEADERS
TO IMPROVE PALESTINIAN LIFE.

RESPONDING TO THESE ATTACKS IS ESPECIALLY
DIFFICULT BECAUSE PALESTINIAN WOMEN AND
CHILDREN ARE OFTEN PLACED AT THE FRONT OF
VIOLENT CROWDS, CREATING A MORAL AND
PUBLIC RELATIONS CHALLENGE FOR ISRAEL.

AT THIS TIME, SOME PALESTINIAN ARABS, LOOKING FOR
AN EVEN HARDER-HITTING AND MORE RELIGIOUS
EXPRESSION OF THEIR ASPIRATIONS, TURN TO ANOTHER
GROUP OF ISLAMIC MILITANTS, HAMAS.

THE DEATH OF ABU JIHAD

ON APRIL 16, 1988, ARAFAT S TOP DEPUTY, HALIL AL-WAZIR (ABU JIHAD),
WHO ORCHESTRATED MANY ACTIONS AGAINST ISRAELI CIVILIANS, IS
KILLED IN TUNIS. THE ASSASSINS, OBVIOUSLY WELL-TRAINED,
APPROACH BY SEA AS AREA COMMUNICATIONS SUDDENLY BLACK
OUT. THE OPERATION BEARS THE MARKS OF THE IDF-MOSSAD.

THE IDF NEITHER DENIES NOR CONFIRMS RESPONSIBILITY,
BUT TO MANY ONLOOKERS, ISRAEL IS THE LIKELY SUSPECT
SINCE ABU JIHAD'S WIFE AND CHILDREN GO UNHARMED
DESPITE BEING AT HOME WITH HIM DURING THE ATTACK.

THE FIRST IRAQ WAR

ON AUGUST 2, 1990, IRAQ'S SADDAM HUSSEIN INVADES KUWAIT. HE THREATENS TO LAUNCH CHEMICAL WEAPONS AGAINST ISRAEL IN RESPONSE TO ANY COUNTERATTACK FROM A U.S.-LED MULTI-NATIONAL COALITION FORCE. ISRAEL ISSUES GAS MASKS TO NEARLY EVERY CITIZEN.

IN THE EARLY MORNING OF JANUARY 17, 1991, AIR STRIKES BY U.S.-LED COALITION PLANES HIT TARGETS IN IRAQ AND KUWAIT. IRAQI SCUD MISSILES SOON BEGIN TO FALL ON CIVILIAN AREAS IN ISRAEL AS PEOPLE PACK THEMSELVES INTO HOMEMADE SEALED ROOMS IN THE EVENT THAT THE SCUDS ARE TIPPED WITH CHEMICALS.

ISRAELI FINANCIAL MARKETS TUMBLE AS TEL AVIV AND HAIFA ARE STRUCK. DESPITE THE 39 SCUD STRIKES, THERE ARE FEW CASUALTIES, BUT THERE IS EXTENSIVE PROPERTY DAMAGE.

THE U.S. STATIONS PATRIOT MISSILE BATTERIES AROUND ISRAEL TO INTERCEPT THE SCUDS, BUT THE PATRIOTS ARE LARGELY UNSUCCESSFUL.

DUE TO ISRAELI-PENTAGON COOPERATION, ISRAEL AGREES NOT TO USE ITS OWN POWERFUL MILITARY IN RESPONSE TO THE ATTACKS SO AS NOT TO DESTABILIZE THE TENUOUS ANTI-IRAQ ALLIANCE WHICH INCLUDES ARAB LEAGUE MEMBERS. SITTING PASSIVELY UNDER THESE CONDITIONS IS A CONTROVERSIAL DECISION FOR MANY ISRAELIS.

THIS TRIP AND OUR STUDY OF ISRAEL'S HISTORY IS NEAR AN END. WE'VE SEEN ZION AS A PLACE OF ANCIENT PROMISES AND MODERN DREAMS AS WELL AS A SITE OF INTENSE STRUGGLE. BUT FROM BIBLICAL TIMES TO THE PRESENT JEWS HAVE SPOKEN ABOUT THE HOPE FOR SHALOM, MEANING BOTH "PEACE" AND "WHOLENESS."

THROUGH THE DECADES, ISRAEL'S EFFORTS TO MAKE PEACE WITH ITS NEIGHBORS HAVE OFTEN BEEN OBSTRUCTED BY ARAB REJECTION AND AGGRESSION. THE ARABS WOULD SAY THAT ISRAEL HAS ALSO MISSED OPPORTUNITIES AND HAS BEEN IN THE WRONG.

PROFESSOR, ISN'T THE BIGGEST PROBLEM THE FACT THAT ISRAEL HAS OCCUPIED DISPUTED LAND FOR MANY YEARS? ISN'T THIS THE ROOT CAUSE TODAY OF THE TERRORISM AGAINST ISRAEL?

SOME TAKE THAT VIEW, BUT THE LAND IN DISPUTE CAME UNDER ISRAEL'S CONTROL AFTER WARS FOUGHT IN HER OWN DEFENSE FROM MAY 1948 THROUGH TODAY.

AND UNTIL 1967, ARABS CONTROLLED EASTERN JERUSALEM, THE WEST BANK AND GAZA. DURING ALL THOSE YEARS, ISRAEL WAS NOT ACCEPTED BY THE ARAB WORLD AND NO PALESTINIAN STATE WAS FORMED. SO, IS THE ROOT PROBLEM "OCCUPATION" OR IS IT THE EXISTENCE OF ISRAEL AT ALL?

WITH HOPE AND TERROR

ISRAELIS FEEL THEIR NATION'S RIGHT TO EXIST HAS BEEN UNDER ATTACK SINCE THE STATE WAS FOUNDED IN 1948. SOMETIMES THE TERM "OCCUPATION" IS USED TO COVER UP A REJECTION OF ISRAEL'S EXISTENCE ALTOGETHER.

IN THE EARLY YEARS OF THE ISRAELI STATE, ARAB GOVERNMENTS CHOSE A HEADS-I-WIN-TAILS-YOU-LOSE STRATEGY. IF THEY DEFEATED ISRAEL IN WAR, WELL AND GOOD. THE JEWISH STATE WOULD COME TO A BLOODY END. BUT WHEN THE ARABS WERE DEFEATED, THEY EXPECTED THE LOST GROUND, TERRITORIES OCCUPIED, TO BE HANDED BACK.

BUT, PROFESSOR, YOU CAN'T DENY THAT PALESTINIAN ARABS, WHO HAVE NOT BEEN REPRESENTED WELL BY ARAB GOVERNMENTS, HAVE BEEN LIVING UNDER OPPRESSIVE CONDITIONS?

YES, THERE HAS BEEN OCCUPATION, ALTHOUGH ISRAEL WITHDREW FROM LEBANON IN 2000 AND FROM GAZA IN SUMMER 2005.

MOST ISRAELIS WOULD REMIND YOU THAT THESE WITHDRAWAL EFFORTS HAVE NOT ENDED THE TERRORISM, FORCING THEM TO RETURN THERE IN RESPONSE TO INCREASED TERRORIST ACTION AGAINST ISRAELI CIVILIANS.

MOST OBSERVERS AGREE WITH YOU THAT THE PALESTINIAN CAUSE HAS NOT BEEN WELL-SERVED BY COUNTRIES LIKE JORDAN, EGYPT, SYRIA AND SAUDI ARABIA. BUT TO ISRAEL IT IS UNCLEAR WHETHER PALESTINIAN ARAB LEADERS ARE READY TO ABANDON WARFARE OR IF THEIR PREFERRED METHOD OF NEGOTIATION IS TERRORISM.

1991–PRESENT

LET'S GET AN OVERVIEW OF THE POLITICAL AND DIPLOMATIC STEPS THAT ADVANCE OR HINDER THE CAUSE OF PEACE IN THIS REGION. WE ARE ALSO OBLIGED TO RECOUNT ACTS OF VIOLENCE THAT TAKE PLACE DURING THIS TIME. SADLY, THERE ARE TOO MANY TO LIST, SO WE COVER A REPRESENTATIVE SAMPLE. MOST OF THE TERROR IS COMMITTED BY ARAB ORGANIZATIONS AGAINST JEWS, BUT A FEW ACTS ARE CARRIED OUT BY A JEW AGAINST ARABS.

3/17/92
ISLAMIC JIHAD/HEZBOLLAH BACKED BY IRAN SETS OFF CAR BOMB THAT DESTROYS ISRAELI EMBASSY - ARGENTINA
22 MURDERED
252 INJURED

2/25/94
SHOOTING BY JEWISH TERRORIST AT CAVES OF PATRIARCHS - HEBRON
39 MURDERED
250 INJURED

JULY 26, 1972
P.M. GOLDA MEIR INVITES EGYPTIAN PRESIDENT ANWAR SADAT TO ENGAGE IN DIRECT NEGOTIATION

OCTOBER 6-23, 1973
YOM KIPPUR WAR

7/18/94
ISLAMIC JIHAD/HEZBOLLAH, BACKED BY IRAN, SETS OFF CAR BOMB, DESTROYS JEWISH COMMUNITY CENTER - BUENOS AIRES
100 MURDERED
250 INJURED

NOVEMBER 19, 1977
PRESIDENT SADAT ARRIVES IN ISRAEL TO DISCUSS PEACE BETWEEN THE TWO COUNTRIES

SEPTEMBER 17, 1978
PEACE ACCORDS SIGNED AT THE WHITE HOUSE BY ISRAEL AND EGYPT FACILITATED BY U.S. PRESIDENT JIMMY CARTER AFTER CAMP DAVID MEETINGS; EMBASSIES ARE ESTABLISHED

10/9/94
ISRAELI SOLDIER NACHSHON WACHSMAN KIDNAPPED AND LATER MURDERED DURING RESCUE OPERATION.
1 RESCUE TEAM MEMBER ALSO MURDERED.

DECEMBER 10, 1978
P.M. MENACHEM BEGIN AND PRESIDENT SADAT ARE AWARDED NOBEL PEACE PRIZES

1/22/95
SUICIDE BOMBINGS - BEIT LID JUNCTION
19 MURDERED
69 INJURED

3/3/96
SUICIDE BOMBING - JERUSALEM BUS
19 MURDERED
7 INJURED

OCTOBER 6, 1981
PRESIDENT SADAT ASSASSINATED BY MEMBERS OF THE MUSLIM BROTHERHOOD

APRIL 24, 1982
THE ISRAELI SETTLEMENT YAMIT IN THE SINAI DESERT IS EVACUATED AND RAZED AS PART OF THE EGYPTIAN ACCORDS

JUNE 5, 1982
WAR IN LEBANON I

MAY 6, 1983
SHORT-LIVED PEACE ACCORDS WITH LEBANON SIGNED

4/4/96
SUICIDE BOMBING - TEL AVIV
14 MURDERED
63 INJURED

3/12/1997
8TH GRADE GIRLS ATTACKED BY JORDANIAN SOLDIER KING HUSSEIN MAKES CONDOLENCE CALLS TO ISRAELI FAMILIES
7 MURDERED
6 INJURED

DECEMBER 8, 1987
INTIFADA I BEGINS

6/30/97
2 SUICIDE BOMBINGS - JERUSALEM
16 MURDERED
178 INJURED

JULY 26, 1990
IRAQ INVADES KUWAIT. BUILD UP TO OPERATION DESERT STORM

SEPTEMBER 25, 1995
OSLO II ACCORDS
SIGNED, EXPANDS
PALESTINIAN
SELF-RULE

OCTOBER 23, 1995
U.S. CONGRESS
RECOGNIZES
JERUSALEM AS ISRAEL'S
"UNITED CAPITAL."
U.S. EMBASSY REMAINS
IN TEL AVIV

3/9/02
Palestinian grenade
attack on boardwalk - Netanya
50 injured

3/2/02
Suicide bombing
Bar Mitzvah - Jerusalem
10 murdered
50 injured

2/8/02
25 year old Israeli woman
stabbed to death by 4 Palestinian
teens - Jerusalem.

OCTOBER 26, 1994
PEACE ACCORDS
SIGNED BETWEEN
ISRAEL AND JORDAN

1/17/02
Suicide bombing
Bar Mitzvah - Hadera
6 murdered
35 injured

JULY 22, 1994
ISRAEL SETS UP FIELD
HOSPITAL IN RWANDA
DURING GENOCIDE; 80
STAFF SENT ON ISRAEL'S
LARGEST MEDICAL
AID MISSION EVER

12/2/01
Suicide bus bombing -
Haifa
15 murdered
40 injured

JULY 1, 1994
ARAFAT ARRIVES
IN GAZA

SEPTEMBER 19, 1993
VATICAN ESTABLISHES
DIPLOMATIC RELATIONS
WITH ISRAEL

12/1/01
Double suicide bombing -
Jerusalem
11 murdered (ages 12-21)
180 injured

9/9/01
Suicide bombing -
Nahariya train station.
3 murdered
90 injured

SEPTEMBER 13, 1993
OSLO ACCORDS SIGNED

• LAND IN EXCHANGE
  FOR CESSATION OF
  PALESTINIAN VIOLENCE

• PLO RECOGNITION
  OF ISRAEL

• IDF TO PULL BACK FROM
  JERICHO AND GAZA

8/9/01
Sbarro Pizza
Jerusalem
15 murdered (7 children)
130 injured

• AID TO PALESTINIANS FOR
  BUILDING INFRASTRUCTURE

• ARAFAT AND HIS
  SUPPORTERS PERMITTED
  BACK IN GAZA

JULY 13, 1992
RABIN ELECTED
PRIME MINISTER

5/9/01
2 young boys murdered -
Tel Tekoa

FALL 1991-WINTER 1992
ISRAEL RE-ESTABLISHES
RELATIONSHIP WITH RUSSIA
AND INITIATES TIES
WITH CHINA

JANUARY 17, 1991
GULF WAR I
OPERATION DESERT
STORM BEGINS,
PLO SUPPORTS
SADDAM HUSSEIN

POST GULF WAR I
NEW PEACE
EFFORTS BEGIN

OCTOBER 30, 1991
MADRID PEACE TALKS

12/12/00
2 Israeli reserve soldiers
lynched - Ramallah.

NOVEMBER 4, 1995
YITZHAK RABIN
ASSASSINATED

JANUARY 5, 1996
YIHYE AYYASH "THE ENGINEER,"
ARCHITECT OF SUICIDE BOMB-
MAKING, RESPONSIBLE FOR
KILLING 50 AND INJURING 340
ISRAELIS, IS KILLED BY BOOBY-
TRAPPED CELL PHONE

3/27/02
SUICIDE BOMBING
PASSOVER SEDER - NETANYA
22 MURDERED
140 INJURED

3/29/02
16 YEAR OLD FEMALE
SUICIDE BOMBING - JERUSALEM
2 MURDERED
20 INJURED

4/12/02
SUICIDE BOMBING -
JERUSALEM
6 MURDERED
60 INJURED

3/30/02
EXPLOSION AT CAFÉ -
TEL AVIV
30 INJURED

AUGUST 7, 1998
ISRAEL SENDS URBAN RESCUE
TEAMS TO ASSIST SURVIVORS
OF U.S. EMBASSY BOMBINGS
IN KENYA AND TANZANIA.
AL-QAIDA TERRORISTS CLAIM
RESPONSIBILITY FOR
THE ATTACKS.

6/1/02
SUICIDE BOMBING -
TEL AVIV DISCO
21 MURDERED
120 INJURED

5/8/02
SUICIDE BOMBING -
JERUSALEM MARKET
15 MURDERED
58 INJURED

OCTOBER 23, 1998
WYE RIVER ACCORDS

• ADDITIONAL ISRAELI
WITHDRAWALS FROM
THE WEST BANK

• PLO COVENANT
MODIFIED; CLAUSE
INCITING VIOLENCE
AGAINST ISRAEL
REMOVED

• PALESTINIAN
PRISONERS FREED

5/19/02
SUICIDE BOMBING -
RISHARDS CLUB
MURDERED
INJURED

5/27/02
SUICIDE BOMB
ICE CREAM PARLOR - PE
BABY, GRANDMOTHER
40 INJURED

MAY 17, 1999
EHUD BARAK ELECTED
PRIME MINISTER

AUGUST 17, 1999
ISRAEL SENDS URBAN
RESCUE TEAMS TO
ASSIST TRAPPED EARTH-
QUAKE VICTIMS IN
TURKEY AND SET UP
FIELD HOSPITALS

7/31/02
EXPLOSION AT
HEBREW UNIVERSITY -
JERUSALEM
8 MURDERED
86 INJURED

SEPTEMBER 4, 1999
BARAK AND ARAFAT SIGN
AGREEMENT TO IMPLEMENT
OUTSTANDING ISSUES OF
WYE RIVER ACCORDS

MAY 23, 2000
ISRAEL PULLS OUT OF
LEBANON, U.N. VERIFIES
PULLOUT ON JUNE 15

6/
SUICIDE BUS BOMBING -
JERUSALEM
19 MURDERED
74 INJURED

JULY 11, 2000
CAMP DAVID II
IN UNPRECEDENTED CONCESSIONS,
ISRAEL OFFERS PALESTINIANS MORE
THAN 90% OF THE WEST BANK AND
CONTROL OVER PARTS OF JERUSALEM.
ARAFAT REJECTS THE OFFER.

SEPTEMBER 28, 2000
FOREIGN MINISTER SHARON
VISITS THE TEMPLE MOUNT;
BEGINNING OF INTIFADA II.

10/22/02
SUICIDE BOMBING -
HADERA
14 MURDERED
45 INJURED

11/15/02
ATTACK ON HEBRON JEWS
WALKING FROM SABBATH
PRAYERS 12 KILLED

MAY 23, 2002
IN A TERRORIST
ATTEMPT TO CREATE A
MEGA ATTACK LIKE 9/11,
TANKER TRUCK
EXPLODES INSIDE
PI GLILOT FUEL DEPOT
TO DESTROY NEARBY
ISRAELI RESIDENTIAL
NEIGHBORHOOD. FIRE
CONTAINED, NO
INJURIES.

SEPTEMBER 2002
ROADMAP TO PEACE
INITIATED BY U.S., RUSSIA,
EUROPEAN UNION AND
U.N. WITH GOAL OF
MOVING ISRAEL
AND PALESTINIANS
FROM VIOLENCE
TO NEGOTIATION

JANUARY 28, 2003
P.M. SHARON
RE-ELECTED

FEBRUARY 1, 2003
SHUTTLE COLUMBIA
DISINTEGRATES KILLING
AMERICAN CREW
AND ISRAEL'S
FIRST ASTRONAUT,
ILAN RAMON

3/5/03
SUICIDE BOMBING -
HAIFA UNIVERSITY BUS
16 MURDERED
30 INJURED

11/21/02
BUS BOMBING, MANY
CHILDREN ON BOARD -
JERUSALEM
11 MURDERED
50 INJURED

APRIL 2002
SECURITY FENCE INITIATED
TO SEPARATE ISRAEL
FROM WEST BANK
PALESTINIAN SUICIDE
ATTACKS. RESULTS IN
DRASTIC DECREASE
IN ATTACKS.

APRIL - JUNE 2002
OPERATIONS DEFENSIVE
SHIELD AND DETERMINED
PATH INSTITUTED TO STOP
PALESTINIAN TERROR
ATTACKS AND DESTROY
THEIR INFRASTRUCTURE

11/   2
SURFACE TO   SILE
MISSES ISRAELI EL AL
PLANE - KENYA AIRPORT.

JANUARY 3, 2002
CAPTURE OF S.S. KARINE A,
SHIP WITH ARMS THAT THE
PALESTINIAN AUTHORITY
PURCHASED FOR
PALESTINIAN TERRORIST
GROUP FROM IRAN
IN VIOLATION
OF AGREEMENTS

11/28/02
SUICIDE BOMBS AT ISRAELI
OWNED HOTEL - KENYA
13 MURDERED
80 INJURED

1/5/03
SUICIDE BOMBING
TEL AVIV CENTRAL
BUS STATION
23 MURDERED
120 INJURED

SEPTEMBER 11, 2001
WORLDWIDE WAR ON TER-
ROR BEGINS ISRAELI DAN
LEWIN, A PASSENGER
AND FORMER ISRAELI
COMMANDO ON AMERICAN
AIRLINES FLIGHT 11, IS KILLED
BY HIJACKERS AFTER HIS
APPARENT EFFORT TO
RESIST BEFORE THE PLANE
STRIKES THE WORLD
TRADE CENTER.

SEPTEMBER 12, 2001
IN AFTERMATH OF ATTACK
ON WORLD TRADE CENTER,
ISRAELI URBAN RESCUE
TEAMS GO ON STANDBY
FOR POSSIBLE RESCUE
ASSISTANCE. ISRAEL
DECLARES NATIONAL DAY
OF MOURNING.

3/30/03
SUICIDE BOMBING -
NETANYA MALL
40 INJURED

MAY 2001
MITCHELL REPORT
STATES THAT SHARON'S
VISIT TO THE TEMPLE
MOUNT DID NOT CAUSE
INTIFADA II. VIOLENCE
BY PALESTINIANS
CONTINUES. REPORT
BECOMES FOUNDATION
FOR ROADMAP
FOR PEACE.

FEBRUARY 2001
ARIEL SHARON ELECTED
PRIME MINISTER

8/19/03
SUICIDE BOMBING -
JERUSALEM
23 MURDERED
133 INJURED

6/11/03
SUICIDE BUS BOMBING
DRESSED AS CHASIDIC JEW -
JERUSALEM
16 MURDERED
80 INJURED

MARCH 6, 2003
QASSAM ROCKET FIRE BRINGS
ISRAELI RE-OCCUPATION OF
PARTS OF GAZA

10/4/03
ARAB-JEWISH OWNED
RESTAURANT - HAIFA
21 MURDERED
60 INJURED

10/15/03
U.S. CONVOY IN GAZA
STRIP BOMBED
3 MURDERED
1 INJURED

MARCH 19, 2003
GULF WAR II
INVASION OF IRAQ

MARCH 22, 2004
HAMAS LEADER
AHMED YASSIN
ASSASSINATED

1/29/04
SUICIDE BUS BOMBING -
JERUSALEM
11 MURDERED
50 INJURED

2/22/04
SUICIDE BUS BOMBING -
JERUSALEM
8 MURDERED
70 INJURED

APRIL 17, 2004
YASSIN'S SUCCESSOR,
ABDEL AZIZ RANTISSI,
ASSASSINATED

NOVEMBER 11, 2004
ARAFAT DIES

FINAL VERSION OF ROADMAP
TO PEACE PRESENTED TO
SHARON AND PALESTINIAN
LEADER MAHMOUD ABBAS

6/28/04
KASSEM MISSILE ATTACK –
SDEROT
2 MURDERED
7 INJURED

DECEMBER 2004
ISRAEL SENDS EMERGENCY
AID AND RESCUE SERVICES
TO SRI LANKA, THAILAND
AND INDONESIA AFTER
DEVASTATING TSUNAMI

9/27/04
TERRORISTS SHOOT PREGNANT
WOMAN AND FOUR DAUGHTERS -
GUSH KATIF

8/31/04
2 SUICIDE BUS BOMBINGS -
BEERSHEVA
16 MURDERED
100 INJURED

9/24/04
MORTAR ATTACK -
GUSH KATIF
1 MURDERED

JANUARY 9, 2005
MAHMOUD ABBAS
ELECTED PRESIDENT
OF PALESTINIAN
NATIONAL AUTHORITY

FEBRUARY 14, 2005
ASSASSINATION OF
FORMER LEBANESE PRIME
MINISTER RAFIK HARIRI.
PUBLIC OPINION BLAMES
SYRIAN GOVERNMENT AND
ITS 14,000 TROOPS
IN LEBANON

JULY 19, 2005
CEDAR REVOLUTION
PRO-SYRIAN GOVERNMENT
IN LEBANON COLLAPSES.
REPLACED BY
MODERATE COALITION
GOVERNMENT.

9/29/04
2 TODDLERS MURDERED
BY KASSEM ROCKETS FROM
GAZA - SDEROT

10/7/04
SUICIDE ATTACKS ON
SINAI HOTELS
27 MURDERED

AUGUST 15-24, 2005
ISRAEL PAINFULLY DISENGAGES
FROM ALL JEWISH SETTLEMENTS
IN GAZA STRIP AND SOME WEST
BANK SETTLEMENTS

THE FIRST FULL BATTLE OF THE 21ST CENTURY BY ISRAEL AGAINST THE IRANIAN PROXY ARMY IN LEBANON RESULTS AT BEST IN A DRAW AND COULD REDUCE ISRAELI DETERRENCE TO OTHER ARAB ATTACKS.

IN TERMS OF ISRAEL'S LESSONS FROM THE WAR, THE ARMY INCREASES TRAINING SIGNIFICANTLY AND ESTABLISHES AN OPPOSITION TRAINING UNIT THAT SIMULATES HEZBOLLAH TACTICS.

IRAN AND SYRIA, WHO CONTINUE TO PROVIDE HEZBOLLAH WITH WEAPONS, COME AWAY UNSCARRED. THE TERRORIST ORGANIZATIONS HAMAS, ISLAMIC JIHAD, AL-QAIDA PALESTINE AND FATAH BEGIN TO DEVELOP SIMILAR OFFENSIVE AND DEFENSIVE INFRASTRUCTURES IN THE GAZA STRIP.

ALSO AT THE END OF 2006 AND THE BEGINNING OF 2007, CONFLICT FLARES IN THE GAZA STRIP BETWEEN PALESTINIAN GROUPS HAMAS AND FATAH. ISRAELI-SYRIAN SECRET TALKS ARE DISCLOSED.

8/4/05
AWOL ISRAELI SOLDIER MURDERS 4 ISRAELI ARABS - SHFARAM
12 INJURED

AUGUST 11, 2006
U.N. APPROVES RESOLUTION 1701 TO ESTABLISH CEASE-FIRE CALLING FOR AN ISRAELI WITHDRAWAL AND END TO WEAPON TRANSFERS TO HEZBOLLAH. KIDNAPPED SOLDIERS REMAIN CAPTIVE. TREMENDOUS DAMAGE TO ISRAEL'S NORTHERN TOWNS. LEBANON'S RECONSTRUCTION SET BACK YEARS.

JULY 12 - AUGUST 11, 2006
HEZBOLLAH FIRES 4,000 KATYUSHA ROCKETS AT ISRAELI CIVILIANS. ISRAEL ATTACKS INFRASTRUCTURE AND HEZBOLLAH STRONGHOLDS IN LEBANON. LARGE NUMBERS OF LEBANESE ARE FORCED TO EVACUATE. ISRAEL FACES STIFF RESISTANCE FROM HEZBOLLAH AND THEIR UNEXPECTEDLY EFFECTIVE ANTI-TANK MISSILES.

8/18/05
4 MURDERED BY JEWISH SETTLER - SHILOH

JULY 12, 2006
LEBANON WAR II
HEZBOLLAH CROSSES INTO ISRAEL, KIDNAPS 2 SOLDIERS. 5 ISRAELIS KILLED DURING UNSUCCESSFUL RESCUE MISSION. ISRAELI RESPONSE IS SEVERE.

8/28/05
SUICIDE BOMBING - BEERSHEVA CENTRAL BUS STATION52 INJURED

12/5/
SUICIDE BO
NETANYA MALL
6 MURDERED
55 INJURED

12/12/05
SUICIDE BOMBING - NETANYA MALL
5 MURDERED
90 INJURED

1/19/06
SUICIDE BOMBING - TEL AVIV CENTRAL BUS STATION
30 INJURED

JUNE 25, 2006
SOLDIER KIDNAPPED BY HAMAS IN RAFAH, 2 SOLDIERS KILLED, 4 INJURED.

SUMMER 2006
IN THE POWER VACUUM LEFT IN SOUTH LEBANON AFTER THE 2000 WITHDRAWAL OF ISRAELI FORCES, HEZBOLLAH HONEYCOMBED LEBANESE VILLAGES WITH MILITANT CELLS AND AMMO DUMPS, OFTEN IN BUILDINGS INHABITED BY CIVILIANS. IRANIAN FUNDING AND SUPPLIES ARMED HEZBOLLAH WITH THOUSANDS OF KATYUSHA ROCKETS AIMED AT ISRAELI CIVILIAN TARGETS.

2/25/05
SUICIDE BOMBING - TEL AVIV CLUB
5 MURDERED
50 INJURED

JANUARY 4, 2006
ARIEL SHARON SUFFERS MASSIVE STROKE

SEPTEMBER 23, 2005 TO PRESENT PALESTINIANS FIRE QASSAM ROCKETS FROM EVACUATED SITES OF GAZA SETTLEMENTS

4/17/06
SUICIDE BOMBING - TEL AVIV FALAFEL STAND
11 MURDERED
40 INJURED

MANAGING TERROR

- ISRAELIS ARE TRAINED FROM CHILDHOOD TO ALERT AUTHORITIES WHEN THEY COME ACROSS SUSPICIOUS PEOPLE AND PACKAGES.

- POLICE AND BORDER GUARDS CONTINUALLY PATROL FOR PACKAGES AND SUSPICIOUS PERSONS.

- MANY CITIZENS BELONG TO A CIVIL GUARD THAT SUPPORTS POLICE EFFORTS.

- MANY CIVILIANS RESPONSIBLY CARRY ARMS FOR SELF-DEFENSE.

- ALL SCHOOL FIELD TRIPS REQUIRE AN ARMED GUARD.

- CUTTING-EDGE MONITORING TECHNOLOGIES AND HUMAN INTELLIGENCE ARE UTILIZED TO PREVENT TERROR OPERATIONS.

- AFTER TERRORIST ATTACKS, THE ORGANIZATION ZAKA WORKS TO ASSURE THAT ALL BODIES ARE TREATED WITH RESPECT AND DIGNITY.

- HOUSES USUALLY HAVE ONE ROOM DESIGNATED AS AN "EMERGENCY SEALED ROOM" TO BE USED IN CASE OF GAS ATTACKS. NEW HOMES HAVE THEM BUILT IN.

- STADIUMS CONDUCT SECURITY CHECKS BEFORE ENTERING.

- ISRAEL HAS THE WORLD'S MOST SOPHISTICATED SECURITY SYSTEMS IN PLACE TO PREVENT AIRLINE TERRORISM, INCLUDING HIGH QUALITY SCREENING AND ANTI-MISSILE SYSTEMS.

- RESTAURANTS/CAFES/HOTELS USE SECURITY GUARDS TO CHECK ALL ENTERING PATRONS. FENCES SURROUND CAFE AREA TO LIMIT ACCESS.

AND LIVING LIFE

- HOSPITALS HAVE QUICK-REACTION SYSTEMS TO ADDRESS MAJOR TRAUMA AND MASS CASUALTIES.

- MAGEN DAVID ADOM (MDA), ISRAEL'S MEDICAL SERVICE, HAS EMERGENCY TEAMS ON TERRORIST ATTACK STANDBY.

- TERROR VICTIMS AND THEIR FAMILIES ARE TREATED BOTH PHYSICALLY AND PSYCHOLOGICALLY FOR THEIR WOUNDS. THE GOAL IS TO MOVE THEM FROM VICTIMS TO SURVIVORS TO THRIVING IN SOCIETY.

- IN MARKETS AND MALLS PACKAGES ARE CHECKED. METAL DETECTORS ARE OFTEN UTILIZED.

- ENTRANCES TO PUBLIC PLACES ARE SECURED BY GUARDS.

- BUS PASSENGERS ARE SCREENED AT MAJOR STATIONS BEFORE ENTERING.

- ISRAELIS OFTEN CARRY MORE THAN ONE CELL PHONE, LISTEN TO THE NEWS EVERY 30 MINUTES AND ARE IN CONSTANT COMMUNICATION WITH THEIR FAMILIES.

- UP-TO-THE-MINUTE SECURITY UPDATES ARE AVAILABLE REGIONALLY BY PHONE.

- TO PREVENT SABOTAGE, IT IS DIFFICULT TO ACCESS ELECTRIC TOWERS.

- ISRAELIS SHARE SECURITY TECHNIQUES WITH ALLIED COUNTRIES THROUGHOUT THE WORLD.

- MILITARY CREWS ARE ON CALL IN CASE OF BUILDING COLLAPSE OR EXPLOSION.

MUCH OF THE TECHNOLOGY DEVELOPED FOR THE MILITARY TRANSLATES TO INNOVATION FOR ISRAELI SOCIETY AND THE WORLD.

CENTRAL JERUSALEM IS ONE OF THE FIRST WIRELESS INTERNET ACCESS CITIES IN THE WORLD TODAY.

NECESSITY IS THE MOTHER OF INVENTION. CAUGHT IN A VISE OF EXTERNAL PRESSURES- MASSIVE IMMIGRATION, LIMITED FUNDING AND A CHALLENGING NATURAL ENVIRONMENT, IT'S NOT SURPRISING THAT ISRAEL QUICKLY BECAME A CENTER FOR ENTERPRISE AND INNOVATION.

DESPITE BEING THE 100TH SMALLEST COUNTRY IN THE WORLD, ABOUT THE AREA OF NEW JERSEY, ISRAEL'S IMPACT ON WORLD TECHNOLOGY IS IMMENSE, AND THAT COMMITMENT TO CUTTING-EDGE TECHNOLOGY CAN BE TRACED BACK TO THE EARLIEST JEWISH IMMIGRANTS TO PALESTINE.

IN AN EFFORT TO RECLAIM SWAMPLAND AND DESPOILED LANDS, THEY BEGAN AN AGGRESSIVE TREE-PLANTING PROGRAM THAT TODAY HAS "RE-GREENED" ONCE- DESERT LANDS.

INNOVATION

THE NATIONAL WATER CARRIER SYSTEM OF AQUEDUCTS, TUNNELS, PIPES AND PONDS WAS BEGUN IN 1953 AND FINISHED IN 1964. IT CARRIES WATER FROM LAKE KINNERET, THE SEA OF GALILEE, 130 KM (81 MILES) TO THE NEGEV DESERT.

TODAY ISRAEL IS ON THE FOREFRONT OF WATER RESOURCE TECHNOLOGY INCLUDING DESALINATION AND WATER RECYCLING.

ISRAELI AGRICULTURAL INNOVATION PRODUCES FASCINATING RESULTS SUCH AS THE INCREASED YIELD OF DATE PALM TREES FROM 38 POUNDS TO 400 POUNDS PER YEAR ON SHORT TREES THAT CAN BE EASILY HARVESTED.

MASHAV, ISRAEL'S PROGRAM FOR INTERNATIONAL CO-OPERATION, PROMOTES GOOD RELATIONS WITH DEVELOPING COUNTRIES BY SHARING ISRAELI EXPERTISE IN AGRICULTURE AND OTHER AREAS.

ISRAELI NOBEL PRIZE WINNERS IN THE SCIENCES

Daniel Kahneman	Economics	2002
Avraham Hershko	Chemistry	2004
Aharon Ciechanover	Chemistry	2004
Robert J. Aumann	Economics	2005

AGRICULTURE IS NOT THE ONLY AREA IN WHICH ISRAELIS CAN POINT TO REMARKABLE ACCOMPLISHMENTS. RESEARCH AND INNOVATION IN TECHNOLOGY, SCIENCE AND MEDICINE MAKE ISRAEL A WORLD LEADER IN THOSE FIELDS AS WELL. SINCE 1988, ISRAEL HAS BEEN AMONG THE FEW COUNTRIES IN THE WORLD WITH SATELLITE CAPABILITY. ISRAEL'S FIRST NUCLEAR REACTOR WAS BUILT IN DIMONA IN THE MID-1950'S.

ISRAELIS ARE RECOGNIZED WORLDWIDE FOR THEIR COMPUTER TECHNOLOGY INNOVATIONS. HUNDREDS OF COMPANIES CHOOSE TO LOCATE RESEARCH AND DEVELOPMENT CENTERS IN ISRAEL TO TAKE ADVANTAGE OF THE HIGH-TECH TALENT POOL THERE.

ISRAELI INNOVATION CREATES AND CONTRIBUTES TO THE TECHNOLOGY FOR ADVANCES THAT ARE PART OF OUR EVERYDAY LIVES INCLUDING CELL PHONES, INTERNET-CHAT TECHNOLOGY AND VIDEO-CONFERENCING.

IN 1974, INTEL CHOOSES ISRAEL FOR ITS FIRST DESIGN AND DEVELOPMENT CENTER OUTSIDE THE U.S. TODAY, INTEL HAS ADDITIONAL FACILITIES IN ISRAEL WORKING ON TECHNOLOGY THAT SIGNIFICANTLY INCREASES THE SPEED AND POWER OF COMPUTERS, INCLUDING THOSE LAPTOPS YOU ALL BRING TO CLASS. MICROSOFT ALSO HAS MAJOR OPERATIONS IN ISRAEL.

OTHER INTERNATIONAL HIGH-TECH POWER PLAYERS AND TECHNOLOGIES DEVELOPING PRODUCTS IN ISRAEL INCLUDE:

- CISCO SYSTEMS (NETANYA) NETWORKING EQUIPMENT FOR THE INTERNET

- MOTOROLA-ISRAEL (TEL AVIV) CELL PHONE TECHNOLOGY

- CHECKPOINT (RAMAT GAN) "FIREWALL" SOFTWARE, THE INDUSTRY STANDARD FOR PROTECTING HIGH TRAFFIC COMPUTER SYSTEMS

- I.C.Q. (TEL AVIV) SOFTWARE, THE FIRST MAJOR REAL-TIME CHAT APPLICATION, PAVED THE WAY FOR AOL INSTANT MESSENGER AND MSN INSTANT MESSENGER

- M-SYSTEMS (KFAR SABA) DISKONKEY, A PORTABLE COMPUTER STORAGE DEVICE THAT WORKS LIKE A HARD DRIVE AND IS SMALL ENOUGH TO FIT ON A KEY CHAIN

Check Point™
SOFTWARE TECHNOLOGIES LTD.

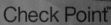

We Secure the Internet.

MOTOROLA®

 intel®

 **icq**® **msystems**

IN 2006, ISRAEL HAD MORE COMPANIES LISTED ON NASDAQ THAN ANY COUNTRY OUTSIDE NORTH AMERICA. AN INDICATOR OF ISRAEL'S ECONOMIC STRENGTH WAS THE PURCHASE BY U.S. INVESTMENT MAGNATE WARREN BUFFETT, THE SECOND RICHEST PERSON IN THE WORLD, OF AN 80% STAKE IN ISCAR, A MACHINE TOOL COMPANY BASED IN THE NORTHERN ISRAEL REGION OF GUSH TEFEN.

ISRAEL HAS MADE SIGNIFICANT CONTRIBUTIONS IN THE FIELD OF MEDICINE AS WELL. FOR EXAMPLE, TEVA PHARMACEUTICALS IS THE WORLD'S LARGEST PRODUCER OF GENERIC DRUGS. MEDICAL RESEARCH TO FIND TREATMENTS AND CURES FOR PARKINSON'S DISEASE, SPINAL CORD INJURIES AND BREAST CANCER HAVE RECEIVED INTERNATIONAL ATTENTION.

WITH DEFENSE BEING VITAL TO ISRAEL, IT'S NOT SURPRISING THAT MANY OF THE MEDICAL TECHNOLOGY ADVANCES PIONEERED BY THE COUNTRY ARE BASED ON THE NEED FOR SECURITY AND THEN SPREAD TO THE CIVILIAN SECTOR. GIVEN IMAGING DEVELOPED INGESTIBLE IMAGING CAPSULES FOR DIAGNOSTIC ENDOSCOPIES THAT ARE BASED ON MILITARY TECHNOLOGY FOR CAMERAS USED IN MISSILES.

ISRAELI MILITARY TECHNOLOGY IS EMPLOYED WORLDWIDE. IN 2006, THE U.S. SPENT $137 MILLION TO UPGRADE BRADLEY REACTIVE ARMOR TILES THAT PROTECT SOLDIERS RIDING IN COMBAT VEHICLES. THE ARMOR PLATING EXPLODES OUTWARD, DIFFUSING THE IMPACT OF INCOMING FIRE. IN 2007, MANY U.S. SOLDIERS ARE SCHEDULED TO BEGIN WEARING LIGHTWEIGHT HELMETS DEVELOPED BY RABINTEX INDUSTRIES, BASED IN HERZLIYA.

LIFE AND CULTURE

PROFESSOR, I HAVE TO ADMIT I'M STILL THINKING ABOUT ALL THE FIGHTING AND LOSS OF LIFE WE'VE HEARD ABOUT TODAY. HOW DOES IT AFFECT THE ISRAELI PEOPLE?

WELL, THERE IS AN INTERESTING FEATURE OF THE ISRAELI NATIONAL CALENDAR WHICH SPEAKS TO YOUR QUESTION. IN ISRAEL THEY OBSERVE THEIR MEMORIAL DAY AND THEIR INDEPENDENCE DAY BACK TO BACK. LIKE MEMORIAL DAYS EVERYWHERE, ISRAEL HONORS ITS FALLEN SOLDIERS IN PUBLIC CEREMONIES AT NATIONAL CEMETERIES. AS ON HOLOCAUST DAY, SIRENS BLOW ACROSS THE COUNTRY AND PLACES OF ENTERTAINMENT ARE CLOSED.

AT SUNDOWN ON MEMORIAL DAY THE MOOD IN THE COUNTRY TURNS QUICKLY FROM MOURNING TO REJOICING AS INDEPENDENCE DAY IS CELEBRATED. PEOPLE LITERALLY FILL THE STREETS WITH SONG AND DANCING FAR INTO THE NIGHT TO CELEBRATE THE 5TH OF IYAR, THE ANNIVERSARY ON THE HEBREW CALENDAR OF WHEN THE COUNTRY'S LEADERS DECLARED STATEHOOD IN 1948.

I THINK THIS ABRUPT TRANSITION BETWEEN THE TWO DAYS SAYS SOMETHING IMPORTANT ABOUT THE EXTREMES OF ISRAELI LIFE, AND THEIR CAPACITY NOT TO ALLOW SUFFERING TO OVERCOME HAPPINESS AND HOPE.

ISRAEL'S POPULATION COMES FROM MORE THAN 100 COUNTRIES ON FIVE CONTINENTS; AS A RESULT ITS CULTURE IS A DIVERSE MIX OF ETHNIC AND RELIGIOUS TRADITIONS, OFTEN MERGING INTO NEW PATTERNS. THE STATE OF ISRAEL PRIDES ITSELF ON MAINTAINING CONNECTIONS TO THE PAST, BUT IN MANY WAYS IT IS A THOROUGHLY MODERN, COS-MOPOLITAN PLACE.

PERFORMING ARTS

BEZALEL ACADEMY OF ART

IS FOUNDED BY RUSSIAN-JEWISH IMMIGRANT BORIS SCHATZ IN 1906. THE NAME BEZALEL IS TAKEN FROM EXODUS 35:30, AFTER BEZALEL BEN URI, WHO OVERSAW THE DESIGN AND CONSTRUCTION OF THE DESERT TABERNACLE. SCHATZ'S INNOVATIVE ACADEMY FUSES JEWISH, MIDDLE EASTERN AND EUROPEAN ART TRADITIONS INTO A DISTINCTIVE NATIONAL ISRAELI STYLE.

HABIMAH THEATER COMPANY

ORIGINATES IN MOSCOW IN 1917, UNDER THE LEADERSHIP OF NAHUM ZEMACH. IN 1926, HABIMAH (THE STAGE) STARTS TO TOUR INTERNATIONALLY, AND IN 1931 IT PERMANENTLY SETTLES IN TEL AVIV. SINCE 1958, HABIMAH HAS BEEN THE NATIONAL THEATER OF ISRAEL.

BATSHEVA DANCE COMPANY

IS FOUNDED IN 1964 BY BARONESS BATSHEVA DE ROTHSCHILD WHO IMMIGRATED TO ISRAEL IN 1958. BATSHEVA IS NOW CONSIDERED TO BE ISRAEL'S PREMIERE DANCE ORGANIZATION. THE COMPANY'S CHOREOGRAPHY WAS INITIALLY MODELED AFTER THE AMERICAN-BASED MARTHA GRAHAM DANCE COMPANY (THE TWO WOMEN WERE FRIENDS). TODAY THE BATSHEVA DANCE COMPANY UTILIZES IT'S OWN, EXPRESSIVE DANCE ROUTINES.

MANY JEWISH IMMIGRANTS TO ISRAEL HAVE BROUGHT MUSICAL TALENT ALONG WITH THEM. IN THE 1980'S AND 1990'S BECAUSE SO MANY JEWS FROM THE FORMER SOVIET REPUBLICS WERE PERFORMERS, THE JOKE WAS THAT IF A RUSSIAN IMMIGRANT CAME OFF THE PLANE WITHOUT A VIOLIN CASE, HE MUST BE A PIANIST!

FROM MOROCCANS TO RUSSIANS, THE MUSIC OF DIVERSE JEWISH
COMMUNITIES HAS FOSTERED MUSICAL EXPRESSION IN THE STATE.
TODAY, ISRAEL HAS MORE THAN 35 MUSIC CONSERVATORIES, AND
EVEN SMALL KIBBUTZIM HAVE SOME SORT OF MUSIC ENSEMBLE.

THE ISRAEL PHILHARMONIC ORCHESTRA IS FOUNDED AS THE
PALESTINE PHILHARMONIC IN 1936, ITS OPENING CONCERT WAS
CONDUCTED BY THE WORLD RENOWNED ARTURO TOSCANINI.

ISRAELI MUSICIANS HAVE MADE THEIR MARK ON THE
WORLD'S CONCERT HALLS. AMONG THE LEADING
NAMES ARE:
Itzhak Perlman
Daniel Barenboim
Pinchas Zuckerman
Gil Shaham

Itzhak Perlman

CALLED ISRAEL'S "FIRST LADY OF
SONG," NAOMI SHEMER HAS COM-
POSED MANY BELOVED SONGS
USING CLASSIC JEWISH TEXTS
AND MODERN HEBREW
POETRY. HER MOST FAMOUS
PIECE, "YERUSHALAYIM SHEL
ZAHAV" (JERUSALEM OF
GOLD), IS ORIGINALLY
RELEASED JUST BEFORE
THE SIX-DAY WAR AND
BECOMES AN INSTANT
ANTHEM FOR THE
COUNTRY. THE
REFRAIN GOES:

*O JERUSALEM OF GOLD,
AND OF BRONZE,
AND OF LIGHT,
 I AM AN INSTRUMENT
 FOR ALL YOUR SONGS*

Daniel Barenboim

CONTEMPORARY
MUSIC IS EVERY-
WHERE IN ISRAELI
CULTURE, TOO.
FROM POP SINGER
SHLOMO ARTZI,
(AS POPULAR IN
ISRAEL AS BRUCE
SPRINGSTEEN IS IN
AMERICA), TO RAP
SENSATIONS LIKE
SUBLIMINAL,
ISRAELIS ENJOY A
WIDE VARIETY OF
MUSICAL GENRES.

Gil Shaham

Shlomo Artzi

HIP-HOP ALSO HAS WIDE APPEAL IN ISRAEL.
ARTISTS FROM SEPHARDIC, ASHKENAZI,
ETHIOPIAN AND ARABIC BACKGROUNDS
BRIDGE CULTURES AMONG JEWISH ISRAELIS,
AND BETWEEN ISRAELIS AND ARABS.

SPORTS & MEDIA

SOCCER AND BASKETBALL ARE CONSIDERED THE NATIONAL SPORTS OF ISRAEL. ALTHOUGH ISRAEL IS LOCATED IN ASIA, IT COMPETES PRIMARILY IN EUROPEAN LEAGUES.

ISRAEL'S MOST FAMOUS AND SUCCESSFUL BASKETBALL TEAM IS MACCABI TEL-AVIV. WINNERS OF NUMEROUS NATIONAL TITLES, THE TEAM HAS CAPTURED THE EUROPEAN CUP FIVE TIMES SINCE 1977.

AMONG ISRAEL'S 23 SOCCER CLUBS, MACCABI HAIFA IS THE MOST SUCCESSFUL WITH 10 CHAMPIONSHIPS AND FIVE NATIONAL CUPS. IT IS ALSO THE FIRST ISRAELI SOCCER TEAM TO QUALIFY FOR THE UEFA (UNION OF EUROPEAN FOOTBALL ASSOCIATIONS). THE ARAB/ISRAELI TEAM, HAPOEL B'NAI SACHNIN WINS THE ISRAEL NATIONAL CUP IN 2003.

ISRAEL'S FIRST OLYMPIC MEDAL IS AWARDED AT THE 1992 SUMMER OLYMPIC GAMES IN BARCELONA, SPAIN, WHEN YAEL ARAD WINS A SILVER MEDAL IN JUDO. TWO DAYS LATER, OREN SMADJA ALSO WINS A BRONZE MEDAL IN JUDO. MICHAEL KALGANOV WON A BRONZE IN KAYAKING IN 2000. AT THE 2004 SUMMER OLYMPIC GAMES IN ATHENS, GREECE, WINDSURFER GAL FRIDMAN BECOMES THE FIRST ISRAELI TO WIN A GOLD MEDAL.

NEWSPAPERS

HAARETZ, OFTEN CALLED THE ISRAELI "NEW YORK TIMES," IS FOUNDED IN 1918. REVISIONIST LEADER ZE'EV JABOTINSKY IS AMONG ITS FIRST WRITERS.

YEDIOT ACHRONOT IS FIRST PUBLISHED IN 1939 AND WITH 55% OF THE MARKET, IS THE MOST POPULAR NEWSPAPER IN ISRAEL TODAY.

MA'ARIV, ISRAEL'S SECOND MOST POPULAR PAPER, IS FOUNDED IN 1948 BY A GROUP OF JOURNALISTS WHO LEFT *YEDIOT ACHRONOT*.

ART, CINEMA AND LITERATURE

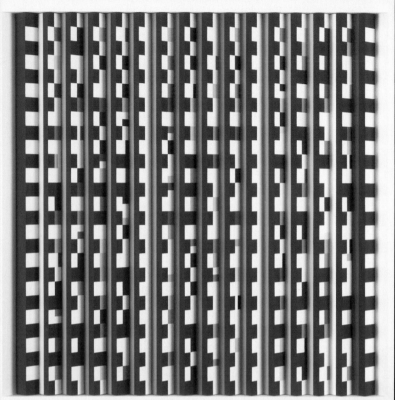

ISRAELI ARTIST YAACOV AGAM IS CREDITED WITH HELPING DEVELOP THE KINETIC MOVEMENT. HIS EARLY WORKS ADD TOUCH AND SOUND TO THE ART. TODAY, HIS WORK IS RECOGNIZED WORLDWIDE FOR ITS COLORFUL GRID PATTERNS THAT SEEM TO CHANGE WITH THE MOVEMENT OF THE VIEWER'S EYE.

ONE OF THE FOUNDERS OF DADAISM, MARCEL YANKO, IMMIGRATED TO ISRAEL IN THE 1930'S WITH A GROUP OF FELLOW DADAISTS. THIS COUNTER-CULTURAL MOVEMENT, BEGINS DURING WORLD WAR I, USING VISUAL ARTS, LITERATURE, THEATER AND GRAPHIC DESIGN TO CHALLENGE PREVAILING ARTISTIC STANDARDS.

ISRAELI AUTHORS AND FILM MAKERS HAVE BEEN RECOGNIZED FOR INNOVATIVE PORTRAYALS OF ISRAELI LIFE AND CULTURE. IN 2005, ISRAELI FILMS RECEIVED A TOTAL OF 18 AWARDS AT INTERNATIONAL FILM FESTIVALS IN COPENHAGEN, MONTREAL, HAMBURG AND CANNES.

ISRAELIS LOVE BOOKS. MORE THAN 8,000 NEW BOOKS ARE PRINTED HERE EACH YEAR. DURING THE ANNUAL HEBREW BOOK WEEK, FAIRS ARE HELD ALL ACROSS THE COUNTRY WHERE MORE THAN 1 MILLION ISRAELIS TYPICALLY BUY OVER 2.5 MILLION VOLUMES DURING THIS PERIOD.

AMONG ISRAEL'S MOST NOTABLE AUTHORS, S.Y. AGNON IS THE FIRST TO WIN THE NOBEL PRIZE FOR LITERATURE (1966), AND AMOS OZ WINS THE GOETHE PRIZE IN FRANKFURT, GERMANY IN 2005.

OZ ALSO RECEIVES THE ISRAEL PRIZE, THE MOST PRESTIGIOUS CIVILIAN AWARD PRESENTED BY THE JEWISH STATE. RECIPIENTS ARE ISRAELI CITIZENS WHO HAVE DISPLAYED PARTICULAR EXCELLENCE IN THEIR FIELD, OR HAVE MADE MAJOR CONTRIBUTIONS TO ISRAELI CULTURE. OTHER WELL-KNOWN WINNERS OF THE PRIZE INCLUDE MUSICIAN NAOMI SHEMER AND JEWISH PHILOSOPHER MARTIN BUBER.

Amos Oz

ARCHITECTURE

IN 1918, SIR RONALD STORRS, THE FIRST BRITISH MILITARY GOVERNOR OF JERUSALEM, ENDORSES A REGULATION STATING THAT THE OUTER WALLS OF ALL NEW BUILDINGS IN JERUSALEM HAD TO BE CONSTRUCTED FROM JERUSALEM STONE, A NATURAL LIMESTONE QUARRIED IN ISRAEL. THIS POLICY CONTINUES TO SET JERUSALEM APART FROM OTHER CITIES IN ISRAEL.

ARCHEOLOGY

MORE THAN 20,000 PLACES IN THIS SMALL LAND ARE REGISTERED AS PROTECTED HISTORICAL SITES. SOME DATE BACK TO PRE-HISTORICAL TIMES; OTHERS ARE FROM AS LATE AS THE MEDIEVAL PERIOD. IN OUR STUDY WE HAVE TOUCHED ON THE BACKGROUND TO MANY OF THESE FINDS.

ONE OF THE MOST FAMOUS ARTIFACTS OF THE PAST FOUND IN ISRAEL IS THE DEAD SEA SCROLLS, AMONG WHICH ARE THE EARLIEST COPIES WE HAVE OF BIBLICAL TEXTS. THEY DATE FROM APPROXIMATELY 200 B.C.E. TO 68 B.C.E. AND INCLUDE THE FULL TEXT OF THE BOOK OF ISAIAH.

THE DEAD SEA SCROLLS ARE HOUSED IN THE ISRAEL MUSEUM ALONG WITH NEARLY 500,000 OTHER OBJECTS OF FINE ART, ARCHAEOLOGY AND JUDAICA.

MUSEUMS

YAD VASHEM

ESTABLISHED IN 1953, SERVES AS A MEMORIAL TO THE MILLIONS OF JEWS AND OTHER HUMAN BEINGS MURDERED IN THE HOLOCAUST. THE FIRST THING ONE SEES ON APPROACHING YAD VASHEM IS THE AVENUE OF THE RIGHTEOUS AMONG THE NATIONS WHICH HONORS NON-JEWS WHO RISKED THEIR LIVES AND THE LIVES OF THEIR FAMILIES TO HELP SAVE JEWS. YAD VASHEM IS A LEADER IN HOLOCAUST EDUCATION, RESEARCH AND DOCUMENTATION.

MUSEUM OF THE JEWISH DIASPORA

SURVEYS THE HISTORY OF THE JEWISH PEOPLE FROM THE TIME OF THE BABYLONIAN EXILE, 2500 YEARS AGO, TO THE PRESENT.

TEL AVIV MUSEUM OF ART

FIRST OPENED TO THE PUBLIC IN 1932 IN THE HOME OF THE CITY'S FIRST MAYOR, MEIR DIZENGOFF. IN ADDITION TO ITS COLLECTION OF MODERN AND CONTEMPORARY ART, THE MUSEUM HOSTS A VARIETY OF PROGRAMS INCLUDING CLASSICAL AND JAZZ MUSIC, THEATER, LECTURES, DANCE, AND CINEMA.

RELIGIOUS CULTURE

PROFESSOR, I'VE BEEN HOPING TO HEAR MORE ABOUT THE DIFFERENT KINDS OF PEOPLES WE'VE SEEN ON OUR TRIP AND THEIR DIFFERENT RELIGIONS AND CULTURES. I KNOW THERE IS A LOT OF STRIFE IN ISRAEL, BUT I'VE ALSO BEEN IMPRESSED WITH HOW ALL THESE GROUPS SEEM TO LIVE TOGETHER IN SPITE OF EVERYTHING.

YES, WE SHOULD TALK ABOUT THE DIFFERENT KINDS OF JEWISH BELIEFS REPRESENTED IN ISRAEL AS WELL AS THE VARIOUS MINORITY FAITHS AND COMMUNITIES.

WHEN THE STATE IS ESTABLISHED, THE GOVERNMENT GIVES JEWISH ORTHODOXY CONTROL OVER PERSONAL STATUS QUESTIONS FOR JEWISH CITIZENS SUCH AS WHO CAN MARRY, SERVE AS A RABBI, OR CONVERT TO JUDAISM. IN PART, THIS MOVE WAS ORIGINALLY A POLITICAL CALCULATION BY BEN-GURION TO BRING ORTHODOX RELIGIOUS PARTIES INTO HIS COALITION. IN RECENT YEARS THIS ARRANGEMENT HAS BEEN CHALLENGED BY SECULAR AND NON-ORTHODOX JEWS.

ISRAELI JEWS HOLD A WIDE AND COMPLEX RANGE OF BELIEFS. THERE ARE MANY DIFFERENT TYPES OF ORTHODOXY. JEWISH DENOMINATIONS LIKE CONSERVATIVE, REFORM AND RECONSTRUCTIONIST ARE SMALL IN ISRAEL, BUT CONTINUE TO GROW. A LARGE NUMBER OF ISRAELIS ARE SECULAR. THE AVERAGE JEW HERE IS RESPECTFUL OF THE TRADITION, BUT NOT NECESSARILY OBSERVANT OF ALL ITS PRACTICES.

THE PUBLIC FACE OF ISRAEL CONTAINS MANY EXPRESSIONS OF JEWISH RELIGION. FOR INSTANCE, THE ARMY SERVES KOSHER FOOD TO ITS TROOPS. FOR MOST OF SOCIETY, THE JEWISH SABBATH IS A DAY OF RELAXATION, AND MOST STORES, OFFICES, BUSES AND PLACES OF ENTERTAINMENT SHUT DOWN. THE RHYTHM OF LIFE IN ISRAEL THROUGHOUT THE YEAR FOLLOWS THE JEWISH CALENDAR AND ITS HOLIDAYS. AT THE SAME TIME, AS YOU'VE NOW SEEN, ISRAEL IS LARGELY AN OPEN, WESTERN-STYLE SOCIETY.

MANY RELIGIOUS OR ETHNIC MINORITIES ALSO
CONSIDER ISRAEL THEIR HOME. IN FACT, AS
OF 2006, OUT OF A POPULATION OF NEARLY
SEVEN MILLION ISRAELIS, THERE ARE MORE
THAN ONE MILLION NON-JEWISH CITIZENS, THE
LARGE MAJORITY OF WHOM ARE MUSLIM.

LIFE FOR ISRAELI ARABS HAS ITS OWN
STORY, AND ISRAEL'S RELATIONSHIP WITH
ITS ARAB CITIZENS WILL BE AN IMPORTANT
PART OF ISRAEL'S NARRATIVE IN THE 21ST
CENTURY. NEVERTHELESS, LET'S COVER A
FEW IMPORTANT FACTS AND IDEAS ABOUT
ISRAEL'S MINORITIES:

ISRAEL'S MINORITY COMMUNITIES

- ARABS, THE OVERWHELMING MAJORITY OF WHOM ARE SUNNI MUSLIMS.

- CHRISTIAN ARABS, CHRISTIANS WHOSE COMMUNITY INCLUDES GREEK
  CATHOLIC, GREEK ORTHODOX, ROMAN CATHOLIC, ARMENIANS AND
  VARIOUS PROTESTANT DENOMINATIONS.

- THE DRUZE, THE SAMARITANS AND THE CIRCASSIANS, WHO ARE NOT OF
  ARAB ABSTRACTION, BUT DO SPEAK AN ARAB DIALECT. THERE ARE ALSO
  A SMALL NUMBER OF KARAITES LIVING HERE, AN OFFSHOOT OF THE
  JEWISH COMMUNITY.

- BAHAI ALSO CONSIDERS ISRAEL THEIR HOME, SPECIFICALLY THE CITY OF
  HAIFA WHERE THEIR INTERNATIONAL HEADQUARTERS IS LOCATED. MANY
  BAHAI FLEE PERSECUTION IN IRAN AFTER AYATOLLAH KHOMEINI TAKES
  POWER. BAHAI PILGRIMAGES TO HAIFA OCCUR ANNUALLY, AS THOUSANDS
  OF BAHAI COME TO VENERATE THE HOLY SITES OF THEIR FAITH.

ISRAEL'S DECLARATION OF INDEPENDENCE PROMISES FREEDOM OF
"RELIGION, CONSCIENCE, LANGUAGE, EDUCATION, AND CULTURE." I
THINK IT'S FAIR TO SAY THAT ISRAEL HAS NOT FOUND THE PERFECT
FORMULA TO COMPLETELY FULFILL THIS DIFFICULT AND NOBLE GOAL.
BUT CONSIDERING THE COMPLEXITIES AND DANGERS OF ISRAEL'S
SITUATION, IT'S ALSO FAIR TO SAY THAT IN MANY WAYS THIS LAND
IS AN INSPIRING MULTICULTURAL TAPESTRY.

WALKING THROUGH JERUSALEM, THE SOUNDS OF JEWISH,
CHRISTIAN AND MUSLIM WORSHIP INTERMINGLE IN THE AIR.
AND THE CITY IS A SITE OF PILGRIMAGE FOR COUNTLESS
RELIGIOUS TOURISTS WHO COME HERE TO SEEK GOD AND
STRENGTHEN THEIR FAITH.

PURSUIT

LET'S CONSIDER RECENT EFFORTS BY ISRAELIS AND ARABS TO RESOLVE THEIR STRUGGLE. THE FIRST TURNING POINT OCCURS IN 1977 WHEN EGYPTIAN PRESIDENT ANWAR SADAT ACCEPTS ISRAEL'S INVITATION TO VISIT JERUSALEM FOR PEACE TALKS.

IN 1978, THE COURAGE AND VISION OF PEOPLE LIKE SADAT AND ISRAEL'S MENACHEM BEGIN LEAD TO THE FIRST PEACE TREATY SIGNED BETWEEN JEWS AND ARABS. AS PART OF THE AGREEMENT, ISRAEL PULLS OUT OF THE SINAI DESERT, SACRIFICING STRATEGIC DEPTH, OIL, MILITARY INSTALLATIONS, AND THE JEWISH TOWN OF YAMIT, ALL FOR A CHANCE TO LIVE IN PEACE.

UNFORTUNATELY, OVER THE YEARS THIS HAS BEEN A "COLD PEACE"–THERE IS LIMITED TRADE, FEW EGYPTIANS VISIT ISRAEL, AND THE ANTI-JEWISH PRESS IN EGYPT REMAINS INTENSE. THE ASSASSINATION OF SADAT ON OCTOBER 6, 1981 BY RADICAL MUSLIMS HIGHLIGHTS THE GRAVE RISKS OF MAKING PEACE.

THROUGH THE 1980'S, EFFORTS ARE MADE TO DISCUSS POLITICAL AUTONOMY FOR PALESTINIAN ARABS. IN 1987, ARAB VIOLENCE BREAKS OUT (THE INTIFADA), AND FOR SOME ISRAELIS, THIS CONFIRMS THAT THEY HAVE NO PEACE PARTNER. FOR OTHERS, IT CONFIRMS THAT PEACE SHOULD BE INTENSIVELY PURSUED.

FROM 1991-1995, ISRAELIS AND PALESTINIAN ARABS NEGOTIATE. CONFERENCES IN MADRID UNDER P.M. SHAMIR CONTINUE IN OSLO UNDER P.M. YITZHAK RABIN, SHIMON PERES AND YASSIR ARAFAT. THORNY PROBLEMS ARISE SUCH AS WATER RESOURCES, STATUS OF REFUGEES AND THE FUTURE OF JERUSALEM.

WITH AMERICAN SUPPORT, TWO COMPLEX AGREEMENTS ARE MADE THAT COULD EVENTUALLY LEAD TO A SEPARATE STATE FOR ARABS. HOPE FOR ARAB-ISRAELI RECONCILIATION BUILDS IN 1994 AS JORDAN SIGNS A FULL PEACE TREATY WITH ISRAEL.

AND DESPITE RABIN'S ASSASSINATION BY A JEWISH EXTREMIST THE NEXT YEAR, THE PEACE PROCESS CONTINUES. PALESTINIAN ARABS GAIN SELF-RULE IN MUCH OF THE WEST BANK AND GAZA. TALKS ARE HELD WITH SYRIA. THIS PROGRESS, HOWEVER, DOES NOT STOP DEADLY ATTACKS ON ISRAELIS.

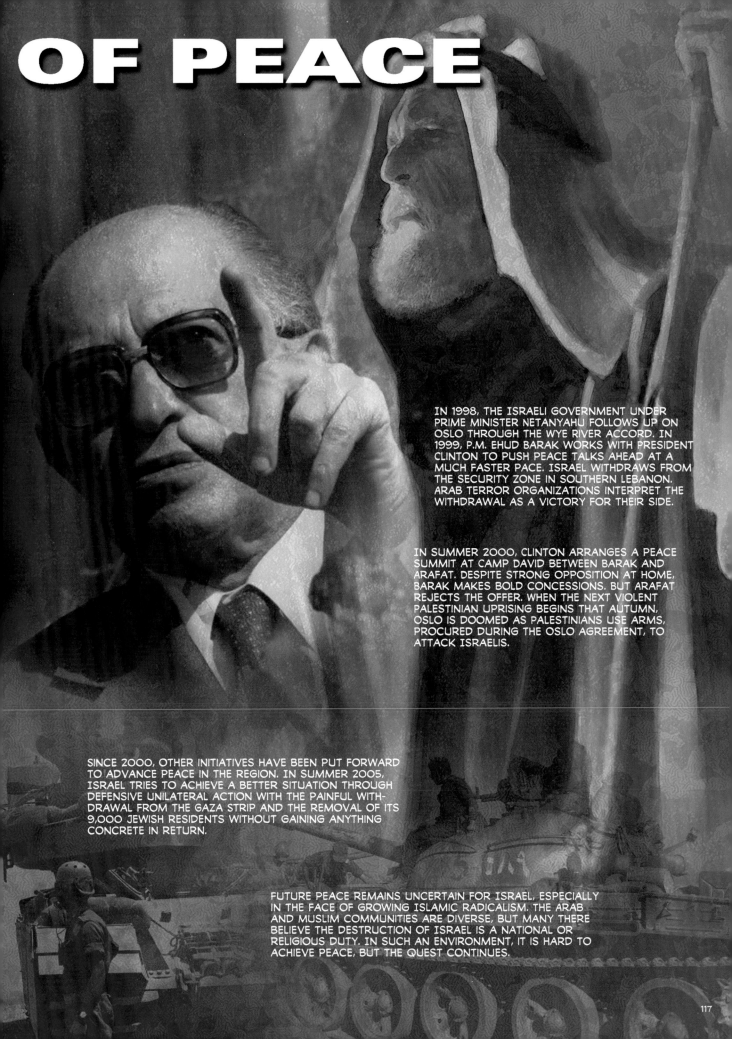

OF PEACE

IN 1998, THE ISRAELI GOVERNMENT UNDER PRIME MINISTER NETANYAHU FOLLOWS UP ON OSLO THROUGH THE WYE RIVER ACCORD. IN 1999, P.M. EHUD BARAK WORKS WITH PRESIDENT CLINTON TO PUSH PEACE TALKS AHEAD AT A MUCH FASTER PACE. ISRAEL WITHDRAWS FROM THE SECURITY ZONE IN SOUTHERN LEBANON. ARAB TERROR ORGANIZATIONS INTERPRET THE WITHDRAWAL AS A VICTORY FOR THEIR SIDE.

IN SUMMER 2000, CLINTON ARRANGES A PEACE SUMMIT AT CAMP DAVID BETWEEN BARAK AND ARAFAT. DESPITE STRONG OPPOSITION AT HOME, BARAK MAKES BOLD CONCESSIONS. BUT ARAFAT REJECTS THE OFFER. WHEN THE NEXT VIOLENT PALESTINIAN UPRISING BEGINS THAT AUTUMN, OSLO IS DOOMED AS PALESTINIANS USE ARMS, PROCURED DURING THE OSLO AGREEMENT, TO ATTACK ISRAELIS.

SINCE 2000, OTHER INITIATIVES HAVE BEEN PUT FORWARD TO ADVANCE PEACE IN THE REGION. IN SUMMER 2005, ISRAEL TRIES TO ACHIEVE A BETTER SITUATION THROUGH DEFENSIVE UNILATERAL ACTION WITH THE PAINFUL WITH- DRAWAL FROM THE GAZA STRIP AND THE REMOVAL OF ITS 9,000 JEWISH RESIDENTS WITHOUT GAINING ANYTHING CONCRETE IN RETURN.

FUTURE PEACE REMAINS UNCERTAIN FOR ISRAEL, ESPECIALLY IN THE FACE OF GROWING ISLAMIC RADICALISM. THE ARAB AND MUSLIM COMMUNITIES ARE DIVERSE, BUT MANY THERE BELIEVE THE DESTRUCTION OF ISRAEL IS A NATIONAL OR RELIGIOUS DUTY. IN SUCH AN ENVIRONMENT, IT IS HARD TO ACHIEVE PEACE, BUT THE QUEST CONTINUES.

WHEN WE LANDED IN ISRAEL A WEEK AGO, WE SAW THE SKYLINE OF TEL AVIV, A SYMBOL OF WHAT IS NEW IN THE LAND. PAST AND PRESENT ARE INTERTWINED IN THIS LAND. OPPOSING BELIEFS FACE EACH OTHER AT ALMOST EVERY TURN. THERE ARE STRUGGLES BETWEEN RELIGIONS AND EVEN AMONG MEMBERS OF THE SAME FAITH.

BUT IN ISRAEL'S STORY, THE IDEA THAT DEEP CONFLICT CAN BE OVERCOME GOES BACK TO THE BIBLICAL PROPHETS. REMEMBER ISAIAH'S BOLD IMAGES OF A FUTURE WHERE WEAPONS ARE RESHAPED INTO TOOLS FOR GROWING FOOD, AND WHERE WOLVES AND LAMBS LIVE IN MUTUAL RESPECT. THESE TEXTS HAVE GIVEN HOPE TO PEOPLE WORKING FOR PEACE.

ISRAEL HAS MADE CONTRIBUTIONS TO THE WORLDS OF SCIENCE, MEDICINE, ART, LITERATURE, MUSIC, AS WELL AS TO RELIGIOUS AND POLITICAL LIFE AND DEMOCRATIC IDEALS IN THE FACE OF THREATS MOST OTHER COUNTRIES CANNOT EVEN IMAGINE.

PROFESSOR, I'D LIKE TO RETURN SOON AND HAVE THE OPPORTUNITY TO SPEAK PERSONALLY WITH PEOPLE WHO LIVE HERE - ISRAELI ARABS, FAMILIES WHO HAVE MADE ALIYAH, ISRAELIS WHO WERE BORN HERE - AND LEARN MORE.

I HOPE YOU WILL RETURN AND CONTINUE TO LEARN HERE ...UNFORTUNATELY, WE MUST SAY OUR GOODBYES FOR NOW TO THE LAND.

IF WE THINK ABOUT THE LONG PATH LEADING TO THE MODERN STATE OF ISRAEL, WHAT DOES IT MEAN THAT THE JEWISH PEOPLE HAVE A NATIONAL LIFE IN THE LAND? FOR SOME RELIGIOUS BELIEVERS IT MEANS THAT THE COVENANT GOD MADE WITH THE JEWISH PEOPLE IS STILL WORKING ITSELF OUT IN HISTORY. ISRAEL IS "AN ECHO OF ETERNITY."

FOR MOST, THE STATE OF ISRAEL MEANS THAT HOPE NEVER DIES. ISRAEL'S NATIONAL ANTHEM, HATIKVA, MEANS "THE HOPE." ISRAEL BEARS WITNESS TO THE POWER OF MEMORY TO HOLD A PEOPLE TOGETHER, AND THE POWER OF COURAGE TO ENDURE THE GREATEST CHALLENGES.

THE STATE OF ISRAEL REPRESENTS THE REUNION OF LAND AND PEOPLE. JEWS RECALL THIS LAND IN THEIR DAILY LIVES AND AT MILESTONE OCCASIONS. AT THE TRADITIONAL WEDDING CEREMONY GOD IS PRAISED FOR "MAKING ZION HAPPY" WHEN HER CHILDREN RETURN, AND THE PASSOVER SEDER CONCLUDES WITH THE HOPE "NEXT YEAR IN JERUSALEM."

FROM THE BEGINNING OF ITS LONG AND DRAMATIC STORY, THE JEWISH PEOPLE FIND HOME IN ISRAEL.

ACKNOWLEDGEMENTS

We are grateful to live in a country where we are free to write and publish a book like HOMELAND. There are many people to thank for their contributions to this project. It was a privilege to work with Marv Wolfman who brought his longtime professional career, vision and mastery of language to bear on this ground-breaking project. Mario Ruiz, "The Friend," whose talent and commitment to this project were without limit, tapped divine forces to bring it to fruition.

Gary Shapiro's vast scholarly knowledge and razor-sharp mind helped to craft HOMELAND and resolve the challenging questions raised by this endeavor. From the outset, Keith Kanter's many contributions pushed us to do the best work possible. It is great to work with a person whose array of knowledge spans the Bible, Talmud, the Wall Street Journal and Green Lantern's oath. Barbara Chandler stepped right in and did an outstanding job keeping the project on track. None are more professional!

Dave Lanphear worked around the clock and responded to the many last minute changes with calm and professionalism. We thank Bill Haase and the Rosenwald Day School Trust for their vision. Thank you to the Nachshon Press Committee, Chuck Friend, Jay Goodgold, Ellen Kenemore, Fred Levy, Paul Saharack, Max Wasserman and Al Winick, for their suggestions, enthusiasm and steadfast support throughout the process.

Our thanks to Rabbi Brad Hirschfeld, Vice President of the National Jewish Center for Learning and Leadership, for making the introductions that led to the project's launch and for the Israel experience. Special thanks to the Community Foundation for Jewish Education of Metropolitan Chicago's Cindy Barnard, Michael Bass, Susan Bayer, Barbara Borden, Ramona Choos, Harry Cohen, Larry Dobkin, Jennifer Flink, Ruth Freedman, Charles Friend, John Geiringer, Jay Goodgold, Sam Grodzin, Donald Hoffman, David Jacobson, David Kahn, Ruth Kahn, Ethan Kahn, Clive Kamins, Robin Katz, Barbara Kaufman, Ellen Kenemore, Karen Kesner, Ellen Leiderman, Fred Levy, Scott Newberger, Morris Oldham, Rhoda Pomerantz, Daniel Ray, Howard Reese, Marc Sacks, Paul Saharack, Marc Slutsky, Maxine Sukenik, Howard Swibel, Max Wasserman, Lynn Weisberg, Al Winick and Geena Cohen Zaslavsky.

We appreciate the support of Dr. Steven B. Nasatir, Dr. Peter B. Friedman and Michael B. Tarnoff of the Jewish Federation of Metropolitan Chicago/JUF. We are grateful to our reviewers, Dr. Mitchell Bard, Dr. Barry Chazan, Dr. Jacob Lassner and Dr. Rafael Medoff, Yizhar Hess, Esq. and Meytal Chernoff for their attention to the facts and details. Many people provided professional expertise and guidance.

Thanks to Barbara Rooks for the initial efforts that helped lay the foundation for the project, and to Gaby Siegal, Dale Davison, Leslie Weiss, Liz Lassner, Etty Dolgin, Cindy Friedman, Leah Polin and Dan Milner for their dedicated hours of research. Lynn Weisberg's and Sid Singer's proof-reading and edits were much appreciated. Special thanks to Yaffa Berman for taking the lead while I was engaged with the project and her commitment to translate and utilize the work in the Hebrew language. Thanks to Amy Kurzawski who handled the expected and unexpected details. Thanks to Nina Chaitin, Shlomit Hoch, Diane Kamil, Sondra Lorig, Yakov Magdel, Jo Ellen Reed and Marcia Seltzer-Tobias for their patience, professionalism and support.

Barry Friedland, InnerWorkings Principal and Marc Suchomel, President of Independent Publishers Group, and their staffs helped us navigate the production and distribution process. Thanks to Rich Goldberg at Fastsigns and Elaine Luckett for their creativity and support. We thank Aaron Cohen, JUF News for his assistance and encouragement. Leah Finkelshteyn, Lisa Hostein, Wendy Margolin, Sari Steinberg, Chanan Tigay and Cliff Vaughn were among the first to tell the public about HOMELAND.

Thanks to Julie Katz, Welsh & Katz, Ltd., Johnnie Allen, Associated Agencies, Inc., and Ken Tornheim and Helen Blovsky, Ostrow Reisin Berk and Abrams, LTD. for their professional expertise. Maggie Thompson provided our first real understanding of the graphic medium and its potential. Thanks to Steve Bergson, Brad Weber, J.T. Waldman, David Levy and Josh Weinberg for their suggestions and encouragement.

We thank Yonatan Gefen for allowing us to open our story with his very fitting poem, and Rona Ramon for her heartfelt letter. Mohammad Darawshe gave us insight regarding the Israeli Arab narrative. Thanks to David Weiss for his invaluable help, research and guidance, and thanks to Aric Berman, Hon. Baruch Binah, Allen Chandler, Tony Chaitin, Hon. Dr. Andy David, Jacob Ner-David, Rabbi Shaul Feinberg, Shulamit Ghildner, Marla Goldberg, Eric Mahr, Dr. Michael Messing, Byron Preiss z"l, David Roet, Leslie Rosen-Stern, Louis Weber and the community's educational leadership for their support.

Thank you to Rabbi Meir Schweiger for the inspiration. Everyone's support and dedication to this project has been invaluable. If we have overlooked anyone in these acknowledgements, please know that your contributions were truly appreciated. Finally, a very special thanks to our families who encouraged us every step of the way.

William J. Rubin, MA/MBA
Executive Editor, Nachshon Press

END NOTES

P. 1 Green Man/Blue Man poem with permission of Yonatan Gefen and Acum, The Sixteenth Lamb, translation: G. Shapiro.
P. 2-18 Stories are primarily from the Hebrew Bible.
P. 5 Hagar leaves Abraham's home twice; once before Isaac's birth, when she runs away after a conflict with Sarai (Sarah), and again after Isaac's birth, when she is sent away. Genesis 16:6, 21:14.
P. 9 "...one opinion claims..." Babylonian Talmud (BT), Sotah 36b-37a.
P. 10 "Two different midrash readings..." BT, Shabbat 88a. See also Exodus 24:7.
P. 13 "A midrash suggests..." BT, Ta'anit 9a.
P. 19 "According to the traditional story..." Letter of Aristeas, 3rd century B.C.E.
P. 21 This page depicts the menorah as it was in the Temple with seven candles. Today, a menorah with eight candles plus a shammash, a candle used to light the others, is used on Hanukkah.
P. 25 Temple vessels, including the menorah, are carried off to Rome and this image is still depicted on the Arch of Titus in Rome.
P. 27 "Rabbinic tradition records..." Berachot 61b. "Rome renames the Land Palestina..." Reich, p.8.
P. 28 "According to rabbinic tradition..." cf. Pirkei Avot 1:1.
P. 32 Poem by Judah Halevi. The Penguin Book of Hebrew Verse, T. Carmi(ed), trans: G. Shapiro, Allen Lane: London, 1981, p.347.
P. 35 Kabbalah chart, Green, p.ix.
P. 36 Glueckel of Hameln Memoirs. Rosamond Fisher Weiss, translated by Marvin Lowenthal, Schocken Books, NY, 1932.
P. 38 "China, India, Barbados, Surinam, Curacao...." Barnavi, p.151.
P. 39 "...24,000 Jews in Palestine..." Gilbert, Atlas of the Arab-Israeli Conflict, p.3.
P. 41 "How many Jews lived..." Gilbert, Atlas of the Arab-Israeli Conflict, p2.
P. 46 "...Christian Zionists..." Sachar, p.106.
P. 47 "Syrian Arabs claim..." Laqueur and Rubin, p.22.
P. 48 "reached into the Arabian Desert..." Dr. J. Lassner review (notes on file with publisher).
P. 49 "...eight Americans..." Dr. R. Medoff review (notes on file with publisher).
P. 50 "Jabotinsky rejects..." R. Medoff review.
P. 51 "...divided into strips..." Dr. M. Bard review (notes on file with publisher).
P. 52 "...1939 Britain's White Paper..." Gilbert, Israel, A History, p.97.
P. 52 "...in 1935, the Nazis implemented..." R. Medoff review.
P. 54 Carmel Plan, Allon, p.96-7.
P. 54 "The Mufti, now living in Germany..." R. Medoff review; see also Myths & Facts, M. Bard, p.192.
P. 55 Hannah Senesh: Her Life & Diary. p.256.
P. 57 King David Hotel bombing warnings, Begin, p.212, Sacher, A History of Israel, p.267, Ben-Sasson, p.1050.
P. 58 Detail of conditions on Exodus ship "...British soldiers using rifle butts, hose pipes and tear gas against the survivors of the death camps. Men, women and children were forcibly taken off to prison ships, locked in cages below decks and sent out to Palestine waters." Gilbert, Israel: A History. p.145.
P. 58 "...Kielce pogroms erupt..." Ben Sasson, p.1046. Compelling description of why Jews could not return to European homes.
P. 59 "Arabs reject partition..." Laqueur & Rubin, p.57-62, Reich, p.51- 52 (the speech) and Lewis, p.363. Truman support, M. Bard review.
P. 60 "Saudi Arabia...reserves to itself..." Reich p.44.
P. 61 Arabs attack convoy at Jerusalem hospital "On 13 April a convoy of doctors and nurses from Hadassah hospital and some faculty from the Hebrew University made its way up to Mount Scopus, in accordance with an agreement with the British military authorities. This convoy was attacked by the Arabs, and its passengers were slaughtered before the eyes of the British forces who stood only a few paces away. They not only did nothing to halt the massacre but prevented Haganah units from extending help to the convoy." Ben Sasson, p.1057.
P. 61 Deir Yasin, Dershowitz, p.81, Gilbert, Israel: A History, p.169, Sacher, A History of Israel p.333.
P. 62 Independence speech by Ben-Gurion, Eban, p453.
P. 63 5708 is the year on the Hebrew calendar, 1948 on the standard calendar.
Jerusalem established as capital. Dr. B. Chazan review (notes on file with publisher).
P. 64 "...K'far Etzion and many Jews...", Dershowitz, p.79, Gilbert, Israel: A History, p.184-185.
P. 64 "...thousands of Arabs end up fleeing..." Sachar A History of Israel, p.331-336, Dershowitz p.78-90, Pappe, p.87-101, Lewis, p.364.
P. 65 El Al security information primarily from "Unfriendly Skies are No Match for El Al," by Vivienne Walt, USA Today, October 1, 2001.
P. 67 Anatoly (Natan) Sharansky was a Soviet political prisoner and later became an Israeli cabinet minister.
P. 68 "...from 1948-1958..." Y.Hess review, notes on file with publisher.
P. 68 Population numbers. Gilbert, Israel: A History, p.257-259, Ben Sasson, p.1076.
P. 68 In 1977, 66 Vietnamese refugees were rescued by Israel after being turned away by other countries.
P. 69 Soviet Union and Argentina immigration numbers, JAFI.
P. 71 As an example of one of the most outstanding campaigns in the country, the Jewish Federation/Jewish United Fund in Metropolitan Chicago (JUF) is a leader among Federations and raises tens of millions of dollars annually for these critical needs.
P. 71 Keren Hay'sod (the foundation fund) provides support for Israel from countries outside N. America. P. 71 Birthright, B. Chazan review (notes on file with publisher).
P. 71 "Since then the U.S. has provided nearly $100 billion in grants and loans." "U.S. Aid to Israel" by Mitchell Bard, Jewish Virtual Library.
P. 77 Arab education information, B. Chazan review, J. Lassner review.
P. 79 Unit 101/202: (pictured) Meir Har-Zion, Arik Sharon, Moshe Dayan, Dani Matt, Moshe Efron, Asaf Simchoni, Aharon Davidi, Ya'akov Ya'akov, Raful Eitan. Y. Hess review.
P. 81 Statistics of troops / tanks, Gilbert, Israel, p.381.
P. 81 "Nassar's promise..." Bard, Myths & Facts, p.78.
P. 81 On June 8, 1967, during the Six-Day War, the U.S. naval intelligence ship "Liberty" was mistakenly attacked by the Israeli air force and navy. Thirty-four were killed and 75 wounded. Israel paid reparations. Thirteen U.S. and Israeli government investigations concluded the attack was a tragic mistake, see Bard, Myths and Facts, p.90.
P. 84 "...troops who fail to prevent..." R. Medoff review.
After the March 11, 1978 attack, Israel launches Operation Litani to push PLO militants out of South Lebanon. In 7 days, 25,000 Israeli soldiers occupy everything south of the Litani except the Lebanese city of Tyre. However, the PLO would reinfiltrate the area and launch hundreds of Katyusha rockets against northern Israel, which leads to the First Lebanon War 4 years later. Reich, p.125.
P. 87 "In the South, Major General Ariel Sharon..." Sacher, History of Israel, p.776.
P. 90 One catalyst for this attack on the infrastructure of the PLO in south Lebanon was the attempted assassination of Israel's Ambassador to Britain, Shlomo Argov on June 4, 1982.
P. 90 J. Lassner provided valuable insight regarding Israel's War in Lebanon I.
Page 91   On February 10, 1983, Emil Grunzweig, a Peace Now organizer was killed by a grenade thrown by a young Jerusalem resident Yona Avrushmi at a rally in front of the Prime Minister's office.
P. 96-101 Events and terrorist attacks obtained primarily from Israel Ministry of Foreign Affairs, Mideast Web, second source Johnston's Archive.
P. 99 Daniel Lewin. 9/11 Commission Report, p.5.
P. 104 "...built in Dimona..." Gilbert, Israel: A History, p.522.
P. 113 Israel book fair numbers, Y. Hess review.
P. 118 "...where wolves and lambs..." "...the wolf and the lamb shall graze together, ..." Is 65:25.
Map of Israel. Carta, Israel: Carta Map and Publishing Co., 2007.

Prime Ministers of Israel (as of 1/1/07): David Ben-Gurion (1948-53, 1955-63), Moshe Sharett (1954-55), Levi Eshkol (1963-69), Yigal Allon (Interim 1969), Golda Meir (1969-74), Yitzhak Rabin (1974-77, 1992-95), Menachem Begin (1977-83), Yitzhak Shamir (1983-84, National Unity Government,1986-92), Shimon Peres (1984-86, National Unity Government, 1995-96, interim P.M. after Rabin's assassination), Benjamin Netanyahu (1996-99), Ehud Barak (1999-2001), Ariel Sharon (2001-05), Ehud Olmert (2005- present, interim P.M. after Sharon's stroke, elected P.M. in 2006).

Presidents of Israel (as of 1/1/07): Chaim Weizman (1948-52), Yitzhak ben Tzvi (1952-63), Zalman Shazar (1963-73), Ephraim Katzir (1973-78), Yitzhak Navon (1978-83), Chaim Herzog (1983-93), Ezer Weizman (1993-2000), Moshe Katsav (2000-present).

We have made every effort to provide accurate information. Any factual errors are the sole responsibility of Nachshon Press, LLC. Please e-mail suggestions or corrections for the second edition, with citations, to wrubin@nachshonpress.com.

PHOTO CREDITS

Photos on these pages with permission of the National Photo Collection, State of Israel:
45, 46, 50, 51, 55, 57, 58, 61,62, 63, 68, 69, 70,71, 72 , 74, 75, 76, 77, 79, 80, 81, 82, 83 ,84, 85, 86, 87, 88, 90, 91, 93, 94, 95, 96, 97, 98, 99, 100, 101, 102, 103, 104, 105, 106, 107, 108, 109, 110, 111, 112, 113, 114, 115, 116, 117.

41	First Zionist Congress. National Photo Collection, State of Israel
44	Kibbutz Degania. Reuven Milon and Jewish Agency for Israel (JAFI)
48	Haganah. Daniel Sieradski and The Haganah Museum, 23 Rothschild Blvd., Tel Aviv
50	Wingate's night squad; National Photo Collection, State of Israel
52	Slovakian militia shaving a Jew's beard. Yad Vashem Film and Photo Archive
52	Jews captured by SS and SD troops during Warsaw Ghetto uprising. USHMM Courtesy of Instytut Pamieci Narodowej
59, 82	United Nations building. Natalia Bratslavsky/123rf.com
63	Altalena burning. National Photo Collection, State of Israel
68	New immigrant family in main square of Yehud. National Photo Collection, State of Israel
68	Sixty-six Vietnamese refugees arrive in Israel after other countries refuse to accept them. National Photo Collection, State of Israel
69	Ma'abarot camp. JAFI
69	Anatol Sharansky and his wife. National Photo Collection, State of Israel
69	Operation Solomon Ethiopian immigrants. United Jewish Communities (UJC)
70	Operation Magic Carpet Yemenite immigrants. National Photo Collection, State of Israel
	Shula ben Shlush from Morocco at new Israeli settlement. National Photo Collection, State of Israel
71	Paving road in Negev from Beersheva to Eilat. National Photo Collection, State of Israel
73	Holocaust remembrance. Isranet News and Media: Edgar Asher.
74-75	Israeli Prime Ministers and world leaders, National Photo Collection, State of Israel
74	Ariel Sharon at Western Wall after being elected Prime Minister. Getty Images: Patrick Baz. Sharon with head wound. Getty Images: Yossi Greenberg
78	IDF Soldiers. Israel Defense Forces.
79	Unit 101/202. Meir Har-Zion, Arik Sharon, Moshe Dayan, Dani Matt, Moshe Efron, Asaf Simchoni, Aharon Davidi, Ya'akov Ya'akov, Raful Eitan. National Photo Collection, State of Israel
86	Soldiers in trenches. Courtesy of Micha Bar Am and Ron Endrino
89	American hostages, U.S. Embassy in Iran. Corbis
89	Ilan Ramon. NASA and National Photo Collection, State of Israel
93	Israeli students adjust gas masks during drill. Brian Hendler/JTA
96	Iraq Invades Kuwait, Desert Storm. AP Photos
97	Rabbi Yisrael Meir Lau and Rabbi Eliyahu Bakshi-Doron with Pope John Paul II. National Photo Collections, State of Israel
98	Israelis mourn Rabin in Malchei Yisrael Square. Brian Hendler/JTA Camp David II. William J. Clinton Presidential Library
99	World Trade Center Twin Towers. AP Photos Karine A. National Photo Collection, State of Israel
	Charred remains of Haifa bus after Palestinian suicide bombing. Brian Hendler/JTA Security Fence. Brian Hendler/JTA Shuttle Columbia Crew. NASA and National Photo Collection, State of Israel
100	Katyusha rocket in backyard of Gaza family. Brian Hendler/JTA
	Young woman carried by Israeli soldiers during evacuation of Gaza settlement of Shirat Hayam. Brian Hendler/JTA
101	Israeli soldiers grieving. Brian Hendler/JTA
	Israeli family and soldiers mourn at gravesite. Brian Hendler/JTA
102-103	Israeli Café. Brain Hendler/JTA
106	Professors Aaron Ciechanover and Avram Hershko. Technion/ISRAEL21c
	Professor Robert J. Aumann. National Photo Collection, State of Israel
	Professor Daniel Kahneman. Denise Applewhite
107	Satellite. Andrey Volodin/123rf.com
108	Children celebrate Purim in Tel Aviv. Brian Hendler/JTA.
109	Batsheva Dance Company. National Photo Collection, State of Israel
110	Daniel Barenboim, Gil Shaham. Dan Porges, National Photo Collection, State of Israel
	Itzhak Perlman, Pinchas Zuckerman, Shlomo Artzi. National Photo Collection, State of Israel
111	Soccer game. Brian Hendler/JTA
112	Agam, Yaacov, Accessioned object, 1987. © 2007 Artists Rights Society (ARS), New York/ADAGP, Paris. Digital Image Photo credit: The Museum of Modern Art/Licensed by SCALA / Art Resource, NY.
114-115	United Jewish Communities (UJC) Photo Archive.